RENAISSANCE DRAMA

New Series 34   2005

Renaissance Drama

New Series 34

Media, Technology, and Performance

Edited by Jeffrey Masten, Wendy Wall, and W. B. Worthen

Northwestern University Press

Evanston 2005

Contents

Editorial Note

T HIS ISSUE OF *Renaissance Drama,* volume 34, devoted to the topic of "Media, Technology, and Performance," is coedited by W. B. Worthen, Wendy Wall, and Jeffrey Masten. The articles displayed here address the interface between drama and its various modes of production over the past four centuries. The volume explores the relationship of drama to other forms of early modern spectacle (pageantry, masques), to the specificities of typography and the economics of the book industry, to the intersection with film and DVD production, and to the way that stage technologies and theatrical economies of the sixteenth, seventeenth, nineteenth, and twentieth centuries define plays and playing. Rather than thinking of the early modern text as something simply reconstituted in its different incarnations, these essays make clear that different media force a rethinking of the text "itself" and of the terms we use to envision, to conceptualize, and even to see the work of drama.

As the essays in volume 34 suggest, *Renaissance Drama,* an annual and interdisciplinary publication, invites submissions that investigate traditional canons of drama as well as the significance of performance, broadly construed, to early modern culture. We particularly welcome essays that examine: the impact of new forms of interpretation on the study of Renaissance plays, theater, and performance; the cultural discourses that shaped and were shaped by drama and the institutional conditions in which it was produced; and the way that performance and performativity functioned both on and off the professional stage.

Renaissance Drama conforms to the stylistic guidelines of the *Chicago Manual of Style* (14th edition), including endnote reference citations. Scholars preparing manuscripts for submission should refer to this book. Please submit an electronic file of manuscripts as an e-mail attachment (saved in rich text, as an rtf file) to renaissancedrama@northwestern.edu, along with three hard copies sent to the address below. For initial review of manuscripts, legible photocopies of any illustrations are acceptable; authors of essays accepted for publication will be responsible for obtaining any necessary permissions. Manuscripts submitted with a stamped self-addressed envelope will be returned. The journal does not accept submissions of essays by fax. Please address all submissions and inquiries to:

> *Renaissance Drama*
> Department of English
> Northwestern University
> 1897 Sheridan Road
> Evanston, IL 60208-2240
> USA

Additional information on submissions, special issues, and forthcoming essays may be found at the Northwestern University English Department Web site, http://www.english.northwestern.edu/.

RENAISSANCE DRAMA

New Series 34   2005

Inoculating the Old Stock:
Shakespearean Chorographies

BARBARA HODGDON

Shakespeare is a model of the theatre that contains Brecht and Beckett, but goes beyond both. Our need in the post-Brecht theatre is to find a way forwards, back to Shakespeare.

—Peter Brook, *The Empty Space* (1968)[1]

Beckett has changed the way we do Shakespeare, the way we act, the way we write and the way we direct in the theatre.

—Peter Hall (1976)[2]

T HAT BRECHT AND Beckett, with Brook as their advance man, have given shape to Shakespeare's late twentieth-century legacy is hardly new news. What Peter Hall marked as the equivalent of a theatrical paradigm shift has accumulated over the ensuing decades, shaping what Bill Worthen calls the force of Shakespearean performance, expanding its power of expression and impact and challenging its traditions.[3] Here, I want to explore how collusions and collisions with Brecht and, especially, Beckett operate within visual regimes of space and light in two Shakespearean performances—Steven Pimlott's 2000 *Richard II* and his 2001 *Hamlet,* both featuring Sam West. Neither a mere "frame" nor a neutral form or container, space is social morphology: it is to lived experience what form itself is to the living organism, and just as intimately bound up with function and structure—and thus with ideology. Serving as a tool of thought and action, space defined, transformed, and mediated by lighting technology and controlled by institutions—in this case, theatrical institutions—is also a means of domination, of power.[4] How, then, do these theater technologies or modes of production facilitate, even force, particular modes of staging, enactment, and spectatorship?

I am less concerned, here, with the presence of the author and the text than with the presences of theater, with the sights and resitings which performance makes possible. For although theater and theory once shared an etymological connection through the idea of sight or spectacle, and by

3

association, with contemplative speculation, that connection gets blocked, in the case of Shakespeare, where the text, operating as a metalanguage somewhat analogous to "the world" as the arbiter of truth in conventional notions of science and theory, intervenes. Taking on an authority it never had in Shakespeare's time, the text has become its own disjunction, a print intervention between histories of performance. Invoking the word to explain—or monitor—the phenomenology of performance often superimposes a textual story that the performance is seen to illustrate and, substituting one pleasure for another, avoids seeing theater's spatial dynamics, which construct their own tight system of stage language.[5] This, then, represents an investigation of how particular modes of production give form to performed Shakespeare and how they contribute to perceiving those performances as aesthetic entities and as cultural events. But before turning to case studies, which represent the most visible sites for observing the processes of filiation, change, and exchange that interest me, a brief historiography—or chorography—is in order to set the scene. And since the performances in question took place at Royal Shakespeare Company (RSC) spaces, *Richard II* in The Other Place, *Hamlet* in the Royal Shakespeare Theatre, these are local histories, maps of specific locations and practices.

In April 1947 at Stratford's Shakespeare Memorial Theatre, six years before the Paris performance of *Waiting for Godot,* its famous opening stage direction—"*A country road. A tree. Evening."*—heralding the death of stage realism, Peter Brook scrapped the scenery for his production of *Romeo and Juliet* except for a single tree and a stand of crenellated wall. As Chorus made a slow exit through the dark, his voice fading, strong white light blazed out suddenly upon a virtually bare orange arena backed by an indigo cyclorama, what Brook later called "the great tent of Mediterranean blue which hangs over every moment . . . from the first brawl in the dusty market to the calm and peaceful cadence in the grave."[6] Once again working on Stratford's main stage in 1962, Brook discarded the complicated rusty iron bridges and staircases designed for his *King Lear,* replacing them with tall, white, coarsely textured screens, set at angles to the proscenium arch. Critics spoke about harsh, cruel, unrelenting light (daylight? the Globe playhouse?) that gave no aesthetic shelter: *Lear* staged not just as theater of the absurd, as Brook (influenced by Jan Kott) claimed, but *Lear* seen in the "blaze of hellish light" illuminating Beckett's *Happy Days.*[7] The locale that, in 1968, Brook would call an "empty space" was, in fact, a space *emptied out*, as though for a kind of theatrical garage sale that already had been theorized—by Adolphe Appia, sculpting stages in light to create a habitus[8] for performance, and by Edward Gordon Craig's visually revolutionary nonrepresentational designs, related, in turn, to an acting revolution through Brecht.[9] Although Craig's "theatre of the future" and Brook's "post-Brecht theatre" both incorporate Shakespeare's presence, each imagines a way forward rather than a return to Elizabethan spaces. Yet there has, I think, been a tendency to speak as though Shakespeare's Globe were the initial minimalist space, an early modern analogue of Brook's empty space, and to fantasize its previous existence (as well as its recent return) as an alternative to what frequently has been demonized as designers' theater or conceptual theater. But at least in its reconstructed, highly decorated mode, the Globe is a visually busy space, far from the bare platform or "wooden O" so mystified as an originary performance space that somehow, magically, will release Shakespearean meanings.[10] Moreover, despite the much discussed and (to my mind) largely illusory discourses of authenticity that mark the space, the performances that take place there inevitably are driven by a legacy that inflects their meanings through contemporary performative behaviors tied to Stanislavski, Brecht—and even to Beckett.[11]

Further spatial ironies hover around the edges of any conversation that links Shakespeare with Brecht and Beckett. For Brecht as well as Beckett—each committed to visions of a "new," radical theater and theater language—are (like Shakespeare?) no longer popular (or, in the case of Brecht, populist) but have achieved classical status. Once, each spoke from the margins, out of a sense of dispossession—Brecht from exile in Hollywood; Beckett a self-exiled Irishman in Paris, writing in French and then translating into English. *Godot*'s 1955 London performance, directed by Peter Hall, met uncomprehending audience response until Kenneth Tynan praised the play; when the following year brought the Berliner Ensemble's *Mother Courage* to London, the shock of renegotiating the relationship between play and its spectators had as much to do with space and its "spare, unrelenting bright light" as with traverse curtains, signage, audience address, or alienation effects. Yet if throughout ensuing decades Brecht's once innovative theatrical vocabulary has collapsed into visual and performative clichés, losing its political edge, Beckett's theater is neither driven by a political project nor dependent, as with Brecht's connection to Stanislavski, on faithfully reconstructing a realistic subtext.[12]

Just as theater is always local and located, contingent and partial,[13] so too is writing about theater, especially when undertaken from a position outside theatrical culture itself, one that straddles theater studies and textual studies. In writing back from performance, I want to try to think as the theater thinks—that is, as process, as coming into being.[14] My subject is what might be called the "other performance," one that conveys my own connection—kinesthetic, intellectual, emotional—to the event. Here too I want to work with a reader as a performance might—playing with the position, status, and kinds of discourse that contribute to it, netting in my own and others' observations as well as evidence, anecdote, theory, and speculation—in order to open up a space, to raise questions of embodiment and enactment, of spectatorship and pleasure, and to attempt to discern how process, performance, and vision are written over (and through) one another in a complex ghosting.[15]

A Room of His Own: *Richard II* at The Other Place, 2000

History decomposes into images, not narratives; I have nothing to say, only to show.
—Walter Benjamin[16]

Bleacher seating faces a wide white-walled space. Fourteen or so white bentwood chairs are placed at intervals around three sides and in two upstage alcoves; a mound of earth, shaped like a newly dug grave, stage right; a rectangular wooden box—like those for croquet mallets or ammo— at center stage, with another chair (painted gold) atop it, a jacket draped over its back, a simple golden circlet on the seat. With spectators ranged as though at surgical grand rounds or on one side in a parliamentary debate, the space resembles a laboratory or operating theater—a place for anatomizing the play. Offering an analogy for a blank page, David Fielding's design—a "white box" reminiscent of Sally Jacobs's gymnasium–squash court for Peter Brook's 1970 *Dream*—sets up a cool spatial geometry, maps a close relation between playing space and audience space.[17] If, on the one hand, its austere architecture reads like déjà vu all over again, a grand theatrical mechanism rethought, it also looks like a rehearsal room. Indeed, this *Richard II* not only refuses to leave rehearsal behind but also encourages its travel into performance, where both processes converge, one layer visible over (or through) the other. And since rehearsal work—as well as decisions about space and light—figure prominently in Sam West's account of bringing the play, and his performance as Richard, to theatrical life,[18] I interleave italicized selections from West's unusually astute gloss on what the cast called "white boxing" with my own narrative/analysis.

At first look, such a spare visual field ruthlessly strips away the play's traditional gilt-and-rapture scenography, heavy with the "theatricalized" ideology of medieval pageantry (and poetry), replacing it with key objects— a chair, a pile of earth, a coffinlike box (*its true nature [not] revealed until the end*)—which not only attained huge resonance in the small space but served doubly as markers of an ordinary workaday world and as theatrical signs. (*Anything that went into the box was thrown into huge relief by the white walls—someone commented that everything had inverted commas around it.*) Only a bit of gold paint, its position onstage—and the spectator—"make" the chair a throne. (*Up to the first day of technical rehearsal we had benches around the walls. By replacing them with chairs, [Pimlott] made the point that the "throne" . . . was just a chair after all . . . and [that] the king is just a man. The ground was England's ground, from which Bolingbroke takes his leave when exiled, but it also stood for the dust of the grave, to the taint of which Richard believes himself immune.*) If Shakespeare was the source of such symbolic emblems, the minimalist theatrical language resonated with Beckett's abstract stage compositions, yet it would be difficult to discern which way the strands of influence—or the frictions between them—run. Certainly, however, both the strategic reimagining of space and the isolated phenomenology of material things strongly signaled a break with previous stagings. Although one of Pimlott's ideas had been to stage the play "on a pile of old costumes from previous RSC productions of the history plays, thereby literally treading on the past,"[19] that gesture toward past performances and to the play's—and England's—historical continuity eventually became an acoustic soundscape which played as spectators took their seats: a Churchill speech, Blake's anthem "Jerusalem," lines from Gilbert and Sullivan's *Iolanthe* ("Bow, bow, you lower middle classes")—voices which, like those within the play, speak from positions of class privilege.

A few moments before curtain time, a figure in elegant modern dress entered and sat in an up-left chair, his head in his hands: the presence of an actor onstage an anticipatory signal, alerting spectators to perceive meaning as located not just in the collage of voices but in the actor's body. Bells rang, and the eclectically costumed cast assembled and faced the seating blocks, where a slight young man in gray pullover and black trousers—hailed into the play from among the audience—entered the playing space through an aisle, walked to the up-right doors and bolted them. (*If I was going through with this, I had to make sure the audience was trapped inside the box with me and wouldn't get out until we'd solved this problem.*) Sitting on the edge of the box, he addressed the audience: "I have been studying how I may compare / This prison where I live unto the world"—the opening of Richard's fifth-act soliloquy, continuing through "Yet I'll hammer it out," then moving to "Thus play I in one person many people" and ending with "Nor I, nor any man that but man is, / With nothing shall be pleased till he be eased / With being nothing." (*This was to be an exploration of the prison that we all are born into, and from which we are only released at the hour of our death. . . . The play seemed . . . to articulate a peculiar sort of existential angst that wasn't specific to Richard—those surrounding him were as vulnerable as he if he lost power, and those succeeding him would come to know in time the poison of the "hollow crown."*) Putting on the crown, the jacket, and a signet ring, West spoke the play's opening words, "Old John of Gaunt," to a white-bearded man in a wheelchair near the box. As he placed one foot on the wooden box, the other actors shifted forward slightly, anticipating his next move, and as he spoke "Then call them to our presence," blinding white lights shot up, enveloping stage and spectators as "Richard" seated himself on top of the box which would become his mirror, his torture chamber, and—dragging it in on his back like a cross—his coffin.

Witnessing, I was present in the moment and also recalling Harry Berger Jr.'s notion of Richard as a special case of performative behavior: that he is speaking and listening to himself and that everything he says from the play's beginning forward is a variation or illustration of "I have been studying." Imagining a stage direction—*Enter Richard alone*—slipped in before the play's first lines, Berger reads the self-dividing, self-confining, self-canceling, and self-coupling rhetoric of the prison soliloquy as framing an action that plays out the consequences of Richard's wishes and thoughts.[20] Yet when this ingenious theory of reading hit firm theatrical ground, there was more to it than Berger had imagined in his philosophy. I heard the lines, as it were, twice: "I have been studying" was precisely what West—not yet playing a role but outside it—had, of course, been doing; now, he locked that study into this elegant forensic space where he would perform Richard II. Given a strategy which puts performer, play, and theater under an anamorphic lens, "character" was called into question from the outset:

not only was West italicizing his own (double) presence but, as Bridget Escolme writes, "slip[ping] back and forth between absorption in the fiction to a knowledge of just where his days will end."[21] Right away, too, the idea of the audience got doubled up; with all attempt at illusion broken, the fourth wall vanished, and "audience" became a principle of interpretation, or another actor. For just as West himself gave up his position outside the fiction to take the throne (an uncanny anticipation of Bolingbroke's action from within it), he solicited those sitting in the bleachers to validate him as both actor *and* character, who also depends on (and appeals to) an onstage audience to ratify (or depose) his authority.

Within this contract of doubled spectatorship, the audience became—or were invited to become—part of nearly every scene: Richard's courtiers at the opening; invited spectators at the lists (1.3);[22] Richard's soldiers (3.2) as well as Bolingbroke's (3.3); the Commons (4.1), during Richard's abdication. (*It meant we could talk and stare at them, and for the most part, get hard stares back.*) Although the idea of having two banquettes on stage to mirror the audience seating was discarded early in the rehearsal process,[23] an unusually detailed prompt copy records those moments when speakers acknowledged both audiences, addressing some lines of a speech to those onstage, others to those offstage, consistently marking the distance between the two. Among multiple instances, both Mowbray and Bolingbroke turned out, inviting support for their positions (1.1; 1.3), and Northumberland warned spectators that "[t]he King is . . . basely led" (2.1.242); such conscious manipulation of the relation between stage and audience not only furthered the notion of performance as dialectic but also, by creating break points where any separation between player and spectator abruptly vanished as the fiction rolled on its edge, risked becoming dangerous. What if the audience acts up? What if it doesn't? At one performance, as Bolingbroke (David Troughton) asked the audience to rise to acknowledge the dead Mowbray (4.1.103–4), he handed the text of the prayer to a vicar in the audience, who then read it; at another, he took a script from a spectator seated in the front row and read the prayer from it; he then returned it (and she returned to reading, as she had been since the start).[24] When the material reality of the theater so reframes a moment, what is being reframed is not just an aspect of the onstage fiction but also the situation of the audience. "In attempting to produce the audience as courtiers or commoners," writes Escolme, "this production stages the potential of its rebellion."[25] Asking spectators to stand makes them accessories to and complicit with Bolingbroke's takeover; a few moments later, when the Bishop of Carlisle attacked Bolingbroke— "What subject can give sentence on his king?"—I, for one, felt embarrassed that I had allowed myself to be implicated, party to his performance. For an instant, a ghost of Essex's notorious 1601 "command performance" appeared, producing something like a New Historicist shiver. Was this also treason? On at least one occasion, some did not rise: taking out a notebook, Bolingbroke wrote down names; not playing along, it seemed, might have consequences.

Simon Kemp's lighting not only further defined this emphasis on doubled spectatorship but also worked to double performance with rehearsal. The fluorescent tube light boxes of Kemp's design both are and are not theater lights: are because they have strong echoes of "workers," the instruments used generally on stage before a lighting plot exists; are not because they never are used to light a production.[26] (*Simon's lighting . . . a bright white political reality lit . . . mostly from above, and a darker world of shadow and plaint . . . was designed to illuminate both [audience and actors] constantly, . . . dissolving boundaries that sometimes let the jam-making classes sit back and let the gilt and splendour wash over them. . . . All special knowledge or hindsight evaporated under the lights.*) Beckett calls light "a unique inquisitor": here, it served to interrogate textual politics.[27] Working not just to accentuate the actor-audience relationship, it also served to segment the action, as though titling or bannering scenes or beats. For most scenes, a bright white state prevailed, but the purple light used for the opening returned, signaling several other moments of textual transpositions, deliberately marking their changed placement outside the flow of the fictional narrative. Following the interval (set between scenes 2 and 3 in act 3), Richard and Bolingbroke entered in fluorescent lavender overhead light (which changed to a green state) to confront each other at center stage, with Bolingbroke speaking some of Richard's lines to Queen Isabel as he goes to prison: "In winter's tedious nights . . . / Tell thou the lamentable tale of me" (5.1.40–44)—a parallel to Richard's opening prologue. Isabel herself (as well as others) appeared more frequently than the text indicates—for example, at the opening scene and throughout the scene at Flint Castle (3.3), the theatrical dynamic affording her a presence and voice that the fiction denies her.[28] (*Blue and purple sidelights threw long shadows, especially accompanying the women in the play, and the sense of existential doom that their being outside the political loop seemed to give them . . . the colour of a nightmare.*) Again under purple light, she spoke the first five lines of Richard's prison soliloquy as a prologue to the Gardeners' scene (3.4), as though oracling Richard's deposition—and her own—before she learned of it; after the Gardener (doubled with John of Gaunt) left, she uprooted the red rose he had planted on the grave mound.

Just as this performance announced its redesign of the logos through lighting technology, the design of the space and the placement of objects within it (together with a neo-Brechtian presentational style) demanded a precision of blocking that gave the word a particular impact. Not only did the theatrical presentation of space itself—which stressed lateral movement toward and away from the central fulcrum of chair and coffin and, briefly, as Richard descends from above to "the base court" (3.3), up and down—incorporate a sociopolitical commentary,[29] but it also was the case that this (not so) "empty" place, affording spectators a privileged position in relation to the fiction, magnified the spatial politics of embodiment and enactment, especially as movements and gestures recurred. At the beginning of act 4, scene 1, Troughton's Bolingbroke—tense, self-insistent, dangerous, occupying considerably more physical and vocal space than West's Richard—repeated the latter's initial gestures: striding in through the audience, bolting the upstage door, putting on the mantle of "the king," and assuming, under bright white light, center stage—the panoptic command post of performative meaning. Political takeover meant taking over theatrical space as well. But he did not keep either long, for once West's Richard entered, wearing a thorned crown of red roses, carrying a white rose, his body wrapped in a flag bearing the cross of St. George—and whistling "God save the king" (*Richard has never had a court fool; he is free now to be his own one*)—that spatial dynamic shifted. Like an animal marking its territory, West strolled the stage, controlling the entire space; moving to the mound of earth at stage right, he refocused attention from Bolingbroke to himself, upsetting the balance of power previously localized at center. Repressing emotion under a facade of mock courtesy and refusing to make the character's sensations those of the spectator, he took off the garland, dropped the rose onto the grave-mound, and spread the flag over it, all the while reading out his pre-scripted lines (spoken like a quotation, a copy of a copy) from Northumberland's paper.

West's performance was witty, ceremonious, dangerous—and mesmer-izing: his moment-to-moment engagement turned the space around him into a force field, so that he seemed to be occupying not just his own body but also the space around it. Rather than making a scene, he was instead showing, with surgical precision, *how the scene was made* and what *made it up:* a series of routines for canceling kingship, their ide-ological seams made theatrically visible in space. Never losing control, West even produced his own pen and, smiling, signed Northumberland's articles with a flourish. Even when he called for the looking glass—here, the upended box—West evinced no romantic self-indulgence: his seemed an ad lib response *to* the text, not an attempt to *incorporate* it. *([The breaking of the mirror] became a conscious desire to cut the crap— lose the glister, and reduce the king's two bodies to one, the real one, the one not constructed of flattery and self-deception. [For a long time we thought Richard's face could appear on a TV screen, through which he would throw the crown.])* Pushing the box over, it became a coffin, the grave gaping beneath it (*Self-knowledge came in an almost euphoric rush*); running his final exchanges with Bolingbroke over the coffin-mirror as stand-up comedy, he turned them both into vaudeville performers.

Rather than conflating actor with role, most critics marked the distance between the two—or between West's performance and their memories of his theatrical predecessors, notably John Gielgud, whose playing has colonized critical discourse to figure Richard as a role requiring a beautiful voice, a "dazzling virtuosity of phrasing and breathing,"[30] and a poeticized self-pity and pathos true to the "elegiac spirit" of the tragedy.[31] Whereas the key to Gielgud's interpretation came after throwing the looking glass to the ground—" 'Tis very true, my grief lies all within; / And these external manners of laments / Are merely shadows to the unseen grief / That swells with silence in the tortured soul" (4.1.295-98)[32]—for West, the climactic line (*the still center of the scene*) was "I must nothing be" (4.1.201). The difference between the two marks a shift from a poetics of interiority on display to a poetics of performance in space, a recodifying of a signature scene that can be attributed not just to changing theatrical fashions in Shakespearean verse speaking across six decades but also in response to an epistemic shift that took shape on RSC stages in the 1960s, where self-consciously Beckettian images of the isolated, alienated subject—in Brook's *King Lear* (1962) or the Hall-Barton *Wars of the Roses* (1964)— first appeared. Pimlott's *Richard II,* however, "spoke" Beckett with a difference. For as Shakespeare entered The Other Place's Beckettian landscape, that context enabled discovering and energizing ways of perceiving that worked to reify the actor's presence, signaled at the outset when West moved from the audience to the stage, from reading a text to performing it—textual critics take note—an emblematic moment of putting actors' *work* on display.

In unanimously praising West and Troughton, critics did acknowledge some sense of this production *as a performance*. Although some considered the space cold and unforgiving and not only desired to have their minds prefurnished with the medievalized stage trappings of divine-right kingship but also missed the opportunity to savor "Richard's tragedy," the play as a long elegy for a lost crown,[33] several even more firmly objected to Pimlott's "blatant monkeying" with the text. Alastair Macaulay, for one, claimed that while he could provide shrewd answers for doing so, they were not Shakespeare's, yet he also confessed that this performance made him "hang on the words" and that the play was "more clear than [he had] ever known it." (How much did his kinesthetic involvement depend on light, which enables hearing as well as sight, and spatial dynamics?)[34] Certainly these were not Shakespeare's "answers," but similar dislocative procedures occur regularly when critics (Berger and myself among them) operate on Shakespearean texts, transplanting passages from their native habitat and displaying them in the museum spaces of essays—a dismemberment not entirely dissimilar to putting bodies on anatomical slabs. Moreover, such apparently invasive procedures worked (as one might say of the body) in the interests of the text—which, as Herbert Blau (ventriloquizing Peter Brook) writes, "*never* quite speaks for itself but might desire any means to make itself understood."[35] If not precisely a ruthless critique of a canonical text—which Blau maintains is more threatening than self-consciously ruptured postmodern forms of performance[36]—these strategies of textual disintegration enabled meanings to move between individual characters: not only did such moves block reading "character" through essentialist-humanist lenses but also revealed how language, working tropically, called attention to the boundarylessness of text which, though assigned to one speaker, was shared out among several. Indeed, "I have been studying"—the mantra of this performance, initiated when West was hailed into the play—interanimated the idea (or theory?) of self-performativity marking this production through to the very end. In the final scene, each noble abruptly delivered his news to Bolingbroke and then left—through doors that led not just offstage but into the car park, beyond the theater—followed by the banished Exton, who echoed Bolingbroke's words at his own banishment: "Where'er I wander, boast of this I can, / Though banished, yet a true-born Englishman" (1.3.308-309). Alone, Bolingbroke bolted the door, took off his coat, put it on the chair, and, sitting on the throne atop Richard's coffin, addressed the audience: "I have been studying how I may compare / This prison where I live unto the world; / And for because the world is populous, / And here is not a creature but myself, / I cannot do it. Yet I'll hammer it out." And the bright lights snapped off.[37]

Radically reevaluating how theatrical culture responds to "Shakespeare-history," this performance not only mounted a direct critique of *Richard II*'s spectacle text but, as Escolme writes, by drawing spectators into "a troubled relationship to 'presence' and to their own presence as subjects," staged the play's debates over England's ownership "as a theatrical struggle for power [taking] place in the here and now of performance."[38] Moreover, the spatial dynamics of spectatorship offered up performance not as passive entertainment but as dialectic, not just echoing Shakespeare but talking back to him. And that idea of dialectic extended from performance into print where, instead of the program's usual narrative synopsis, Brechtian banners signposted each scene (further vestiges of the rehearsal process?). The program also offered another, even more pointed, meta- or paranarrative for this performance, a line from *Waiting for Godot*—"They give birth astride a grave, the light gleams an instant, then it's night once more"—a gloss for West's Richard as well as Troughton's Bolingbroke, sitting on grave ground, "Allow[ed] . . . a little scene, / To monarchize . . . and farewell, king." For, like Didi and Gogo, both actor-characters were trapped in a bleak, unforgivingly lit space, playing out routines, putting their hats on and off interchangeably, repeating themselves (and each other), ending where they began—still "hammer[ing] it out"—and waiting to come back tomorrow. "Shall we go? Yes, let's go." *They do not move.*[39] If Brecht had ghostwritten the processes shaping performance, it was Beckett's clowns who supplied an even more pertinent "theory"—or technology—of reading which made that performance legible. Invoking two major twentieth-century dramatist-theorists to reengage with the historicity of past performances, this *Richard II* had reassembled its text in space and light to re-create Shakespeare as installation art, giving it the aura of a "new"—and newly topical—play.

King of Infinite Space, Bounded in a Nutshell: *Hamlet* at the RST, 2001

A whole history remains to be written of *spaces*—which would at the same time be a history of *powers* . . .
—Michel Foucault, "The Eye of Power" (1977)[40]

ROS [*at footlights*]: How very intriguing! [*Turns.*] I feel like a spectator—an appalling business. The only thing that makes it bearable is the irrational belief that somebody interesting will come on in a minute. . . .
—Tom Stoppard, *Rosencrantz & Guildenstern Are Dead* (1967)[41]

At the Royal Shakespeare Theatre, the RSC's main stage has been transformed, stretched across the theater's entire width and pushed forward beyond the proscenium over the first few rows of the stalls; a *hanamichi*—the Kabuki theater's "flower path"—extends from the rear stalls through the seating to downstage right, leading into a vast echo chamber with pale gray paneled walls receding toward a large upstage center door. Closed-circuit television cameras and two searchlights mounted on tripods stage right and left (a backpack leaning against one) and set at the proscenium constitute the only objects on this stark, chilly playing field, its space further defined by a high-tech lighting rig: five rows of wall-mounted spotlights on tracks flank stage left and right, affording infinite mobility along the tracks as well as enabling modulations of color without using gels—a technology developed for rock concerts and making its theatrical debut here.[42] Thirty-two photographs, accompanied by dated notations from the diary of Auditorium Project Manager Peter Bailey, banner the tops of the souvenir program's pages, mapping the phases of constructing this space, a process that constitutes perhaps the boldest remodeling of a theater that, over the years, has undergone perennial changes aimed at effecting a closer relationship between actors and audience and improving sight lines. In addition, repeated attempts to mask, minimize, or eliminate the proscenium arch recently failed altogether when, ironically enough, architectural consultants determined that it was the structural component which supported the entire building. ("Don't clap too hard," says *The Entertainer*'s Archie Rice, "It's a very old building.")[43] Alison Chitty's design emphasizes its thrust, which demarcates a broad forestage from a narrower upstage area, a spatial grammar analogous to the locus and *platea* of the early modern platform stage and which also resonates with the mental memory theater designs of Robert Fludd or John Willis.[44] Just as, in such a "virtual" mental theater, how one stores ideas or images depends on where the mind's eye is positioned in facing it, in the material theater, physical space also is psychic space. And just as Foucault's image of the eye of power suggests a relation of power to theatricalized space, this stage, lit by technologies of surveillance, sets up a panoptic dynamic that forces attention to what it means to *be there:* only the presence of bodies—those of spectators as well as performers—repossess the space from a near total abstraction, a stilled arena for waiting, for being observed, completely open to view—and to appearance.

"Clean, bleak, modernist"; "minimalist heaven"; "cliché-free, anti-romantic, visually spare and politically vivid"; "watching the play under laboratory conditions"; "we are occupying a modish Neverland of Elsinore, a white box zone, a Spartan gymnasium where the play is a workout session for the hero's racing mind":[45] reviewers called up descriptors which pointed a marked synchrony between Pimlott's *Hamlet* and his *Richard II*—and with working at the extremities of theatrical space. Yet whereas The Other Place's small-scale "white boxing" took place in a space wider than it was deep, the newly remodeled stage was all about deep space—*a place without any visible character*" reminiscent of Stoppard's *Rosencrantz & Guildenstern Are Dead* and of its ancestor, *Godot,* where there is nothing to do but wait ("What should such fellows as I **DO** crawling between earth and heaven," read one program sound bite, bannering photographs of West's Hamlet in various poses).[46] If this was *like* Beckett-space, it also was Beckett blown up to *Hamlet* size and inflected by Brecht's spatial dynamics and aesthetics of visibility—a space, as Patrick Carnegy puts it, for "theatrical experiment and maybe even self-discovery."[47]

From its initial theatrical sign, in which preset wall spots snap off and the stage right tripod-mounted klieg light turns its eye on the audience, searching through it and ranging around the stage space, probing its recesses, this *Hamlet* translates its famous first line, "Who's there?" into an acknowledgment that draws spectators closer to, if not placing them precisely within, the fictional space. ("It's a production," writes Susannah Clapp, "which makes you think about what it is to be an audience.")[48] And, following the Ghost's appearances, where blue-purple light accompanies his passages forward and back across the stage, changing to violet-red to signal dawn's cockcrow, it does so most expressly at several key points in the narrative, the first of which occurs as full white light blazes out on

Claudius's press conference, his black-suited sycophants advancing toward the audience, strung out in a line, applauding him: "For all, our thanks" goes out to the house, inviting spectators' complicity. Although only Nicholas de Jongh mentions the connection (and mistakes Ethan Hawke for Kevin Bacon),[49] this moment sets up a series of echoes with Michael Almereyda's film (2000): indeed, this performance, especially given the agency it assigns to lighting technologies, not only calls attention to the porous boundaries between theater and cinema but also exists in an in-between space between the two, as though it wants to be something other than it is. It seems entirely appropriate that such a hybrid form should unfold in a building conceived and constructed during a time when more cinema houses than theaters were being built,[50] a physical space that, given its near-constant redesign, is always trying to refashion itself anew. And to the extent that this *Hamlet* is "like a film," it also is like a black-and-white film, not just in the washed-out grays of the set but in the costume palette, which ranges from dark grays to black: as in a tinted silent film,[51] the only color comes from Peter Mumford's lighting, marking shifts of time, mood, and mode, texturizing essential movements and gestures and shaping the politics and psychology of character.

Yet except insofar as it sets up a "close-up" forestage space that travels toward a (Wellesian) deep-space background, there is nothing cinematic about this *Hamlet*'s opening spatial geometry. Lighting carves and separates downstage from upstage areas, functioning at times like a Brechtian half curtain; because the area in front of that curtain is the primary acting space—reminiscent of the carpet Peter Brook uses as the field where the actor is "to play"—the dynamic generates the sense that the action occurs in front-curtain areas chiseled out of a much larger space, an undiscovered (and unplayed upon) country, home of matters unseen, a void that intensifies Hamlet's existential dilemma. Some entrances through the upstage center door, accompanied by rising spots, bring light to this otherwise darkened space, and for the Ghost's appearances, white forestage light plays against blue-purple upstage light (old Hamlet's signature color), casting shadows. When Hamlet and the Ghost meet, their scene is played at the interface between upstage and forestage, marked by the proscenium thrust; as the Ghost leaves, Hamlet is spread out on the floor: suddenly, there is no depth at all to stage space, its shadings of gray and black resembling a Rothko painting.

Claudius's welcoming speech marks the forestage as a formal space, one which West's Hamlet refuses to occupy. At his initial appearance, he sits, cross-legged and hunched over, on the *hanamichi,* in audience space— like us, an observer. Wearing a black hooded sweatshirt, running shoes, and black jeans, he draws in, as Ethan Hawke's Hamlet does in Almereyda's film, the visual and aural regimes of youth culture: disaffection, hard rock music, athleticism, radical politics. Minus its original function as a passageway on which audience members might offer actors *hana* (presents), here, the *hanamichi* lends the relationship between stage and spectator a special proximity that recalls Meyerhold's idea of a "conditional theatre," one which would overcome the limitations of the naturalistic stage, which positions actor and spectator in two separate worlds, those who act and those who receive.[52] As in the Kabuki theater, the walkway serves to establish the nature and attitude of a character by isolating him from the field of theatrical interest onstage. If his position alone enhances his alterity by situating him within a social context, the borrowed technology also forces attention to the outer edges of as well as to the interface between two spaces, generating the illusion that the actor can choose whether or not to enter the fiction. Half outside, half inside the action, he is not bound to realistic considerations of time; his movement is slowed down so that his entrance into the psychological action becomes deliberate, offered up for contemplation, forcing a split focus that charges both audience space and stage space as participant collaborators in the theatrical event. Yet although West's Hamlet enters *from and through* audience space as his Richard II had done the year before, unlike *Richard II,* this performance does not force the same kind of participatory activity on its spectators but gestures toward its complicity by exploiting the *hanamichi*'s unique ability to enable an actor to bring a character into sharp focus over an acting area that binds audience space to stage space. Pointedly, its use is reserved for those who are most closely connected to Hamlet—his doubles, Laertes and Fortinbras, and his friend Horatio—and those who (like him) figure the play's theatricality, the troupe of players.

Just as the *hanamichi* privileges the interconnection between audience and stage space, so too does the consistent use of the wide forestage. Although this use of space and light stands in relation to Terry Hands's structural formalism—as in the 1977 *Henry VI* trilogy ("Many lights make Hands work," ran the backstage joke)[53]—that suspended actors in light-created spaces, holding their performances in an aesthetic dynamic that challenged spectatorial engagement, here, technologies of light work in an even more deliberately anti-illusionist manner. Because the lighting insists on each scene for itself, there's a distinct sense that this *Hamlet* is less a composed action than a selection of apparently random elements placed together so as to comment on each other, recalling Brecht's notion that the essential principle of blocking, as in cinema, is montage.[54] The souvenir program echoes this emphasis on decomposed narrative and on performance *in* and *of* space. Incorporating rehearsal as well as production stills, positioning rehearsal shots beside plot synopses, source materials or scholarly essays— Germaine Greer on "Hamlet and Heroic Doubt" and Frank Kermode's "New Words for a New Theatre"—and setting off production stills on a double-page spread, it charts the exchange and resistance between image and text, performance and critical opinion to initiate a visual-verbal dialectic, suturing image and discourse, seeable and sayable, which serves not merely as a structuring of knowledge and power but as a conversation between two histories—that of the play as read and as performance.[55] More par- ticularly, the semiotics of the double-page photo collage, with blocks of white space between photographs, replicates the "space-y," airy look of the remodeled stage; and neither the photographs themselves—representing key moments or emblematic tropes, aptly enough, precisely the strategy of silent Shakespeare films[56]—nor the quotes that accompany them obey narrative sequence. Furthermore, rather than the familiar captioning pro- tocols that over-read image *as* text to enforce meaning, the text citations function as threads on which the images are strung, floating among them as touchstones, mantras, Brechtian banners that call attention to the spaces of performance and to the performers themselves.[57]

Especially in those scenes taking place on the forestage, with light spilling out over the first rows of the stalls, additional circles of light mark out the areas in which intimate scenes occur, so that the space itself appears reduced, blocked out into separate "rooms" within a potentially larger acting space. Not only does this tight, precise control serve to fix the spec- tator's gaze, forcing the look toward a precise moment of performance, but scenic choreography consistently expresses sharp conflicts between movement and immobility, suggesting an extreme tension of being, and that is further enhanced by the almost complete absence of objects: the first furniture—two chairs and a wardrobe—does not appear until Hamlet lectures the players; the chairs remain for Gertrude and Claudius at the play and return for the final scene, together with a table. While watching his performance of *The Man Who,* based on Oliver Sacks's work, Peter Brook recalls looking at the set of one table and a few chairs on a very small stage and thinking, "How curious—that's all one needs to do Hamlet."[58] When, for example, Hamlet hears of the Ghost from Horatio, lighting casts huge shadows on the upstage wall, creating frames within frames, magnifying the actors and enhancing the sense that both are watchers and watched, put under a lens in this laboratory-like space. Repeatedly, too, stage pictures funnel down to a "still life" tableau in which two or three seemingly alienated figures speak to one another across ten to fifteen feet of stage space: expressing the difficulty these people have in reaching one another, the strategy also throws language into high relief, so that words, like light, become a spatial agent, a means to close the distance that separates them.

Nowhere is this sense of spatial isolation more painfully obvious than in how this *Hamlet* stages Ophelia, to whom the narrative—and this staging—accords the most limited range of action. Consistently, the configurations of space and light strongly mark her discomfort and entrapment, whether by pinning her against a wall, moving slowly forward, or by setting off her figure with greenish light, marking her melancholy as well as (perhaps) prefiguring her death by water. Lit by suffused light against the darkened upstage area, she becomes an ignored presence for Hamlet's "To be or not to be" soliloquy; during their following encounter, played on the forestage, several side-mounted spots, toned blue, capture the mood of their exchanges, darkening as Hamlet leaves. As Ophelia speaks her brief soliloquy, she's close to the lip of the forestage, her kneeling figure now brightly lit, confined in a tight narrow space and surrounded by an aura of greenish-blue light which darkens as, ignored by her father and Claudius, she slowly exits through the upstage center door, darkness closing in around her. When she next appears, lights come up on a spatial tableau resembling a Delvaux painting (such as *The Echo* [1943] or *The Sleeping City* [1938])—a haunted deep-perspective space in which courtiers are poised, as though in eerie stop-motion, creating a kind of "forest" of uncomprehending figures, who either turn away or seem not to notice her, through which she wanders in dreamlike madness to stand, at one point, on the forestage area which, later, will reveal the trap (and her grave) before the scene disperses in a series of long, slow exits.

If, throughout, an outer landscape of light and space figures the inner landscape or dynamic of a character or scene, that is most expressly so with Hamlet himself. Although this performance does unusual justice to

the interrelations between Hamlet and other characters, *Hamlet* is, as
Peter Brook writes, "a uniquely centralist play."[59] Just as lighting reinforces
Hamlet's encounters with others from his first entrance on the *hanamichi,*
highlighting his estrangement from Elsinore's cold corporate world, stressing his theatrical importance yet political impotence (Michael Billington
writes, "Defining Elsinore instantly throws Hamlet's dilemma into sharp
relief: you don't just rush off and kill a protected presidential figure like
Claudius"),[60] an equally striking moment occurs when, striding barefoot
down the walkway reading a book (an echo of West's "studying" in *Richard
II?*), he traverses the entire stage space, slamming straight into the upstage
wall. Spots at stage right and left travel down and up, tracking his sidelit figure so that he appears half in shadow, a double man, there and not there—
"mad"—or sane. And because he so rarely probes this darkened space, the
moment carries astonishing force—a theatrical, even emetic, release of
energy. In this space where Hamlet has no way to do anything but author his
own (theatrical) actions, a narrative of light traces out and underscores his
subjective experience: here, the technologies within which the performer
works not only distinguish performative discipline from human depth but
also intensify focus on the privacy of Hamlet's intellectual experience,
privileging the twists and turns of his thought. For this stage—whether
conceived as "infinite space" or "nutshell"—is, after all, Hamlet's mental
theater, a place where the lip of the forestage is almost exclusively "Hamlet-
space" (Susannah Clapp dubbed it "Hamlet's 'sterile promontory'"):[61] a
brightly lit frontal arena ideally suited for soliloquy, played directly to the
audience as urgent, confrontational arguments, not lyrical set pieces, his
gaze probing the house as he talks, gun—or cigarette—in hand. (Writes
Michael Coveney, "He runs from the depths of the stage to recite To Be
Or Not To Be—making no pretence to disguise its aria-like oddness and
intensity.")[62]

   The conjunction between forestage space and Hamlet's (famous) interiority, of course, comes as no surprise: Hamlet would be less than
"himself"—whatever the spatial configuration surrounding him—did he
not in some way play *to* (and even with) the audience. What does surprise, however, are instances where that forestage space expands, frankly
acknowledging spectators' presence. At the players' entry, for instance,
the houselights come up, turning the entire space askew and, as in a
De Chirico painting, channeling perspective vision to open an avenue of
thought. The momentary spatial distortion has its payoff in the "rogue and

peasant slave" soliloquy when, at "The play's the thing," all the lights blaze out, marking his epiphany: caught momentarily in the crossbeams of two spots, his thought literally seems to illuminate the space, commanding it from its very center. As he turns from the audience and walks rapidly to the upstage door, the side spotlights rake at his heels and, just when he slams through the door, snap out, his exit marking the first of two intervals. Although such blackouts, whether at an exit or entrance, can work to shift dominance from actor to designer, here, Hamlet's long walk-up, the lights following him, gives him command over the technology, generating a thrilling moment when everything comes together: actor, language, and space converging with and punctuated by the aid of an essentially cinematic technology—a sudden cut to black.

In this *Hamlet,* the play indeed is "the thing." It is, remarked Brecht, the duty of theater to speak to the eyes;[63] or, as Hamlet (famously) puts it, "the purpose of playing . . . was and is, to hold as 'twere the mirror up to nature"—a line given pointed emphasis when, as Hamlet lectures the players, gathered around him in what resembles (one supposes) an RSC rehearsal, the houselights come up and the actors swing around to stare directly at the spectators, forcing their look in a moment that risks overdetermining their complicity. Here, what is being staged is less a collaborative exchange between actor and audience than a confrontation between them. The play which follows represents the apotheosis of this Hamlet's romance with theatrical technologies. Just as, in Almereyda's film, Ethan Hawke's " 'The Mousetrap'—A Film by Hamlet" offers a media allegory that sutures footage from home video, silent Shakespeare films, and cartoons into a memory bank,[64] West's Hamlet and his troupe of players (Benedict Nightingale calls them "performance-art rowdies")[65] stage an electrotechno-rock light show, a Sensurround media environment with heavily miked sound that assaults ears as well as eyes, deliberately offensive to its onstage audience. Here, too, Hamlet's "mirror" is a video camera: filming from the lip of the stage, Horatio captures the reactions of Gertrude and Claudius; their images, projected on a screen set in a frame, eclipse the actors' performances, pointing to the ways in which media technologies currently replace and revise theatrical image-making as well as to the circulation back and forth between both kinds of cultural performances. In this performance space lit by crossbeams of blue, green, and red light, Claudius's call for lights, captured in a zoomed-in image by Horatio's camcorder, seems ironic, a sign of his disorientation and desperation; at his abrupt exit, Hamlet applauds, the sound of one hand clapping an echo and critique of Claudius's own performance.

Given the spectacular collusions of light, space, and performers throughout, what is striking about this *Hamlet*'s final scene is that such high-tech effects are startlingly absent. Suddenly, it's like one has arrived at the point in *Rosencrantz & Guildenstern Are Dead* where the Player, instructing the Spies (by order of a stage direction) to "*die at some length rather well*," tells Ros and Guil, "Audiences know what to expect, and that is all they are prepared to believe in."[66] The joke, of course, is the old one: it's a tragedy; they *do* all die in the end. But there is a method here to how the theatrical authority given over to space and light which has functioned to support both individual performers and the performance called *Hamlet* seems to be withdrawn during this scene, setting up a friction between two fictions or, perhaps better, between the authority previously accorded to technologies of space and light and (for lack of a better term) "Shakespeare's *Hamlet*." Bright light fills the stage; at the mass entrance, the court applauds, as they had done for Claudius's initial appearance; and Hamlet busies himself cleaning up the stage, making sure the surface is clear of obstacles, setting up yet another theatrical action. The fight, extremely aggressive, has some finely tuned touches: as weapons get dropped after Laertes nicks Hamlet, Claudius returns the poisoned sword to Hamlet, added insurance that neither combatant will survive; dying, Claudius crawls toward Gertrude, but Hamlet shoots him before he can reach her. At the shot, the lighting draws in, encircling Hamlet and Laertes at center; emptying the cup, Hamlet throws it on the floor as an offstage cannonade sounds; speaking to Horatio, he gives an appalled laugh (Michael Dobson writes, "in a sort of comic disbelief that any day could turn out so spectacularly badly as this one has").[67] At Hamlet's death, a bandolier-clad Fortinbras, the complete military man, strides down the walkway to sit on a chair brought to center stage: all eyes turn toward him, and one courtier begins to clap; following a momentary pause, the entire court joins in, surrounding his figure as the lights go down.

Compared to the use of stage space elsewhere, these moments seem ordinary—pointedly flat, deliberately anticlimactic. The stage littered with bodies, seen in flat light, stands in stark contrast to the court scene over which Claudius presided initially—his own crime hidden, blanked out by a clean, well-lighted space and enthusiastic support for a new regime. Here, the courtiers' applause sounds mechanical, and as they close in around Fortinbras—perhaps the most concentrated massing of bodies this performance has staged—neither their responses nor the patness of Fortinbras's language seem adequate, and nothing suggests that this regime change introduces either a new story or a newly lit space. As Ros puts it in Stoppard's play, "That's it, then, is it? . . . What was it all about? When did it begin?"[68] At its close, this *Hamlet* has little to say: there is only the sense that the near-infinite stage space has contracted and that Hamlet's—and *Hamlet*'s—great reckonings are now indeed confined to the size of a little room, seen by fading light.

Coda

> To experience this Now on many levels, coming from
> Previously and
> Merging into Afterwards, also having much else now
> Alongside it.
> —Bertolt Brecht, "Portrayal of Past and Present in One"[69]

In part, these case studies, which point to how visual technologies of space and light carry value, respond to Worthen's call to "recognize the contingent relationship between Shakespearean drama and other kinds of performance with which it shares the stage."[70] That both stagings take place "in between" the spaces mapped by Shakespeare, Brecht, and Beckett points to the porous boundaries which mark theatrical thinking. What seems to be happening in these performances—and others, such as Declan Donnellan's *As You Like It* (1995) and Sam Mendes's recent *Twelfth Night* (2002)—is that a kind of time accelerator has occurred, so that echoes of Brecht and Beckett appear in highly condensed form, especially within the visual regimes of Shakespearean performances. I have called them echoes, yet it perhaps might be more precise to say that these collisions and exchanges effect a creolizing process, a theatrical coloniality, constituitive of modernity, a process through which "the other"—whether marked as Brecht or Beckett—not only becomes naturalized to the colonizer's mandates of (theatrical) power but enables playing Shakespeare back— and forward—through a high modernist present. Somewhat ironically, inoculating Shakespeare with touches of Brecht and Beckett in the night may offer a hedge against what some mainstream as well as academic critics have feared, the (re)immersion of Shakespeare into mass culture, subject to the whims and appetites of a commodity-driven marketplace where anything goes and where, according to critics such as Kate McLuskie, the plays become empty vessels, "stripped . . . of [their] textual specificity and historical particularity."[71] Yet grafting Shakespeare's plays to theatrical technologies of space, lighting, and acting resonant of and with a modernist aesthetic does not eradicate their previous nature, nor does it assault the form itself or change its individual syntactic, semantic, and pragmatic rules.[72] Rather, as Hamlet's metaphor suggests, inoculating the old stock makes its old virtues more visible by enabling a rediscovery of spatial and specular dynamics that shed new light on past stagecraft and conventions that might not be out of place at Shakespeare's Globe.

Notes

1. Peter Brook, *The Empty Space* (Harmondsworth, U.K.: Penguin, 1968), 96.

2. Hall's comment, spoken after a performance in 1976, is quoted in Rosemary Pountney, *Theatre of Shadows: Samuel Beckett's Drama 1956-76* (Gerrards Cross, U.K.: Colin Smythe, 1988), 163.

3. See W. B. Worthen, *Shakespeare and the Force of Modern Performance* (Cambridge: Cambridge University Press, 2003).

4. I draw here from Henri Lefebvre, *The Production of Space,* trans. Donald Nicholson-Smith (Oxford: Blackwell, 1991), 93-94.

5. See Peter Holland, "Space: The Final Frontier," in *The Play Out of Context: Transferring Plays from Culture to Culture,* ed. Hanna Scolnicov and Peter Holland (Cambridge: Cambridge University Press, 1989), 45-62. For an audiovisual database of theatrical design which includes VRML models of key theater spaces and covers all professional productions of Shakespeare in Stratford and London between 1960 and 2000, see http://www.pads.ahds.ac.uk.

6. See Barbara Hodgdon, "Absent Bodies, Present Voices: Performance Work and the Close of *Romeo and Juliet*'s Golden Story," *Theatre Journal* 41, no. 3 (October 1989): 349. Beckett wrote the first page of *Waiting for Godot* on October 9, 1948, the last on January 29, 1949—see David Bradby, *Waiting for Godot: Plays in Production* (Cambridge: Cambridge University Press, 2001), 15. The play was staged first on January 5, 1953, in Paris and appeared two years later (August 3, 1955) in London, directed by Peter Hall.

7. Samuel Beckett, *Happy Days* (London: Faber and Faber, 1963), 9,11. See Peter Brook, *The Shifting Point: Theatre, Film, Opera 1946-1987* (New York: Harper and Row, 1987), 89; see also Dennis Kennedy, *Looking at Shakespeare: A Visual History of Twentieth-Century Performance,* 2d ed. (Cambridge: Cambridge University Press, 2001), 171-75; see also Charles Marowitz, "Lear Log," *Tulane Drama Review* 8, no. 2 (Winter 1963): 6-22.

8. For the notion of habitus, see Pierre Bourdieu, *Language and Symbolic Power,* ed. John B. Thompson, trans. Gino Raymond and Matthew Adamson (Cambridge, Mass.: Harvard University Press, 1991).

9. Stanton B. Garner Jr., *Bodied Spaces: Phenomenology and Performance in Contemporary Drama* (Ithaca, N.Y.: Cornell University Press, 1994), 57; Brook, *Shifting Point,* 42.

Appia put the actor at the top of the scenic hierarchy, followed, in order, by space, its three dimensions put at the service of the actor's plastic form; light, which articulates the performance image; and, a distant fourth, painting.

10. See Worthen, *Shakespeare and the Force of Modern Performance*, 29. Worthen writes of the illusion that the Globe's framing structure itself, and thus performances within it, will "release the behaviors that originally made the plays 'work' from their captivity in the text" and so "reclaim the original theatrical force of a playwright's writing."

11. See W. B. Worthen, *Modern Drama and the Rhetoric of Theater* (Berkeley and Los Angeles: University of California Press, 1992), 10.

12. Bradby, *Waiting for Godot*, 209.

13. See James Clifford, "Introduction: Partial Truths," in *Writing Culture: The Poetics and Politics of Ethnography*, ed. James Clifford and George E. Marcus (Berkeley and Los Angeles: University of California Press, 1986), 11-12.

14. I draw here from Herbert Blau, *The Dubious Spectacle: Extremities of Theater, 1976-2000* (Minneapolis: University of Minnesota Press, 2002), 295, 318-19.

15. I borrow the last phrase from Tim Etchells, *Certain Fragments: Contemporary Performance and Forced Entertainment* (London: Routledge, 1999), 22-23.

16. Cited in Susan Buck-Morss, *The Dialectics of Seeing: Walter Benjamin and the Arcades Project* (Cambridge, Mass.: MIT Press, 1991), 220, 73.

17. Although *Dream*'s white box has been repeatedly hailed as innovative, its heritage goes back to Christopher Morley's design for William Gaskill's 1966 *Macbeth* at the Royal Court, which featured an empty white box covered in sandpaper. Brook simply removed the sandpaper. "The set," writes Brook, "is the geometry of the eventual play, so that a wrong set makes many scenes impossible to play, and even destroys many possibilities for the actors" (*Empty Space*, 113).

18. Sam West, "Richard II," *Players of Shakespeare 6*, ed. Robert Smallwood (Cambridge: Cambridge University Press, forthcoming). My thanks to Robert Smallwood for sending me West's text before its publication. Half of West's narrative is concerned with the genesis of theatrical choices, intimate knowledge that is rarely available to outsiders except as isolated anecdote.

19. See "Questions of Leadership: Sam West talks to Paul Williams," *Plays International* (March 2000): 10-11.

20. Harry Berger Jr., unpublished (at this writing) excerpts, additions to his essays on *Richard II* in *Making Trifles of Terrors: Redistributing Complicities in Shakespeare* (Stanford, Calif.: Stanford University Press, 1997). My thanks to Berger for sharing these excerpts. In a conversation with Sam West, he indicated that neither he nor Pimlott had read Berger's essay. For another perspective on this prologue, see Alan Dessen, *Rescripting Shakespeare: The Text, the Director, and Modern Productions* (Cambridge: Cambridge University Press, 2002), 83-85.

21. Bridget Escolme, *Talking to the Audience: Shakespeare, Performance, Self* (London and New York: Routledge, forthcoming). My thanks to Escolme for permission to cite her work in manuscript.

22. Citations to Shakespeare are from *The Norton Shakespeare*, ed. Stephen Greenblatt, Walter Cohen, Jean E. Howard, and Katharine Eisaman Maus (New York and London: W.W. Norton, 1997).

23. See Stage Manager's Reports, February 2, 2000. Records at the Shakespeare Centre Library, Stratford-upon-Avon.

24. Stage Manager's Show Reports, May 18, 2000, and May 1, 2000. Records at the Shakespeare Centre Library, Stratford-upon-Avon.

25. Gay McAuley, *Space in Performance: Making Meaning in the Theatre* (Ann Arbor: University of Michigan Press, 1999), 110; Escolme, *Talking to the Audience.*

26. My thanks to Peter Holland for this information.

27. Samuel Beckett, *Collected Shorter Plays* (London: Faber and Faber, 1984), 158.

28. See Escolme, *Talking to the Audience.* Escolme also mentions this point, remarking that "the presence chamber of the theatre offers the queen a voice that the king's fictional presence chamber cannot permit her."

29. Anne Ubersfeld, cited in McAuley, *Space in Performance,* 18.

30. Michael Redgrave, speaking of Gielgud's 1937 *Richard II* and quoted in Gyles Brandreth, *John Gielgud: A Celebration* (Boston: Little Brown, 1984), 68.

31. Charles Spencer, review of *Richard II, Daily Telegraph* [London], March 31, 2000; reprinted in *Theatre Record* 20, no. 7 (2000): 432.

32. Review of *Richard II, Times* [London], September 7, 1937; reprinted in John Gielgud with John Miller, *Acting Shakespeare* (1991; reprint, London: Pan Books, 1997): "[A]ll his playing is a movement towards this climax, and, after the fall, a spiritual search beyond it. . . . [T]he growth of the man in his despair of this world is felt to be a real growth" (118-19).

33. See the following reviews of *Richard II:* John Peter, *Sunday Times,* April 9, 2000; Robert Butler, *Independent on Sunday,* April 2, 2000; and John Gross, *Sunday Telegraph,* April 2, 2000; all reprinted in *Theatre Record* 20, no. 7 (2000): 434-35.

34. Alastair Macaulay, review of *Richard II,* London *Financial Times,* March 31, 2000, reprinted in *Theatre Record* 20, no.7 (2000): 433.

35. Blau, *Dubious Spectacle,* 302.

36. Herbert Blau, *To All Appearances: Ideology and Performance* (New York and London: Routledge, 1992), 81.

37. At some performances, including the production's press night, Troughton spoke the opening lines of *1 Henry IV,* "So shaken as we are, so wan with care"; at any one performance, the choice of whether to echo Richard, bookending the play with his lines, or to point forward to the next "installment" was left up to the actor. Stage Manager's Show Reports note several variations: on May 5, 2000, "Coat off, hang on throne, sit on coffin facing front. Speech goes to 'I'll hammer it out.' No crown." And on May 15, 2000: "Another new ending for Mr. Troughton, incorporating most of the others—jacket off, sitting on coffin, 'I have been studying,' then getting up, putting the crown on, sitting on the throne and doing the scream." The prompt copy records two other possibilities: after Exton's transposed lines, Bolingbroke speaks, "Lords, I protest my soul is full of woe . . . / In weeping after this untimely bier" (5.6.45-52) and then screams; alternatively (although light prompt copy markings suggest that this ending may have been rehearsed but not played), Bolingbroke follows Exton's transposition with "In winter's tedious nights sit by the fire . . . / Tell thou the lamentable tale of me" (5.1.40-44), Richard's response to his queen on the way to the Tower. Prompt Copy Ref. No. RSC/SM/1/2000.R123, at the Shakespeare Centre Library, Stratford-upon-Avon.

38. Escolme, *Talking to the Audience.*

39. Samuel Beckett, *Waiting for Godot* (New York: Grove Press, 1954), 61.

40. Michel Foucault, "The Eye of Power," in *Power / Knowledge: Selected Interviews and Other Writings 1972-1977*, ed. and trans. Colin Gordon (New York: Pantheon Books, 1980), 149.

41. Tom Stoppard, *Rosencrantz & Guildenstern Are Dead* (New York: Grove Press, 1967), 41.

42. My thanks to Peter Holland for this information.

43. John Osborne, *The Entertainer,* no. 7 (London: Faber and Faber Ltd., 1957), 59. For the ongoing debate over physical space and spaces at the RSC, both in Stratford and London, see Miriam Gilbert, "The Leasing Out of the RSC," *Shakespeare Quarterly* 53, no. 4 (Winter 2002): 512-24.

44. John Willis, *The Art of Memory* (London: W. Jones, 1621). Imagine a mental theater, writes Willis, "wide open to our view," with a stage "one yard high above the level of the ground whereon we stand" (3): "Such a fashioned Repositorie are we to prefix before the eyes of our mind, as often as we intend to commit things to memory, supposing ourselves to be right against the midst thereof, and in the distance of two yards there from" (8). See also Frances Yates, *The Art of Memory* (Chicago: University of Chicago Press, 1966).

45. See the following reviews of *Hamlet* by William Shakespeare: John Peter, Sunday *Times* [London], May 6, 2001; Charles Spencer, *Daily Telegraph,* May 4, 2001; Michael Billington, *Guardian,* May 4, 2001; John Gross, *Sunday Telegraph,* May 6, 2001; Michael Coveney, *Daily Mail,* May 4, 2001; all reprinted in *Theatre Record* 21, no. 9 (2001): 567-71.

46. Stoppard, *Rosencrantz & Guildenstern,* 11 (opening stage direction).

47. Patrick Carnegy, review of *Hamlet,* London, *Spectator,* May 12, 2001; reprinted in *Theatre Record* 21, no. 9 (2001): 572.

48. Susannah Clapp, review of *Hamlet,* London, *Observer,* May 6, 2001; reprinted in *Theatre Record* 21, no. 9 (2001): 568.

49. Nicholas de Jongh, review of *Hamlet,* London, *Evening Standard,* March 5, 2001; reprinted in *Theatre Record* 21, no. 9 (2001): 567-68.

50. See Sally Beauman, *The Royal Shakespeare Company: A History of Ten Decades* (Oxford: Oxford University Press, 1982), 113. "On a clear day," commented Baliol Holloway in 1934, "You can just about see the boiled shirts in the first row. It is like acting to Calais from the cliffs of Dover."

51. See, for instance, Paolo Cherchi Usai, *Silent Cinema: An Introduction* (London: BFI, 2000), 23-27.

52. I draw here from Erika Fischer-Lichte, *The Show and the Gaze of Theatre: A European Perspective* (Iowa City: University of Iowa Press, 1997), 120-21, 139. Borrowings from Asian theater seem, these days, de rigueur—one more indicator of a theatrical nomadism that crosses global borders, networking and interconnecting disconnected moments of communication and practices.

53. My thanks to Carol Rutter for this phrase.

54. See Maarten van Dijk, "Blocking Brecht," in *Re-interpreting Brecht: His Influence on Contemporary Drama and Film,* ed. Pia Kleber and Colin Visser (Cambridge: Cambridge University Press, 1990), 123-24.

55. See Michel de Certeau, *Heterologies: Discourse on the Other,* trans. Brian Massumi (Minneapolis: University of Minnesota Press, 1986), 196. The distinction between perfor-

mance and reading, of course, is a perennial feature of review discourse, where critics measure what a particular staging does over and against their own mental performance.

56. On the key scene, key phrase technique, see, for example, William Uricchio and Roberta E. Pearson, *Reframing Culture: The Case of the Vitagraph Quality Films* (Princeton, N.J.: Princeton University Press, 1993), esp. 87–95.

57. For more on the semiotics of the program and on theatrical stills, see Barbara Hodgdon, "Photography, Theater, Mnemonics; or, Thirteen Ways of Looking at a Still," in *Redefining Theatre History: Theorizing Practice*, ed. W. B. Worthen and Peter Holland (Houndmills, U.K., and New York: Palgrave, 2004).

58. Cited in Margaret Croyden, *Conversations with Peter Brook 1970–2000* (London: Faber and Faber, 2003), 255.

59. Brook, quoted in Croyden, *Conversations*, 258.

60. Billington, review of *Hamlet*, 569.

61. Clapp, review of *Hamlet*, 568.

62. Coveney, review of *Hamlet*, 567.

63. Van Dijk, "Blocking Brecht," 128.

64. On media allegory, see Peter S. Donaldson, " 'All Which It Inherit': Shakespeare, Globes and Global Media," *Shakespeare Survey* 52 (1999): 183–200. See also Katherine Rowe, " 'Remember Me': Technologies of Memory in Michael Almereyda's *Hamlet*," in *Shakespeare the Movie II*, ed. Richard Burt and Lynda E. Boose (London and New York: Routledge, 2003), 37–55.

65. Benedict Nightingale, review of *Hamlet*, London, *Evening Standard*, May 4, 2001; reprinted in *Theatre Record* 21, no. 9 (2001): 571.

66. Stoppard, *Rosencrantz & Guildenstern*, 84.

67. Michael Dobson, "Shakespeare Performances in England, 2001," *Shakespeare Survey* 55 (2002): 299.

68. Stoppard, *Rosencrantz & Guildenstern*, 125.

69. Bertolt Brecht, "Portrayal of Past and Present in One," in *Poems 1913–1956*, ed. John Willett and Ralph Manheim, with Erich Fried (New York and London: Methuen, 1976), 307–8.

70. W. B. Worthen, "Shakespearean Performativity," in *Shakespeare and Modern Theatre: The Performance of Modernity*, ed. Michael Bristol and Kathleen McLuskie, with Christopher Holmes (London and New York: Routledge, 2001), 133.

71. Kathleen McLuskie, "Shakespeare and the Millennial Market: The Commercial Bard," *Renaissance Drama* n.s. 30 (1999–2001): 170.

72. I draw here from Fischer-Lichte, *Show and Gaze of Theatre*, 156.

Reading Occasions

STEPHEN ORGEL

I BEGIN WITH a printed piece of frozen pageantry. In 1579, the famous work we call Saxton's *Atlas* was published, adorned with a splendid portrait of Queen Elizabeth (see figure 1). It contained maps of all the counties of England and Wales and was a landmark in a number of ways. It was not only the first attempt at a comprehensive mapping of Britain; it was also the first national atlas ever undertaken anywhere. It was scientific, based on refined surveying techniques that had only recently been introduced into general practice, and consequently its maps are extraordinarily accurate. It served, indeed, as the basis for all English county maps until the end of the next century.

Saxton did not call his book an atlas. That term for a collection of maps was first used for Mercator's atlas of the world, published in 1595: *Atlas, or Cosmographical Meditations on the Structure of the World and its Image as Constructed.* Not only was Saxton's book not an "atlas," it had no title at all—it is not even clear that, until the project was well under way, he even thought of it as a book. And having no title, it also had no title-page. The volume instead was issued with three leaves of introductory matter: the frontispiece, an index of the maps to be found within, followed by a chart of noble and governmental coats of arms—the symbology of the nation's ruling elite—facing a list of the cities and towns named on the maps. The third of these leaves was not included in the book until 1589, ten years after the original edition.

31

FIGURE 1. Frontispiece to Saxton's *Atlas of England and Wales, 1579.*
Reproduced by permission of the Folger Shakespeare Library.

The frontispiece engraving is unsigned, but it can be ascribed on stylistic grounds to Remigius Hogenberg, who also engraved a number of the maps. It shows Queen Elizabeth in a complex architectural façade combining elements of the triumphal arch and the pageant stage. The technical term for this structure is "pegma"; the word literally means "structure," and it was used for both the stages on which allegorical tableaux were presented and the analogous emblems and impresas that were increasingly popular throughout the age. In a large central niche, the queen is enthroned between two heroic male figures: Astronomy, left, holding a celestial sphere; and Geography, right, with a terrestrial globe and compass. On the plinths below them are the female figures of Fortitude with her column, on the left, and Prudence with a serpent and looking glass, on the right. Tudor roses adorn the outer sides of the molding. On the throne itself, lions sit at the front bearing shields with the initials *E/R,* and atop the chairback, two male figures in classical armor stand guard. In a cartouche in the middle, Peace, naked, with an olive branch, embraces Justice, clothed, with a breastplate and carrying a sword; behind Justice, Cupid or a putto carries a set of scales. Above these, two putti carry wreaths, and the royal arms appear in the center, supported by the crowned lion of England and griffin of Wales. Below the whole composition, within cartouches, a Latin poem praises Elizabeth's "true faith" and freedom from the "blind error" that afflicts the warring nations on the Continent. On either side of this poem are two more personifications of geography and astronomy: on the left, a cartographer draws a map of England; on the right, an astronomer observes a comet with a cruciform sighting instrument.

There is, as I say, no title page to Saxton's volume, and no title, only this speaking picture declaring the queen the central symbolic figure in the work. Indeed, she fills not only the space normally occupied by the title but the space of author, artist, and engraver as well—Saxton's name appears nowhere, just as the elaborate and beautiful plate is unsigned. Whose atlas is this, then? Richard Helgerson has shrewdly anatomized the changing sense of proprietorship surrounding this monumental work.[1] In fact, Saxton's name does appear, marginally, on all the maps—"Christophorus Saxton descripsit"—but in all but ten cases, that is, in twenty-four out of the total of thirty-four, it was an afterthought, added to maps that had originally been issued without it. The earliest references to the work in progress, by Raphael Holinshed and William Harrison in 1577, refer to the maps not as Saxton's but as Thomas Seckford's. Seckford was Queen Elizabeth's Master of Requests; he was a lawyer and, in various capacities, a civil servant. It was he who employed Saxton, a surveyor, to map the counties of England and Wales; he paid Saxton's expenses and a salary, and the completed maps belonged to him, and thus they all display his arms and motto. To refer to the atlas as Seckford's, therefore, is entirely appropriate within the Renaissance patronage system—no more anomalous than referring, as we still do, to the Sistine Chapel and the Teatro Olimpico rather than the Michelangelo Chapel and the Teatro Palladiano.

But in 1574, both Saxton and Seckford obtained another patron. The queen granted Saxton a lease of royal lands in Suffolk in consideration of his expenses sustained in his survey. From that time on, all the maps bore, in addition to Seckford's shield, the royal arms. Other monetary grants came from the Crown in the following year, and in 1576, the queen's interest was manifested in a more immediately practical way: a royal order commanded all persons of authority in Wales to assist Saxton in his survey and specifically "to see him conducted unto any tower, castle, high place or hill to view that country," to see that he was attended "by two or three honest men that knew the country," and was conducted between towns by a horseman who spoke Welsh and English.

But the most important royal grant came in 1577, when Saxton was given a monopoly on the publication and sale of his own maps for a period of ten years. This grant did more than assure the recovery of his and Seckford's expenses; it gave Saxton complete control over the production and dissemination of his work—the book was now legally his alone. By 1595, Abraham Ortelius, acknowledging his indebtedness to a distinguished predecessor, refers to the maps as Saxton's. And in 1579, the year the volume was published, the royal patron elevated the surveyor to the gentry, granting him a coat of arms. The grant explicitly appropriates to the queen the sole patronage of the cartographer, "who by special direction and commandment from the queen's majesty hath endeavored to make a perfect geographical description of the . . . realm." Seckford disappears; his servant has become the queen's gentleman.

The frontispiece, therefore, representing Queen Elizabeth as patron of cosmography, is an emblem both of the royal will and of a large financial investment on the part of the Crown. It is important to observe that this splendid engraving does not simply constitute a dedication, a bid for patronage of the sort that Spenser solicits for himself by offering *The Faerie Queene* to Elizabeth, on the verso of its 1596 title page, "to live with the eternity of her fame," the poet riding to immortality, so to speak, on the royal coattails. Saxton's frontispiece is not a dedication at all; it shows, on the contrary, Elizabeth taking control of the book of England and expresses, in the fullest sense, the Crown's image of itself. A. B. Hind cites good evidence that she was actively involved in the design of the frontispiece.[2] That is why it is significant that the preliminary leaf with the armorial bearings of the county aristocracy was not included until 1589 and was not part of the original plan. The work asserted that the land was the queen's.

What are the subtexts and implications of this imagery? Certainly the Crown had a vested interest in subsidizing an accurate survey of the realm. A Crown surveyor had been on the royal payroll since 1515, and after the dissolution of the monasteries in 1535, the importance of the office greatly increased. Mapmaking now in the most direct way enabled the monarch's authority. Helgerson shows how Elizabeth too used Saxton's cartography as an instrument of policy, asserting her political authority over a realm that was still deeply imbued with feudal and prenational assumptions. That may help explain a curious fact about Saxton's maps, one that has received very little attention: although they were employed by court officials (e.g., by Burleigh, a principal subscriber) to provide a detailed knowledge of the country, and especially of the location of its great estates, the maps are in fact relatively impractical, in the sense that though they show both topographical and a variety of man-made features—great houses, castles, parks, and the like—they include no administrative units smaller than the counties (the hundreds are not indicated), and more significantly, they do not show roads. Hind is puzzled by this lack of detail and suggests that it "probably reflects the undeveloped state of the country," but that claim is nonsense.[3] English maps had indicated roads for centuries, and Charles Bricker writes of the early fourteenth-century Gough map of Britain that its "road distances and land configurations were so accurate that they set a standard unsurpassed until the late 16th-century"[4]—until, that is, fourteen years after Saxton's atlas, when John Norden included roads in his *Speculum Britanniae,* the next atlas of Britain, published in 1593. Printed maps of England regularly included roads thereafter. The roads were finally added to Saxton's maps in the 1640s, during the civil war, to enable their use by rebellious armies contesting their original creator's royalist bias.

Elizabeth's pegma, then, was addressed to a small and specific audience, with the queen herself at its center, as she was the center of the national spectacle. But, as the addition of the prefatory armorial bearings and of the roads to Saxton's maps imply, audiences have their own purposes. Theater is a two-way affair, action and reaction. In the case of festival modes, especially when the pegma takes life, the interaction with the audience (or more properly, with the several different audiences such shows address) is far more complex, essential—and palpable—than it is in the case of books or even of drama in performance. The difference between Queen Elizabeth's enthusiastic and carefully crafted response to the pageantry that celebrated her accession and James's delayed, reserved, and grudging one to his is notorious, and in both cases the response itself is performative, part of a show for the much larger audience of spectators who line the route. It is also, probably more significantly, a performance for the audience that foots the bill—in the case of civic pageantry, the guilds, city fathers, Inns of Court, or private magnates, for whom the production is an investment; and the responses of both the chief actor-spectator and the civic audience should be considered in that context, as the return on the investment.

When King James balked at participating in London's pageant celebrating his accession, both the refusal and the response to it were matters of public policy, and the whole project could not simply be abandoned. The entry had originally been planned for July 1603 to coincide with his coronation. But the plague was raging, and the entry was repeatedly postponed—so long that the seven triumphal arches, which had been erected along the route at great expense, had to be dismantled and stored. James finally consented to submit to what he made clear he considered an ordeal in March 1604. Arthur Wilson recalled the occasion half a century later:

The King, with the Queen and Prince . . . rode from the Tower to Whitehall; the City and Suburbs being one great Pageant, wherein he must give his ears leave to suck in their gilded Oratory, though never so nauseious to the stomach. He was not like his Predecessor, the late Queen of famous memory, that with a wel-pleased affection met her peoples Acclamations. . . . He endured this days brunt with patience, being assured he should never have such another.[5]

James hated and feared crowds, and he had no talent for manipulating them. His biographer, David Harris Willson, quotes a visitor to the court who reported that "the King . . . would swear with passion, asking his attendants what the people would have. He was told they came of love to see him. 'Then would he cry out in Scottish, "God's wounds! I will pull down my breeches and they shall also see my arse." ' "[6]

It is clear why it was important for the City to put on this show, a public declaration on the one hand of allegiance and support and on the other of the royal dependence on the commercial and financial powers of the kingdom. But when the king resisted, what was in it for the City and the guilds to force him to give the performance, as he eventually did with very bad grace? Obviously this performance was not for the king's benefit; the king became, unwillingly, an actor in a larger drama presented by the City, the central element of which was precisely the City's ability to produce the king as a participant in the pageantry. The show was ultimately less a celebration than a show of force.

Festivals, pageants, and masques are probably a better index to the complex nature of Renaissance theater than drama is. Understanding these social and celebratory forms requires us to take seriously not only plot, character, style, and the constraints and economics of the theater business but also the often arcane but nevertheless ubiquitous forms of Renaissance philosophy and symbolism, the demands of patronage, the nature of artistic collaboration, and most important, the presence of an active and specific audience. Dealing with celebratory works only through the surviving speeches and descriptions, moreover, constantly reminds us of how much in these quintessentially Renaissance forms—and by implication in all artistic forms of the period—is lost to us: spectacle, music, choreography, complex symbolism; most of all, the participation of identifiable patrons and performers who also constitute, in a real sense, what is being cele-brated.

The most elaborate and highly developed of these entertainments was the court masque; and the masque was, in a sense, what much of Renais-sance art was all about. It was more of a game than a show, an expression of aristocratic identity and privilege, with the masks providing a degree of freedom, even if only notional, from the constraints of place, office, and self. We inevitably approach such works through their texts. But the texts tell us far too little—for the most part, they are concerned with intentions, purposes, and meanings. They rarely tell us about the social and political contexts, which are generally what we have wanted to use them as evidence for; and they are especially unforthcoming in cases where things went wrong, which for my purposes are the most interesting cases. Campion is almost alone in acknowledging failure—in this case the failure of the scenic machinery in *Lord Hay's Masque,* "either by the simplicity, negligence, or conspiracy of the painter," as he puts it, thereby exculpating himself, but at the same time acknowledging how little control the text has over the performance.[7] Our evidence in such instances is almost invariably the evidence of report and gossip, which is characteristically more interested in performance than intention, performers than scripts, audiences than performers.

Sir John Harington's satiric account of the masque of Solomon and the Queen of Sheba, devised for the entertainment of James and Christian IV on their visit to the Earl of Salisbury at Theobalds in 1606, is a case in point. It has become a touchstone for the indecorum of the Jacobean court, and since the text of the masque does not survive, Harington's letter has in effect become the masque. I am quoting rather more of the account here than usual, since I want to focus on some things that are generally overlooked:

After dinner the representation of Solomon his temple and the coming of the Queen of Sheba was made, or (as I may better say) was meant to have been made, before their majesties, by device of the Earl of Salisbury and others [note that credit for the "device" belongs to the patrons, not the poet and architect]. But, alas! . . . The lady who did play the Queene's part did carry most precious gifts to both their majesties; but forgetting the steps arising to the canopy, overset her casket into his Danish majesty's lap, and fell at his feet, though I rather think it was in his face. Much was the hurry and confusion. Cloths and napkins were at hand, to make all clean. His majesty then got up, and would dance with the Queen of Sheba; but he fell down and humbled himself before her, and was carried to an inner chamber and laid on a bed of state; which was not a little defiled with the presents of the queen which had been bestowed on his garments; such as wine, cream, jelly, beverage, cakes, spices, and other good matters.

The account continues to tell how most of the speakers bungled their parts through incompetence or drunkenness. King James, moreover—this is worth stressing—was decidedly uncooperative:

Victory, in bright armor . . . presented a rich sword to the King, who did not accept it, but put it by with his hand; and . . . did endeavor to make suit to the king . . . but after much lamentable utterance, she was led away like a silly captive and laid to sleep in the outer steps of the anti-chamber.

Harington concludes that "I never did see such lack of good order, discretion and sobriety as I have now done."[8]

This is all that survives of a masque embodying King James's most deeply felt persona, the Solomonic monarch, and the only masque recorded from his reign on a biblical subject. He could not have been ignorant of the text. Why did the king refuse the sword of Victory?—he must have known it was to be presented. Was he, like Harington, simply so offended by the indecorum that he withdrew from the game? Or was there a deeper meaning that Harington missed, the pacifist king refusing the martial image—was this even perhaps part of the show? Even in masques where nothing goes wrong, what spectators see often differs significantly from what inventors intend.

Jonson's, Daniel's, and Campion's texts describe—or prescribe—a court that moves in perfect order, like the movement of the spheres. Andrew Sabol, who has done more than anyone to rescue the ephemeral music of this most ephemeral form, says of the dances that in them "the masquers function always as an identically accoutred group, moving simultaneously in sober splendor."[9] I cite this not because it seems to me egregiously incorrect (though it does), but because it remains so completely within the terms provided by the poets' texts. If we look beyond the texts, we get quite a different picture. From Inigo Jones's costume designs and his annotations to them we learn how much freedom the royal and noble participants in these supreme assertions of aristocratic community and independence had in presenting themselves. Jones made the costume designs, but he was an employee, working to order, paid not to dictate but to realize the intentions of his employers. The costumes were the property of the ladies and gentlemen masquers, made for them by their own dressmakers and tailors, or in some cases provided by the Crown. They were based on Jones's designs, but the aristocratic masquers felt free to adapt the final outfits to their own taste. A startling piece of evidence is preserved in the material relating to Jonson's *Hymenaei*. Jonson describes the ladies' garments in detail: the masquers were to be identically dressed, in a very elaborate costume with a richly embroidered double skirt. Now it happens that three ladies who danced in the masque had their portraits painted in costume. Two accord closely with Jonson's description; the third lady, however—Lucy Countess of Bedford—wears not a double but a single skirt. That was how this noble masquer preferred to appear.[10]

Here is another example of aristocratic independence: when at the performance of Jonson's *Love Restored* on Twelfth Night 1612, the lords went to take out the ladies to dance the revels, John Chamberlain reports, "beginning [with the ladies] of Essex and Cranbourne, they were refused, [which set an] example to the rest, so that [the lords] were fain to dance alone and make court to one another."[11] The only way we know about what must have been a real fiasco is from Chamberlain's letter: Jonson is understandably silent about it. Gossip here is of the essence. At this remove, it is very difficult to know what the problem was. The Countess of Essex (who was not yet the notorious divorcée) and Viscountess Cranbourne were sisters, Frances and Catherine Howard, daughters of the Earl of Suffolk—stars of James's court, daughters of a powerful and very influential peer. Suffolk apparently was embarrassed by their behavior, but since the rest of the ladies followed their lead, the problem they perceived cannot have been theirs alone. Martin Butler has suggested to me, plausibly, that the lords, most of whom were Scots, were seen by the Howard ladies as upstarts and insufficiently aristocratic, and if this is correct, the incident gives us a good insight into the limits of protocol and the extent of courtly privilege and independence at such events. But this cannot be the whole story: What happens when the audience refuses to play its part? The work was jointly sponsored by the king and Prince Henry, and the Scottish masquers were members of their households, so the ladies were offending not merely the déclassé lords but their royal patrons as well. One can imagine circumstances in which such behavior would have been considered deeply disruptive, even perhaps treasonable—like Cordelia's behavior at the opening of *Lear*—but if we understand Chamberlain correctly (the letter is not entirely legible), all the apologies were directed at the mortified parent, Suffolk; Chamberlain says nothing about the reaction of the king and prince. In short, the implications of this affair seem more private than public. And yet, the whole point of the masque— any masque—was precisely that public assertion of aristocratic solidarity: everybody joins in the game celebrating the glories of the Crown and court. But even the gossips seem to be silent about what happens when they don't. Is this because nothing happens, or is the lacuna simply in our evidence—or in what we must, perforce, treat as evidence?

A somewhat different kind of example is offered by *Pleasure Reconciled to Virtue*. This looks to us, from the text and designs, like one of Jones's most ingenious scenic inventions, and it includes some of Jonson's best masque poetry. Both poetry and stagecraft, however, were declared unimpressive by those contemporary spectators whose reactions have survived; and indeed, neither poetry nor stagecraft was central to the experience of the original audience—what remains to us of the masque, the text and three drawings, represents only the smallest part of the evening's entertainment. It was the dances that mattered most, especially to King James, the crucial member of the Jacobean audience, who particularly enjoyed watching the revels. On this occasion, the Venetian envoy reported that when the dancing was about to end, the king broke out in a rage, shouting, "What did you make me come here for? Devil take all of you, dance!"; upon which George Villiers, the recently ennobled Marquess of Buckingham, James's current favorite, leaped up and gave an impromptu performance of astonishing virtuosity and thereby restored the king's good humor.[12]

Dancing of one kind or another occupied most of the time a court masque took to perform; a text of fifteen pages or so would normally occupy several hours in production, and the choreography and music were quite as carefully planned as the poetry, costumes, and stagecraft. The masquers themselves rehearsed their choreographed dances for months. Dance in the instance just described, moreover, is not simply a way of pleasing the king; it is more significantly a way of managing him, and for Buckingham in his rise to favor and power, his skill at this courtly accomplishment constituted a potent political talent.

The most compelling and effective element of these entertainments is thus lost to us. While the political aspect of court masques and ballets has been clear for decades, the specifically political content of the dances has only begun to be investigated—here the work of Margaret McGowan and Mark Franko has been particularly enlightening.[13] The relation of dance to text is one that is always in question and sometimes directly adversarial, two theatrical elements that were either in collaboration or conflict but always basically independent of each other. As Franko especially shows, dance has a subversive potential that is only imperfectly restrained by the forms of drama and conventional theater.

Dance is in one sense always subversive in court masques because the text is the monarch's; in courtly forms, as in the country as a whole, royal authority expressed itself through control of the word. But dancing is both nonverbal and an aristocratic prerogative, one of the defining features of the social elite that surrounded the monarch, and it could only partly and intermittently be contained by the royal will. (It is to the point that James did not participate in the dancing.) In this context, Frances and Catherine Howard's refusal to dance and Buckingham's impromptu performance are not flukes but of the essence, assertions of aristocratic independence in the very presence of sovereign authority.

Court masques are invariably topical in some way, though their application is often sufficiently localized so that it is difficult at this distance to discern it. But drama in the period too can be seen as part of the larger spectacle of ceremonial theater, and here the subject of the play is rarely the point, though it is, much too often, assumed to be. Several generations of critics have worked hard to make *The Tempest* an allegory of the Palatine wedding because it was performed at court as part of the festivities preceding that event. But there were fourteen plays performed to entertain the celebrants; if *The Tempest* was selected for its relevance, or revised to make it so, what about the other thirteen? They include *Othello* and *The Maid's Tragedy,* plays that are certainly relevant to marriage, though one would hope they were not chosen for their putative relevance to this particular one. In fact, the point is probably less the relevance of plays than the relevance of theater—the texts, that is, have very little to do with it.

There are cases, of course, where the text has everything to do with it— hence the institution of theatrical censorship in the period. When the Earl of Essex subsidized the Lord Chamberlain's Men for a revival of *Richard II* in 1601, he was banking on the efficacy of a play about the overthrow of a weak and histrionic monarch to energize his own revolutionary performance. This strategy is always treated as a major miscalculation, but it is not clear that this assessment is correct: Londoners did not flock to join him as he marched to Whitehall the next day, but the performance had not been for their benefit. It had been for him and his supporters, to galvanize their resolve. The tragedy was not that it failed but that it worked. And when, some months later, Elizabeth said to William Lambarde, "I am Richard II, know you not that?" and continued, "this tragedy was played forty times in open streets and houses," she articulated how real the power and danger of civic theater was in the age.[14] "Forty times" is no doubt hyperbole (the biblical "forty"?), and the houses are both playhouses and Essex's palace in the Strand. But those open streets constitute a civic fantasy in which the whole city becomes a stage where the monarch is mimed and deposed. Surely this queen imagined the threatening tragedy being performed not at the Globe but in the public streets, because she herself repeatedly took to the streets, in splendid pageantry, to assert and confirm her authority. The city, the realm, was for Elizabeth a theater.

The relevance of the text to the political situation is clear-cut here; and this sort of relevance was always seen as a danger in the period—that is, what was dangerous about theater was precisely the possibility of its relevance. Was a play about Sejanus produced in the first months of King

James's reign not really a play about the new king's favorites? Was the subtext of ancient history not really popery and treason? And even when the mimetic element is not so highly charged, there is, for us, a strong temptation to see in the very fact of a highly theatricalized court and of royal patronage for the stage a key to the playwrights' invention. Our reading of *A Midsummer Night's Dream* has assumed for the past century and a half that it must have been composed to celebrate an aristocratic wedding and that Elizabeth would most probably have been in the audience. This assumption may be correct, but what such a reading occludes is the dark side of the play's marriages, the emphasis on cuckoldry and changes of heart and kinky sexuality—what Oberon wants from his wife is not domestic happiness and a nuclear family but the lovely Indian boy; to punish her for not complying, he engineers his own cuckoldry, putting her to bed with another man who is also an animal. Perhaps most striking in an Elizabethan context is the denial of patriarchal authority in the play, Theseus's overruling of Egeus's right to dispose of his daughter in marriage. And if Elizabeth was in fact in the audience, did she really like the trope of the little western flower, which is transformed into the agent of indiscriminate lust by her own programmatic virginity? Because Elizabeth is protected from Cupid's arrow, rampant libido is set loose in the land; men are unfaithful to their loves and women can be made to lust after animals. Is this all really complimentary and celebratory? Possibly it is, but then compliment and celebration have dark sides that we have failed to take into account.

Similarly, we read *Macbeth* as a royal drama because it is on a Scottish theme and Banquo was James's ancestor. But the play is hardly an obvious candidate for the king's favor: Banquo in the chronicles is an ancestor one would very much rather forget. He is fully in complicity with the murder of Duncan; and in any case his connection with the royal line does not emerge until two centuries later, when a descendant of Banquo's who was a steward in the royal household married into the royal family— hence the family name of Stuart, Scots for "steward." Had James's lineage been the subtext, Shakespeare would have produced a version of *Twelfth Night,* with Malvolio replacing Sebastian. Far from explaining the choice of subject in *Macbeth,* Banquo is a major problem, and Shakespeare had to do a good deal of obfuscating and revising to sanitize him sufficiently to protect the play from charges of sedition and lèse-majesté. What makes the story relevant to James is not Banquo but the witches, a subject on which the king's expertise was an important part of his public persona; and that is, obviously, a very different story.

King James avoided the streets and hated to be on public display, but his sense of the royal situation was the same as Elizabeth's. "A King," he wrote to Prince Henry in *Basilicon Doron,* effectively quoting Elizabeth, "is as one set on a stage, whose smallest actions and gestures, all the people gazingly do behold."[15] A king is an actor in the most public of performances. But this version of the royal advice comes from the second edition of the treatise, published after James ascended the English throne. In the first edition, the sentence reads, "A king is as one set upon a *scaffold.*" The king's emendation of the ambiguous word surely reveals the danger James must have felt to be inherent in the royal drama. It was a danger that was not merely linguistic, and as Charles was to learn, it could not be eliminated through judicious emendation.

Notes

1. Richard Helgerson, "The Land Speaks: Cartography, Chorography, and Subversion in Renaissance England," in *Representing the Renaissance,* ed. Stephen Greenblatt (Berkeley and Los Angeles: University of California Press, 1988), 327–61; see esp. 328ff.

2. A. B. Hind, *Engraving in England in the Sixteenth and Seventeenth Centuries,* vol. 1 (Cambridge: Cambridge University Press, 1952), 73.

3. Ibid., 18.

4. Charles Bricker, *Landmarks of Mapmaking* (Oxford: Phaidon, 1976), 89.

5. Arthur Wilson, *The History of Great Britain, Being the Life and Reign of King Iames the First* (London, 1653), 12–13.

6. David Harris Willson, *King James VI and I* (Oxford: Oxford University Press, 1967), 165.

7. Thomas Campion, *Lord Hay's Masque,* in *The Works of Thomas Campion,* ed. Walter Davis (New York: Doubleday, 1967), 222.

8. John Nichols, *The progresses, processions, and magnificent festivities, of King James the First,* vol. 2 (London, 1828), 72–73.

9. Andrew Sabol, *Four Hundred Songs and Dances from the Stuart Masque* (Providence, R.I.: Brown University Press, 1977), 12.

10. See the relevant paintings in Stephen Orgel and Roy Strong, *Inigo Jones* (London: Sotheby Parke-Bernet; Berkeley and Los Angeles: University of California Press; 1973), 104, 114, figs. 8–10.

11. Norman Egbert McClure, ed., *The Letters of John Chamberlain,* vol. 1 (Philadelphia: American Philosophical Society, 1939), 328. The letter is partly illegible, and the words in brackets are supplied.

12. Orgel and Strong, *Inigo Jones,* 283.

13. See especially Margaret McGowan, *L'art du ballet de cour en France, 1581-1643* (Paris: CNRS, 1963); and Mark Franko, *Dance as Text: Ideologies of the Baroque Body* (Cambridge: Cambridge University Press, 1993).

14. See the account in Peter Ure, ed., *Richard II* (London: Methuen, 1956), lix.

15. Quoted in C. H. McIlwain, ed., *Political Works of James I* (Cambridge, Mass.: Harvard University Press, 1918), 43.

Quid ais Omnium? *Maurice Kyffin's 1588* Andria *and the Emergence of Suspension Marks in Printed Drama*

ANNE HENRY

DAMPLAY: You have heard, Boy, the ancient Poets had it in their purpose still to please the people.
PROBEE: I, their chief aime was—
DAMPLAY: *Populo ut placerent:* (if hee understands so much.)
BOY: *Quas fecissent fabulas.* I understand that sin' I learn'd *Terence,* I' the third forme at *Westminster.*[1]

I N THIS EXCHANGE from the induction to Ben Jonson's *The Magnetick Lady; Or Humors Reconciled,* Damplay disparages modern playwriting for its inferiority to the dramatic compositions of the ancients and assumes that those associated with the theater, such as the boy, are so lacking in learning that they would fail to understand, never mind identify, these few words from Terence. The boy, however, remembers well his lessons from Westminster School and completes Damplay's line as well as providing its source. This brief exchange not only testifies to the centrality of Terence's work to the Renaissance curriculum but also points to Jonson's own experience, as he had been schooled at Westminster. The Latin words in this opening are in turn from a dramatic induction: that is, the prologue to Terence's *Andria,* where Terence complains about the interfering criticisms of his own contemporary Damn-play (a context lost on Jonson's ignorant critic, who, it turns out, has little command of Latin himself).[2] But this exchange also reveals a feature of the printed play text that we might take for granted. Damplay interrupts Probee intending to expose the boy's lack of learning, and in the 1640 *Workes* of Ben Jonson (where this play was first printed), that interruption is marked with a dash. Damplay, no matter how damning of modern plays, thus occasions the use of a still relatively new dramatic symbol that he wouldn't have seen in any Latin book: the suspension mark, or dash.

Suspension marks, or as they come to be known, marks of ellipsis, so

47

fundamental to dramatic writing, have been little explored by historians of punctuation. But it is possible to date the earliest suspension marks in English printed drama to 1588, where they appear in an edition of Terence's *Andria* translated by Maurice Kyffin and printed by Thomas East. There a series of hyphens are used on three occasions to mark an incomplete utterance (see figure 1). In these three examples, the speaker's words remain suspended; the sentence is incomplete due to the interruption of another speaker or, in the second example, because the speaker chooses to interrupt himself. A repeated conversational occurrence is marked consistently with a series of hyphens. The variation in the number of hyphens also reveals careful consideration of the notation as the use of three rules in the first instance, as opposed to four in the second and third, can probably be explained by the concurrent use of an additional point, the question mark. Throughout this essay I will be concentrating on the last of these exchanges (figure 1c) as I examine the emergence of the mark in Kyffin's *Andria* and its adoption and transformation in later dramatic texts. It is from the opening of act 5, scene 3, where Simo calls his son Pamphilus out of the house of his lover, Glycerium, and expresses fury that Pamphilus has deceived him into believing that he would give up Glycerium and marry the daughter of Chremes. The phrase that is curtailed in the Latin is *Quid ais omnium*, translated in the 1912 Loeb edition as follows:

SIMO: Is this credible? Of all the—
CHR. [*interrupting*]: Come now, get to business, don't abuse him.[3]

If readers haven't realized by the punctuation mark alone that Simo hasn't finished what he is saying, the stage direction "[*interrupting*]" provides a further textual signal. But of course when Jonson was at Westminster, or Damplay at his own hypothetical school, the boys would not have had such aids to comprehension when reading their Latin versions of the *Andria*. So how was such an exchange marked in printed Latin works before and during the sixteenth century?

Malcolm Parkes tells us in *Pause and Effect: An Introduction to the History of Punctuation in the West* that in very early printing, three marks of punctuation in particular were used:

The earliest printers reproduced the forms of the marks of punctuation which appeared in the manuscripts used for copy. The punctuation of the *editio princeps* of Augustine's *De civitate Dei* produced by Sweynheim and Pannartz in 1467 (at

OW that I haue made all things in a readines foʒ my daughters marriage, I am come againe that I may caufe her to be fent foʒ . But what haue we here? In good faith it is a childe : woman didʃt thou lay this fame childe here?

lookes af- ✱My. Whether is this fellow gon?
Dauus. Chr. What, wilt thou not aunf were me?
My. Alack he is no where in fight, wo is me (pooʒe wench) the fellow is gon his waies, and left me here.

w Dauus ✱Da. Good Loʒd of heauen, what hurleburley is *s a long.* yonder at the market? how much people is there at ftrife? without it be that coʒne be at a high pʒice, I wot not in the woʒld what to make of it.

My. I pʒay you firra, why did you leaue me here all alone?

Da. How now, what tale is this of a rofted hoʒfe? Nay but heareft thou me Myfis, whofe childe is this? oʒ who bʒought it hether?

My. Art thou well in thy wits, that afkeft me this queftion?

Da. Whom then fhould I afke, feeing here is no body els?

is he faith ✱Chr. I marueil whence it fhould be?
mfelfe. Da. Wilt thou not tell me what I afke?
mes muft My. Ahlas.
ppofed to Da. Come thy way hither on my right hand.
d a loof My. Thou raueft, dydʃt not thou thy felfe? - - -
ing vnto Da. Hufht, be not fo hard foʒ thy eares as to fpeake *e talke* one woʒd moʒe than I fhall afke thee.
eene My. Thou rayleft.
s and , *and yet* Da. Whence is this childe? fpeake out aloud.
ewing My. From among you.
fe vnto

Da.

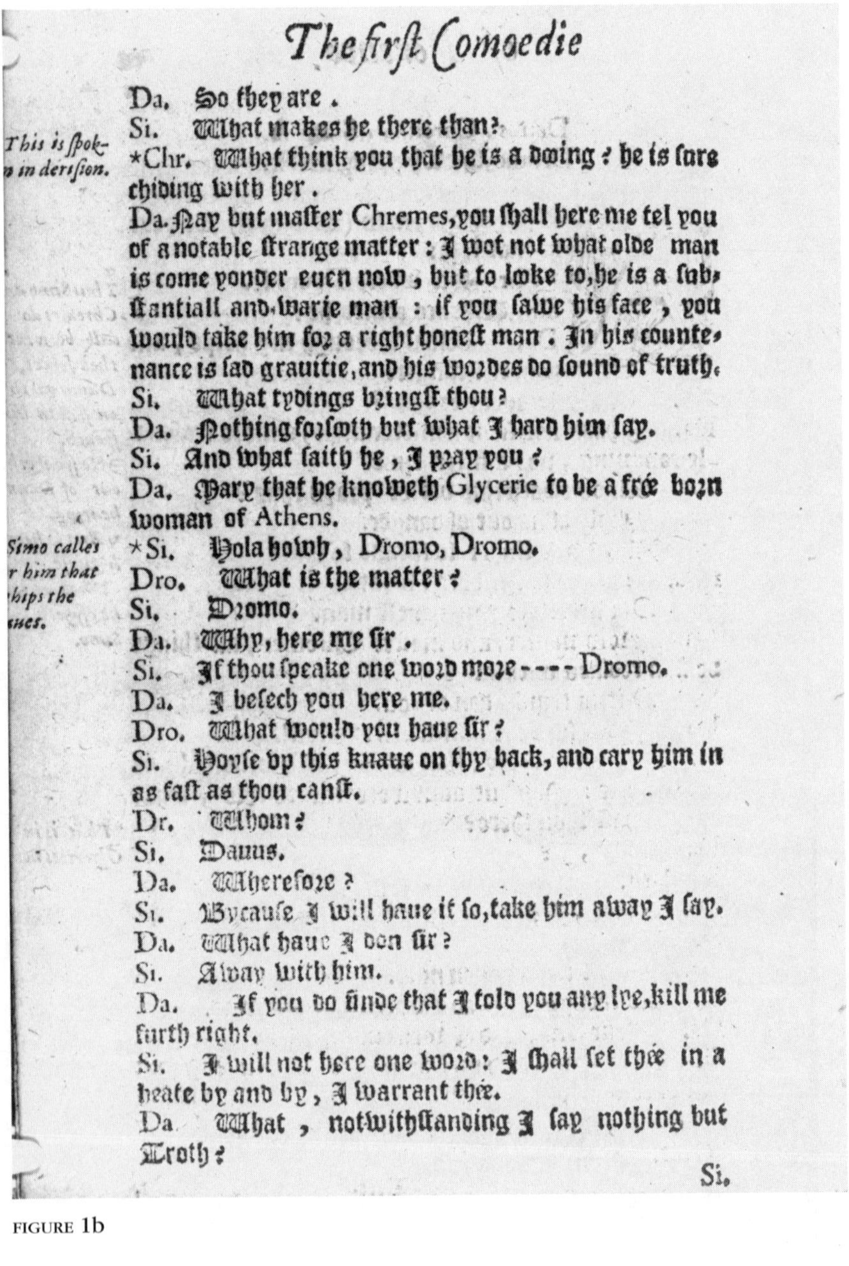

The first Comoedie

This is spok-
n in derision.

Da. So they are .

Si. What makes he there than?

*Chr. What think you that he is a doing ? he is sure
chiding with her .

Da. Nay but maister Chremes, you shall here me tel you
of a notable strange matter : I wot not what olde man
is come yonder euen now , but to loke to, he is a sub-
stantiall and warie man : if you sawe his face , you
would take him for a right honest man . In his countenance is sad grauitie, and his wordes do sound of truth.

Si. What tydings bringst thou ?

Da. Nothing forsooth but what I hard him say.

Si. And what saith he , I pray you ?

Da. Mary that he knoweth Glycerie to be a free born
woman of Athens.

Simo calles
r him that
hips the
nes.

*Si. Hola howh , Dromo, Dromo.

Dro. What is the matter ?

Si. Dromo.

Da. Why, here me sir .

Si. If thou speake one word more ---- Dromo.

Da. I besech you here me.

Dro. What would you haue sir ?

Si. Hoyse vp this knaue on thy back, and cary him in
as fast as thou canst.

Dr. Whom ?

Si. Dauus.

Da. Wherefore ?

Si. Bycause I will haue it so, take him away I say.

Da. What haue I don sir ?

Si. Away with him.

Da. If you do finde that I told you any lye, kill me
furth right.

Si. I will not here one word : I shall set thee in a
heate by and by , I warrant thee.

Da. What , notwithstanding I say nothing but
Troth ?

Si.

FIGURE 1b

of Terence.

Si. Yea neuerthelesse, sirra see thou that he be kept
fast fettered : and hearest thou me? binde his hands and
feete together , ✳ Now sir go to : By God if I liue this
day to an end , I will teach thee and him both , what
danger it is for the one of you to beguile his master ,
and for the other to deceiue his father.

Chr. Tush man, be not in so great a rage.

Si. O Chremes, do you not pitie me, to see what re-
uerend regard my sonne hath towards me ? and that
I should take somuch trauaill for such a sonne? Well go
to Pamphilus : Come out here Pamphilus , Is there no
shame in thee ?

ᵛ He speake Dromo.

✳ He turnes speach to Dauus and Pamphilus.

Act. 5. Scen. 3.

The Argument.

SIMO sharply rebuketh his sonne : who confessing his fault , submit-
teth himselfe wholy vnto his fathers pleasure . Chremes en-
deuoreth to appease thextreame Rage of Simo.

Pamphilus, Simo, Chremes.

Who calles me ? O I am vndone , it is
my father.

Si. What saiest thou? thou arrand - - - -

Chr. Fie , go to the matter , and cease
your euill language.

Si. Yea as though there could be any
name to ill for this fellow . Now sirra , do you say the
same to ? Is Glycerie free bone of this Citie ?

Pamph. So it is reported.

Si.

the press they had set up in the monastery of St Scholastica at Subiaco), follows exactly that of the fifteenth-century manuscript from which they printed the text; the manuscript is still preserved in the library of the monastery. Most printers used three pauses represented by the *punctus, virgula* and *interrogativus,* but other marks depended on the nature of the book to be printed.[4]

Richard Pynson was first to print the plays of Terence in Latin in England, between 1495 and 1497. The three marks of punctuation described by Parkes are employed, as well as the double punctus (the mark we would now recognize as the colon) to mark a medial pause and the apostrophe for the elision of letters. In the *Andria, Quid ais Omnium* is punctuated with a terminal *interrogativus,* or question mark.[5]

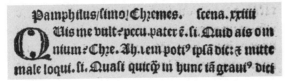

FIGURE 2

This use of a terminal question mark (*Quid ais omnium?*) becomes and remains the standard punctuation of this phrase in Latin editions of Terence long after the introduction and dissemination of other punctuation marks and well into the eighteenth century, including, for instance, Bentley's edition of Terence of 1726.

There are a few exceptions to this standardized punctuation in printed editions of the *Andria.* One example might be an edition from Lyons printed in 1552 which is marked: *quid ais? omnium.*[6] Likewise, occa-sionally the phrase is punctuated, as in the following example from Paris (1572), with a terminal point, *quid ais omnium.*[7]

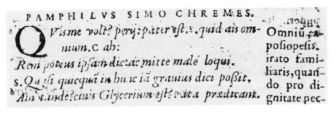

FIGURE 3

This final version, *Quid ais omnium* followed by a period (or, in British us-age, a full stop), emphasizes very well the possible problems in identifying these three words as a self-contained, as opposed to interrupted, unit, and such was particularly the case by this date, when readers' understanding of punctuation was changing. Readers were used to seeing more varied punctuation in their texts, and by the 1570s, when this last example was printed, the new repertory of punctuation marks was fully standardized through the dissemination of common printing types, making the comma, colon, period, question mark, exclamation point, and parenthesis (both rounded and square brackets) common to European grammars and orthographies. There was also a new attention to the function of punctuation as syntactic as well as elocutionary.[8] The reader unskilled in Latin (a schoolboy, for instance) *might* perhaps be misled by the period and seek to make a complete sentence from the Latin fragment: *Quid ais* (what do you say) *omnium* (of all things): What do you say of all things? What do you make of all this? Significantly, the *Editio Princeps* of 1470 (Strasburg, A. Rusch) supplies the putative absent word: *nequissime:*[9]

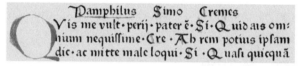

FIGURE 4

However, the scholastic gloss that began to fill the margins of the printed Latin text from the incunabulum period onward prevented the unskilled Latinist from misreading the words for long, and it did away with the necessity of completing the sentence by pointing out explicitly to the reader that Simo hasn't finished what he was intending to say. The most celebrated Terentian scholia were those of Donatus, who comments on *Quid ais omnium* as follows:

This is the third aposiopesis. It is for the degradation of character and is the aposiopesis of the angry father, when for the sake of dignity he does not find a reproof for the fault. And "quid ais" is not a question but a verbal assault. And that he says "omnium" is an ellipsis, indicating many things.[10]

Here, attention is drawn to two figures: aposiopesis and ellipsis. The rhetorical aposiopesis (from ἀποσιωπεῖν, meaning "to maintain silence") is associated with the representation and motivation of the speaker who cannot complete his words through anger. Ellipsis (from ἐλλείπειν, "to come short"), a figure traditionally conceived of as both grammatical and rhetorical, is here referred to more generally: the omission of words in certain circumstances being noted as highly expressive. In his *Ars Major,* Donatus refers to ellipsis as one of the *cetera vitia,* grammatical "vices," which are to be disapproved of unless they be redeemed by means of poetic license. Quintilian had used the same noun for both aposiopesis and ellipsis—*vitia*—blemishes or faults, a notion which then becomes the figure of "defect" in English rhetorics such as Puttenham's 1589 *The Arte of English Poesie.* The idea of aposiopesis or ellipsis as a figure of linguistic defect adds a further joke to Chremes's interjection, *ac mitte male loqui* (and cease your bad language); in preventing Simo from calling his son a bad or rude name in this moment of comic censorship, he instead causes him to commit a linguistic vice. Appropriately, in Isaac Casaubon's annotated Terence, now held in the University Library at Cambridge, *male loqui* has been underlined heavily.[11]

When Terence's Latin began to be translated into the vernacular languages, the interruption of *Quid ais omnium* was also translated and adapted for a new reading public. In a 1542 Paris edition of the play translated into French, there is no punctuation mark employed at all.[12]

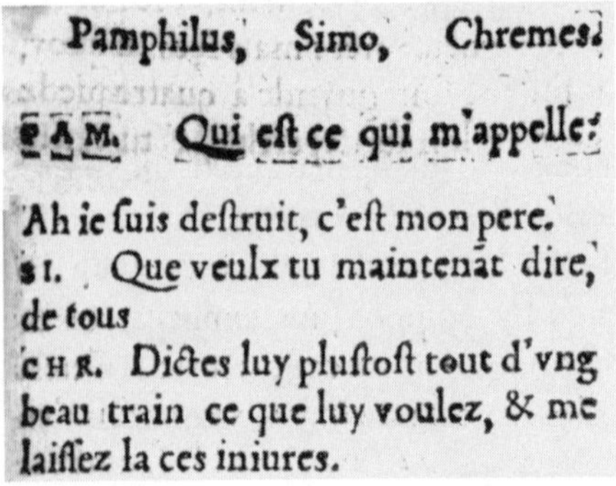

Pamphilus, Simo, Chremes.

PAM. Qui eſt ce qui m'appelle?

Ah ie ſuis deſtruit, c'eſt mon pere.

SI. Que veulx tu maintenãt dire, de tous

CHR. Dictes luy pluſtoſt tout d'vng beau train ce que luy voulez, & me laiſſez la ces iniures.

FIGURE 5

The absence of a period might simply be a compositor's error. But on the other hand, it could be seen as evidence of growing attention to the syntactic value of punctuation. That is, rather than representing the fact that Simo's speech ends, the omission of punctuation reflects the absence of a conclusion to his utterance: absence replicates absence. In versions of Terence translated into English before 1588, no such point is made. In the 1520 *Terens in Englysh,* this is literally the case: there is no mark of punctuation at the end of Simo's utterance, but this, unlike the 1542 French translation, is common to the majority of turns in the play.[13]

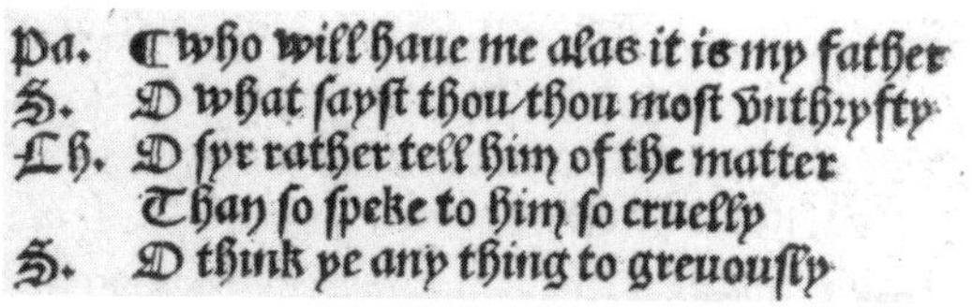

Pa. Ꞇ who will haue me alas it is my father
S.   O what sayst thou thou moſt ꝟnthꝛyfty
Ch. O ſpꝛ rather tell him of the matter
     Ꞇ han ſo ſpeke to him ſo cruelly
S.   O think ye any thing to greuouſly

FIGURE 6

In fact, no play written in English before 1588—as a translation or as an original piece of writing—and included in Greg's chronological listing of plays in *A Bibliography of the English Printed Drama to the Restoration* has marks of suspension such as those that appear in Maurice Kyffin's *Andria*.[14] In Kyffin's text, we have evidence that someone thought an incomplete sentence worthy of a particular type of marking. So why does this mark appear at this date and in this play? And what is its effect?

Before going on to look at the principles behind Kyffin's translation, which he outlines in his preface, it is necessary to situate the emergence of suspension marks within some broader cultural trends and preoccupations. First, the development of suspension marks within the vernacular can be understood within the context of linguistic debates of the day regarding the reform of written English, in particular to bring it closer to spoken speech. Such debates are well documented, and the emergence of suspension marks certainly chimes with their concerns. John Hart, for instance, in his 1569 *Orthographie* called for the development of symbols along phonetic principles: "to mark what voice shoulde be sounded at some time being written, and in another place be left out, and the place marked to be unsounded: [. . .] And for distinction and pointing, to give the reader knowledge the nearest a man to pronounce the writing, as the writer would speake it."[15] The 1588 *Andria*'s suspension marks signal for grammatical and oral purposes the fact that Simo's words remain "unsounded." Richard Mulcaster in his *Elementarie* (1582) might have been less convinced that language should or even could be reformed phonetically but agreed that the language in its current state could be helped "in particulars." Nonetheless, he pointed out the pragmatic and economic constraints on even that: "bycause the printing charact being once cast in metle, what difficultie is there afterward?"[16] By the 1580s, any major reform of the language was economically unviable, because printers would be far from willing to replace their type and were, anyway, dependent on imported continental matrices for casting type until the early eighteenth century.[17] This latter fact sheds light on Kyffin's *Andria* in which hyphens, already existing in the compositors' case, are placed together and transformed into a symbol of suspension, a new mark of punctuation. Roger Chartier, in *Publishing Drama in Early Modern Europe,* does point out, "The role of copy editors and proofreaders in the graphic and orthographic systemization of the vernacular tongues (including punctuation) was far more decisive than the propositions for the reform of orthography advanced by those writers who wanted to impose an 'oral writing' entirely governed by pronunciation."[18] That is certainly the case, but nonetheless, debates about the reform of the written language did reflect and create an environment which cultivated the possibility of typographic innovation along oral principles.

Such systematization as described by Chartier was certainly being carried out by printers. Malcolm Parkes states, "By the 1580s there is clear evidence that compositors were responsible for introducing punctuation marks—especially the semi-colon—to replace others indicated in an author's copy."[19] One can't assume that the suspension marks that appear in the 1588 *Andria* appear through the translator's own initiative; it is possible that the printer, Thomas East, could have been responsible for the unusual pointing of the 1588 *Andria.* East is largely known as a printer of music and generally associated with the work of William Byrd, and one cannot but wonder whether East's skill as a printer of music made him sensitive to the importance of rests or pauses in linguistic as well as musical texts. As Charles Butler would put it in 1636 in *The Principles of Musik,* "As the Ditti is distinguished with Points, [Period, Colon, Semicolon, and Comma;] so is the Harmoni, answering unto it, with Pauses and Cadences," giving the example that "Minim- and Crotchet-rests" answer to "Semicolons, Commas, Breathings, and Sighs" (brackets in original).[20]

Whether such was the case or not, the mise-en-page of the 1588 *Andria* was certainly indebted to changes in the typography and layout of drama that were evolving over the course of the sixteenth century. The result was to facilitate the reader's movement around the page and minimize ambiguity, so that the printed page took on something akin to the immediacy and the visual and oral clarity of the dramatic performance. To take Henry Medwall's *Nature* (1534), for instance, entrances and exits, the names of speakers, and direct speech were all printed in black letter; the paraph was the only means of locating stage directions amid the dense verse but was occasionally omitted and was also used to mark speakers and divisions between stanzas.[21] But by 1568, a play such as *Jacob and Esau* was typographically organized with a system of clear textual signaling and increased leading for clarity and display: the text has act and scene divisions marked in large roman type (Thomas Norton and Thomas Sackville's *Gorboduc* was the first play in English to be so divided);[22] the main text is in black letter, song (with its different sound) in italic; the names of speakers are set left, as are stage directions, which are differentiated by means of roman type.[23]

T. Howard-Hill's essay "The Evolution of the Form of Plays in English during the Renaissance" traces this evolution of the dramatic mise-en-page in fine detail, describing the combination of the native and classical traditions for the layout of dramatic texts during the sixteenth century. Whereas the "classical editions employ nothing recognizable as stage directions until late in the century," in English school texts "the editors were manifestly influenced by native practice," in particular by providing stage directions.[24] Although Howard-Hill doesn't refer to the use of suspension marks, their appearance in 1588 supports his conclusion, "In the 1590s printed editions of plays evince most of the physical formalities to which modern readers have become accustomed from their twentieth-century editions."[25] The 1588 *Andria* was written explicitly for the schoolroom and reflects this trajectory toward visual clarity: the page is easy to navigate, with differentiating typefaces and considerable leading which opens up the page spatially. The marginal gloss of the classical tradition is replaced with simple explanatory notes in italic type for the purpose of textual clarification, as Kyffin himself puts it, to instruct the reader as to "any dowtfull speeches of the speakers: as whether they speake unto him that spake last before, or else to the audience, or to themselves" but which also act as a form of stage direction (see figure 1 a–c).[26]

Not a great deal is known about Maurice Kyffin, even though he was, as William Sherman points out in his entry on Kyffin in the *Dictionary of Literary Biography,* "one of Renaissance England's exemplary scholar-soldiers."[27] Kyffin was born in North Shropshire, was a friend and student of John Dee, and from the beginning of the 1580s was tutor to the sons, William, Henry, and Thomas, of Thomas Sackville, Lord Buckhurst. He traveled with Lord Buckhurst to the Low Countries in 1587 and then served there in military action in 1591; he died in 1598 while acting as surveyor general of the musters in Ireland. Other than his translation of Terence, Kyffin is particularly known for two pieces of writing: *The Blessedness of Brytain,* a poem published in 1587 to commemorate the Queen's Accession Day, and his celebrated 1594 translation of Bishop Jewel's *Apologia Ecclesia Anglicanae* into Welsh.[28] The fact that Kyffin "was completely at home in the literary atmosphere of the Sackville household,"[29] as another commentator has surmised (most probably correctly), is reflected in the fact that it was during this period of his career that the translation of Terence originates. The warm dedication to Henry and Thomas Sackville and then separately to their brother William tells us that it was they who encouraged him to translate Terence into English. The purpose of Kyffin's translation was explicitly to help "all young Students of the Latin Tong,"[30] and the text is published with a commendatory verse by William Camden, the great antiquarian and schoolmaster at Westminster (and there the teacher of Ben Jonson).

In the preface, Kyffin laments the fact that Terence is "diuersly misunderstood,"[31] where he also tells us that he first attempted to translate Terence into verse but abandoned this work at the very final stages as he felt that such a medium failed to capture the style of Terence's comedy. Instead, he has deliberately adopted the language of "common speech."

My cheefest care hath bin, to lay open the meaning of the Author, especially, in all hard and difficult places of this Comoedie, and to utter the same, in such apt, plaine, and familiar words, as are most meete, for this low stile and Argument:[32]

Kyffin certainly had his eye on the glosses to Terence, at one point commenting on scholarly tradition, "commonly in all bookes of Terence, this place of Andria [. . .] is noted thus in the margine,"[33] and T. W. Baldwin has demonstrated that Kyffin would have used an edition of Terence printed on the Continent, narrowing down his Latin source to an edition which would have contained "the prefatory matter of Donatus and Melanchthon, the notes of Muretus-Fabricius, the marginal notes to the text which had been built up from Melanchthon, and the arguments of Adrianus Barlandus."[34] He goes on to identify such an edition as published in Paris in 1572 by Jerome de Marnef and Guillaume Cavellat, which is, in fact, the Parisian Terence reproduced earlier in this essay (figure 3) to demonstrate *Quid ais omnium* punctuated with a period. If this *was* the edition that Kyffin used, then he would have had to negotiate the problems of how to translate this terminal point into the vernacular, without the accompanying gloss of *Omnium* as aposiopesis. By removing the gloss, *Quid ais omnium* might be a "hard and difficult place" for the unskilled translator;[35] but *like* the learned gloss, the suspension marks inform students translating from the Latin that complete syntactic structures should not be sought in the original text.

In her 1996 book *Medieval Reading: Grammar, Rhetoric and the Classical Text,* Suzanne Reynolds urges us to see glosses "as the written vestiges of a reading undertaken by experts for those who are not experts, that is to say, as a reading by a teacher for his pupils." She continues: "The glosses are merely the written traces of a much fuller reading practice and what is more, they are part of a shift in the history of reading itself, away from the solitary rumination of monastic *lectio* to the more public forum of the classroom."[36] Kyffin's text also bears the traces of the classroom but reveals a different shift in the history of reading: that is, the aposiopesis or ellipsis is translated from the more abstract or scholarly principle pointed out in Latin in the margin of the play, or known from the rhetorical or grammatical textbook, into a mark of punctuation incorporated into the body of the play. It becomes a textual approximation of living speech capturing its contingencies and curtailments. The tradition of Latin study is continued in the notation of a figure, but this translation from verbal description to a graphic symbol continuous with the alphabetic code representing direct speech also carries with it the suggestion that the figure is being transformed from an artful departure from ordinary language (marked outside the text) into a feature central to the conception of "common speech" (within the text). We might therefore interpret the marking of suspension in this play as combining the tradition of Latin study with its emphasis on the comprehension of figures, with a commitment to everyday language. The suspension marks are pragmatic, aiding the student's comprehension, while also emphasizing the larger linguistic and dramatic point that everyday speech does not always emerge in complete grammatical units. Although Kyffin explicitly didn't translate the play for performance,[37] the marks do also act as a form of stage direction, informing the reader of dramatic motivation and aiding delivery. The use of a clear visual symbol warns the reader of omission, eliminating the need to double-check comprehension and making the meaning of the characters' words more immediate and dramatically present. Kyffin also interprets Terence's play as one of contraries—"he opposeth seuerall speakers, of seuerall natures, and contrary condicions, one to another"[38]—and thus one might interpret the marks as a symbol of division intrinsic to the play's meaning. As one character cuts across another or breaks his own words in midsentence, the series of rules act out a drama of contradiction and antithesis. The marks grammatically and dramatically elucidate the text but also have a figurative value in their own right.

However one might speculate on the factors that contributed to the emergence of suspension marks in 1588, there is extremely strong evidence for their popularity: from this date onward, it becomes extremely difficult to find a play printed in English which fails to mark suspension or interruption, using either a series of hyphens or a dash. Whereas in the 1588 *Andria* there are three occurrences of the mark, in the 1627 *Andria* translated by Thomas Newman for students at St. Paul's there are twenty-nine, thus the Latin is increasingly interpreted as subject to interruptions and omissions. In fact, Newman emphasizes the use of aposiopesis and ellipsis (here "eclipsis") in his preface to argue for the very suitability and propriety of translating the classics into English; it is the careful deployment of these figures that protects the reader from "bad language":

> There will perhaps some be found who on their good faiths will protest that this generall licentiousnesse of turning Latine bookes into English, carries with it much inconvenience. [. . .] But in *Terence* is no such danger. In those few passages where his matter beares any ranke sent or sence, you shall find it hushed by some modest close *Eclipsis,* or stopping *Aposiopesis;*[39]

One notable exception to this proliferation of suspension marks, however, is Richard Bernard's 1598 Latin-English *Terence in English.* Bernard clearly had Kyffin's translation of the *Andria* open in front of him when he prepared the *Andria,* as much of Kyffin's translation is there word for word.[40] However, Bernard doesn't adopt the punctuation in the same way. That is, no series of hyphens or any equivalent marks are used in Bernard's text. Alongside the Latin *Quid ais omnium* is written the Latin gloss "aposiopesis," but in the English, as in the earlier 1542 French edition, the incomplete sentence is left without a punctuation symbol:[41]

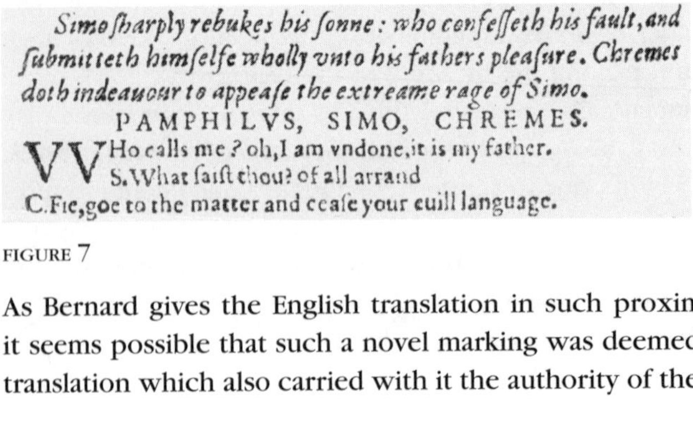

Simo sharply rebukes his sonne: who confesseth his fault, and submitteth himselfe wholly vnto his fathers pleasure. Chremes doth indeauour to appease the extreame rage of Simo.
PAMPHILVS, SIMO, CHREMES.
VV Ho calls me? oh, I am vndone, it is my father.
      S. What saift thou? of all arrand
C. Fie, goe to the matter and cease your euill language.

FIGURE 7

As Bernard gives the English translation in such proximity to the Latin, it seems possible that such a novel marking was deemed unsuitable for a translation which also carried with it the authority of the Latin source.

In 1540, Estienne Dolet, in his *La Punctuation de la Langue Francoyse,* commented on the untranslatability of punctuation.

Although all languages have different means of speaking and writing, without exception, they have only one system of punctuation.[42]

The standardization of common printing types throughout Europe meant that this statement is by and large accurate. But not entirely; printers might have the same marks in their case but could use them in different ways. In England, a series of hyphens and, with increasing frequency, the dash were most commonly used to mark omission. Although the choice between these marks would depend on what was available at any given time to the compositor, this broad trend can be seen in Ben Jonson's work, say, where among larger revisions from the quarto texts to the 1616 folio, the printing of which Jonson oversaw himself, series of hyphens are in general replaced by the bold straight line of the dash. In France, on the other hand, dramatic instances such as *Quid ais omnium* were being translated differently. *Points de suspension*—that is, a set of periods rather than a dash or a series of hyphens—become the conventional mark of omission in French texts, and although these marks seem to become a standard feature of the dramatic text rather later than in England, they are certainly well established by the 1630s.[43] By Madame Dacier's 1688 edition of Terence, both the French translation and the Latin text are marked with these *points de suspension,* or suspension points:[44]

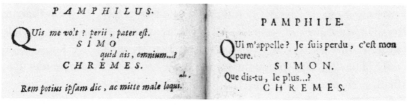

FIGURE 8

This particular Terentian interruption of *Quid ais Omnium* is in fact singled out by French linguistic philosophers. In his 1676 *L'Art de Parler,* Pierre Lamy expressed his disapproval of rhetorical figures in that they disrupt the natural order of language and reveal the speaker's thoughts to be unclear. But, he argues, passion, being a state of extreme agitation and disorder, has a "peculiar language" of its own which is expressed in figures such as ellipsis. So in this respect figures become permissible and "natural" forms of expression. This is from the first English translation of 1676:

ELLIPSIS.

A violent passion never permits us to say all that we would: The Tongue is too slow to keep pace with the swiftness of its motions; so that when a Man is cool in Discourse, his Tongue is not so full of words, as when he is animated by passion. When our Passions are interrupted, or diverted another way, the Tongue following them, produces words of no reference or analogy with what we were saying before. The old Man in *Terence* was so inrag'd against his Son, that he could utter only the word *Omnium;* his passion was too violent to permit him to go through with his Exprobration, or to call him as he intended, *Omnium hominum pessimus. Ellipsis* is the same thing with *Omissio,* or *Defectus.*[45]

Some time later, Dumarsais, in his 1730 work *Des Tropes,* writes that figures are inherent to the most quotidian uses of language[46] and refers explicitly to Terence's *"Quid ais omnium . . .* What do you say you most . . ." Here, writes Dumarsais, "it is clear that it's necessary to supply some of the words to finish expressing a thought which the vivacity of passion makes understood," and such figures are "very ordinary in the language of men. We call this figure Ellipsis, that's to say, omission."[47] Ordinary in the language of men or, as Kyffin had put it, "common speech." This moment of dramatic exchange from Terence is singled out as a means of understanding the way in which "ordinary language" can be understood and represented. The mark of punctuation, in turn, reveals to us the representation of emotion on the page.

   Throughout this essay I've referred to the typographic symbols that are its subject as "marks of suspension" or "suspension marks," but it is possible to look forward to the term "ellipsis marks" by which we know them today. I have so far avoided the term "ellipsis" to describe the punctuation mark as it appears in early translations of Terence as both the figures of aposiopesis and ellipsis are identified in Latin commentaries on the text. However, as Lamy's writing suggests, "ellipsis" began to be the more familiar term to describe omissions in speech, perhaps as rhetorical training waned, and certainly, in England, as vernacular grammars proliferated. More important, the term "ellipsis" does begin to be associated with marks of punctuation. The *Oxford English Dictionary* cites the earliest use of the term "ellipsis" to describe a mark of punctuation as Lindley Murray's 1824 *English Grammar.* Murray describes the use of the dash "when some letters in a word, or some words in a verse are omitted," and it is pointed out by the *OED* that the ellipsis in this sense is often "confused" with "eclipsis" (from ἐκλείπειν, "to leave out"). Etymologically linked to the eclipse, the omission of words leaves a dark place in the text.

However, the first identification of ellipsis as a punctuation mark is much earlier than 1824 and occurs in Charles Butler's 1633 *The English Grammar or the Institution of Letters, Syllables, and Words in the English Tongue*. Butler, like Murray much later, refers to the "eclipsis" as a mark of citation—"Eclipsis signifyeth de elision of woords in de beginning or ending of a vers or sentenc[e] cited in our writings"—and identifies the following two marks as signs of "eclipsis":[48]

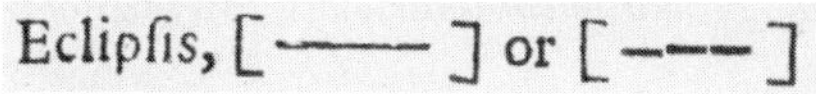

Eclipſis, [———] or [———]

FIGURE 9

It is fitting that Butler was the first to identify the mark: a disciple of Ramus, he advocated the organization of thought and communication along visual and spatial principles and was also, as Walter Ong describes him, "a bold innovator" in spelling and typography himself.[49] He was particularly alert to typographic practice and textual notation, proposing the use of a reformed phonetic alphabet, and, as described earlier, was interested in correlations between musical and linguistic forms. It must be stressed, though, that Butler was referring to "eclipsis" as a mark of textual transcription, to signal words left out from citations—words omitted but retrievable in full from elsewhere—rather than, as he puts it, to show "Ton[e], Sound or Paus." Nonetheless, these very marks (a continuous rule or series of hyphens) were at the same time proliferating in dramatic texts to indicate words withheld by a speaker, unuttered and unrecoverable, though suggested, but also supplying for the reader those dialogic features Butler dissociated from the mark: tone, sound, and—pause.

Notes

I am grateful to Andrew Taylor for his helpful comments on an earlier version of this essay.

All illustrations are used by permission of the British Library (figures 1a–c: c.34.e.26; figure 2: c.4.g.13; figure 3: 11707.aaa.5; figure 4: G.9530; figure 5: c.97.a.19; figure 6: c.34.e.33; figure 7: 11707.c.22; figure 8: 11707.bb.7; figure 9: c.40.e.3).

1. Ben Jonson, *The Magnetick Lady; Or Humors Reconciled* (London: for R. Bishop, sold by Andrew Crooke, 1640), 6.

2. The full citation from Terence's prologue is as follows: "When the playwright first steered his thoughts towards authorship, he supposed his sole business was to see that his plays pleased the people. He now finds that it turns out otherwise, for he spends his time in writing prologues, not to describe the plot but to answer the abuse of a malevolent old playwright." Terence, *The Lady of Andros*, trans. John Sargeaunt (Cambridge, Mass.: Harvard University Press, 1912), 7.

3. PAM: Quis me volt? perii, pater est.

SIMO: quid ais, omnium . . . ?

CHR.:   ah,

rem potius ipsam dic ac mitte male loqui.

Ibid., 94.

4. Malcolm Parkes, *Pause and Effect: An Introduction to the History of Punctuation in the West* (Aldershot, U.K.: Scolar Press, 1992), 50.

5. *Comoediae sex Andria, Eunuchus, Heautontimorumenos* (London: R. Pynson, 1497), fol. Diir.

6. *Petri Menenii Lugdunensis Commentaria in P. Terentii Andriam et Eunuchum* (Lyons: J. Tornaesium and G. Gazeium, 1552).

7. Terentius [*Comoediae*] *a M. Antonio Mureto [. . .] emendatus* (Paris: Jerome de Marnef, & Guillaume Cavellat, 1572), 81.

8. See Walter Ong, "Historical Backgrounds of Elizabethan and Jacobean Punctuation Theory," *PMLA* 49 (1944): 349–60; Parkes, "The Impact of Printing: A Precarious Balance between Logical and Rhetorical Analysis," in *Pause and Effect*, 87–96; and John Lennard, "Punctuation: And—'Pragmatics,'" in *Historical Pragmatics: Pragmatic Developments in the History of English*, ed. Andreas H. Jucker (Amsterdam and Philadelphia: John Benjamins Publishing Co., 1995), esp. 68–69.

9. *Terenti Affri poete comici* [Strasburg: J Mentelin, 1470], unfoliated.

10. 2. QUID AIS OMNIUM ἀποσιώπησις tertia. et est ad deformationem personae. 3. *Et* est irati familiaris ἀποσιώπησις, cum pro dignitate peccati non inveniat convicium. 4. *Et* "quid ais" non est interrogantis sed invehentis. 5. *Et* est ἔλλειψις multa significans, quod ait "omnium." See Paul Wessner, *Aeli Donati quod fertur commentum Terenti accedunt eugraphi Commentum et Scholia Bembina* (Leipzig: B. G. Teubner, 1902), 241.

11. *Terentius a Antonio Mureto [. . .] emendatus* (Lyons: Lodovicum Cloqueminum, 1576).

12. *Première Comédie de Térence, intitulée l'Andrie, nouvellement traduicte de Latin en François* (Paris: A Roffet, 1542), ivv–ivir.

13. *Terens in Englysh* ([Paris: P. le Noir?], 1520), Diiv. Here "thou most uthryfty" corresponds with "nequissime," although the Latin text provided in *Terens in Englysh* does not follow the *Editio Princeps* in including this word.

14. W. W. Greg, *A Bibliography of the English Printed Drama to the Restoration* (London: Bibliographical Society at the University Press, Oxford, 1939–59; reprinted London: Bibliographical Society, 1970).

15. For clarity, throughout this essay ellipsis points added by the author of the present essay appear in brackets. John Hart, *An Orthographie* (1569), in Stockholm *Studies in English 4,*

ed. M. T. Lofvenberg and Alarik Rynell (Stockholm: Almquist and Wiksills Boltryckeri-A.B., 1953), 185. First published as *The Opening of the Unreasonable Writing of Our Inglish Toung* (1551).

16. Richard Mulcaster, *The First Part of the Elementarie which entreateth chefelie of the right writing of our English tung* (London: T. Vautroullier, 1582), 107.

17. S. H. Steinberg, *Five Hundred Years of Printing*, new ed., revised by John Trevitt (London: British Library and Oak Knoll Press, 1996), 78. First published in 1955.

18. Roger Chartier, *Publishing Drama in Early Modern Europe: The Panizzi Lectures, 1998.* (London: British Library, 1999), 15.

19. Parkes, *Pause and Effect,* 53.

20. Charles Butler, *The Principles of Musik* (London: John Haviland, 1636), 97.

21. Henry Medwall, *Nature* (London: printed by William Rastell, 1534).

22. T. H. Howard-Hill, "The Evolution of the Form of Plays in English during the Renaissance," *Renaissance Quarterly* 43, no. 1 (Spring 1990): 112–45.

23. Anon., *A newe mery and wittie comedie or enterlude, newely imprinted, treating upon the historie of Jacob and Esau* (London: Henrie Bynneman, 1568).

24. Howard-Hill, "Evolution of Form," 135.

25. Ibid., 144.

26. *Andria. The first Comoedie of Terence, in English,* trans. Maurice Kyffin (London: T. E[ast] for T. Woodcocke, 1588), Aiiiiv.

27. William Sherman, *Dictionary of Literary Biography: Sixteenth-Century Non-Dramatic Authors,* ed. David A. Richardson, 2d ser., 136 (Washington: Gale Research International, 1994), 214.

28. Gabriel Harvey praises Kyffin's writing in *Pierces Supererogation: Or A New Prayse of the Old Asse. A Preparative to certaine larger Discourses, intituled Nashes S. Fame* (London: imprinted by John Wolfe, 1593), 190–91.

29. E. D. Jones, *Maurice Kyffin's Account of Lord Buckhurst's Embassy to the Netherlands, 1587* (Aberystwyth: National Library of Wales, 1963).

30. *Andria,* trans. Kyffin, Aiiir.

31. Ibid., Air.

32. Ibid., Aiiir.

33. Ibid., Aiiiv.

34. T. W. Baldwin, *Shakspere's Five-Act Structure* (Urbana: University of Illinois Press, 1947), 341.

35. Though this isn't included in Udall's *Floures,* which Baldwin argues Kyffin also used. *Floures for Latine speaking selected and gathered oute of Terence,* 2d ed. (Imprinted at London: In Fletestrete [by Thomas Powell], in the house late Thomas Berthelettes, 1560).

36. Suzanne Reynolds, *Medieval Reading: Grammar, Rhetoric and the Classical Text* (Cambridge: Cambridge University Press, 1996), 29.

37. "And therefore, it was no part of my meaning, to tra[n]slate the same, as a thing either pleasant to be played, or very delightful to bee read." Though this doesn't of course preclude the translation from being either. *Andria,* trans. Kyffin, Aiv.

38. Ibid., Biiir.

39. *The Two First Comedies of Terence called Andria, and the Eunuch newly Englished by Thomas Newman* (London: printed by G. M. and are to bee sold at the house of M. Fenricus, 1627), A2v.

40. See Baldwin, *Shakspere's Five-Act Structure*, 343.

41. *Terence in English. Fabulae Comici*, trans. R[ichard] B[ernard] (Cambridge: Johannis Legat, 1598), 94.

42. Si toutes langues generalament ont leur differences en parler & escripture, toutesfoys non obstant cela elles n'ont qu'une punctuation seulement.

    Estienne Dolet, *La Punctuation de la Langue Francoyse* (Lyon: Estienne Dolet, 1540), 21.

43. Ellipsis points don't become a conventional feature of English print until the nineteenth century.

44. *Les Comedies de Terence, traduites en Francois, avec des Remarques, par Madame D[acier]*, vol. 1 (Paris: Denys Thierry and Claude Barbin, 1688) 170-71.

45. [Lamy, Pierre,] *The Art of Speaking: written in French by Messieurs du Port Royal* (London: W. Godbid, 1676), 104-5.

46. "[I]l n'y a rien de si naturel, de si ordinaire, et de si comun que les Figures dans le langage des homes." C. C. Dumarsais, *Des Tropes ou des diférens sens dans lesquels on peut prendre un même mot dans une même langue*, 3d ed. (Paris: Paschal Prault, 1775), 2. First published in 1730.

47. Dans l'Andriène de Térence, Simon se croyant trompé par son fils, lui dit, *Quid ais omnium . . .* Que dis-tu le plus . . . vous voyez que la proposition n'est point entière, mais le sens fait voir que ce père vouloit dire a son fils, *Que dis-tu le plus méchant de tous les homes?* Ces façons de parler dans lesquelles il est évident qu'il faut supléer des mots, pour achever d'exprimer une pensée que la vivacité de la passion se contente de faire entendre, sont fort ordinaires dans le langage des homes. On apèle cette figure *Ellipse,* c'est-à-dire, *omission.*
    Ibid., 6.

48. Charles Butler, *The English Grammar, or, The Institution of Letters, Syllables, and Words in the English Tongue* (London: William Turner, 1633), 63.

49. Ong, "Punctuation Theory," 358. See also Ong, *Ramus, Method, and the Decay of Dialogue* (Cambridge, Mass.: Harvard University Press, 1958).

Select Bibliography

Baldwin, T. W. *Shakspere's Five-Act Structure*. Urbana: University of Illinois Press, 1947.

Butler, Charles. *The English Grammar, or, The Institution of Letters, Syllables, and Words in the English Tongue*. London: William Turner, 1633.

———. *The Principles of Musik* (London: John Haviland, 1636).

Chartier, Roger. *Publishing Drama in Early Modern Europe: The Panizzi Lectures, 1998.* London: British Library, 1999.

Dolet, Estienne. *La Punctuation de la Langue Francoyse*. Lyon: Estienne Dolet, 1540.

Dumarsais, C. C. *Des Tropes ou des diférens sens dans lesquels on peut prendre un même mot dans une même langue*. 3d ed. Paris: Paschal Prault, 1775.

Greg, W. W. *A Bibliography of the English Printed Drama to the Restoration*. London:

Bibliographical Society at the University Press, Oxford, 1939-59; reprinted London: Bibliographical Society, 1970.

Hart, John. *An Orthographie* (1569). In Stockholm *Studies in English* 4, ed. M. T. Lofvenberg and Alarik Rynell. Stockholm: Almquist and Wiksills Boltryckeri-A.B., 1953.

Howard-Hill, T. H. "The Evolution of the Form of Plays in English during the Renaissance." *Renaissance Quarterly* 43, no. 1 (Spring 1990): 112-45.

Jones, E. D. *Maurice Kyffin's Account of Lord Buckhurst's Embassy to the Netherlands, 1587.* Aberystwyth: National Library of Wales, 1963.

[Lamy, Pierre.] *The Art of Speaking: written in French by Messieurs du Port Royal.* London: W. Godbrid, 1676.

Lennard, John. "Punctuation: And—'Pragmatics.'" In *Historical Pragmatics: Pragmatic Developments in the History of English,* ed. Andreas H. Jucker, 65-98. Amsterdam and Philadelphia: John Benjamins, 1995.

Mulcaster, Richard. *The First Part of the Elementarie which entreateth chefelie of the Right Writing of our English Tung.* London: T. Vautroullier, 1582.

Ong, Walter. "Historical Backgrounds of Elizabethan and Jacobean Punctuation Theory." *PMLA* 49 (1944): 349-60.

———. *Ramus, Method, and the Decay of Dialogue.* Cambridge, Mass.: Harvard University Press, 1958.

Parkes, Malcolm. *Pause and Effect: An Introduction to the History of Punctuation in the West.* Aldershot, U.K.: Scolar Press, 1992.

Reynolds, Suzanne. *Medieval Reading: Grammar, Rhetoric and the Classical Text.* Cambridge: Cambridge University Press, 1996.

Sherman, William. "Maurice Kyffin." *Dictionary of Literary Biography: Sixteenth-Century Non-Dramatic Authors,* ed., David A. Richardson, 2d ser., vol. 136, pp. 214-16. Washington: Gale Research International, 1994.

Steinberg, S. H. *Five Hundred Years of Printing.* London: Faber and Faber, 1959.

Natural Authorship

RICHARD PREISS

> The guiltie goddesse of my harmfull deeds,
> That did not better for my life prouide,
> Then publick meanes which publick manners breeds.
> Thence comes it that my name receiues a brand,
> And almost thence my nature is subdu'd
> To what it workes in, like the Dyers hand . . .[1]

S HAKESPEARE IS OFTEN taken to be confessing here a regret for the social limitations his livelihood imposed upon him—the "public means" of professional theater, which, even as it brought him considerable wealth, also steeped his poetic renown in the taint of vulgar trade. Whether we read it as an unrequited yearning for literary respectability or as an unapologetic affirmation of his craft, the passage is a bellwether for the Shakespeare later generations have wanted to imagine: the artist as alternately a prisoner and a product of the commonness (in both senses of the word) of his institutional medium have swapped places with every shift in critical ideology and taste. That we read the passage at all, however, argues at least two media implicit in its meditation. In the context of a book of poetry strikingly called *Shake-speares Sonnets,* that is—a phrase repeated in running titles—it is tempting to see the "brand" "my name receiues" not just as a figurative blemish but more immediately as the physical impress of type on paper, the printing *of* a name rather than upon it. Such a reflexive twist momentarily insinuates a redemptive narrative within the reprobate one: concurrent with its indenture and anonymity, seemingly, the "public means" of commercial playwriting can also yield ("thence comes it") equally public marks of credit and distinction—a solace that actually sharpens the subtle contrast with "*almost* thence my nature is subdu'd." The "Dyers hand" becomes *visible* as his, in other words, precisely as it mingles in the heterogeneity of "what it works in." The *Sonnets* were of course not a collection initially conceived for the press; as nondramatic work to boot, it can be only dimly that they allegorize here an inverse dynamic between stage and page in which they themselves took no part. But by 1609 Shakespeare had recently witnessed the printing of several other, theatrical, texts that seem to illustrate exactly this correlation of obscurity and individuality across two domains, texts likewise contrived for communal use but professing a far more singular agency upon publication. What "harm" in that?

The history of criticism in early English drama has unfolded, as is often observed, largely within a dichotomy of performance and print. Texts to be read versus scripts to be acted: respective mantras of the postromantic New Bibliography and the theater-oriented critical reaction of the past few decades, even as polar binaries these axioms haunt one another—in quartos inextricable from "bad" actors' memories, in the textual reifications of "stagecraft" commentary.[2] They attest to the slipperiness of local thinking about where (because, surely, always *some*where) dramatic authority must be vested. Perhaps the most salutary by-products of this vexed reception heritage, then, have been investigations into how such authority first came to be so narrowly constructed in the early modern period. In a print environment that hitherto had scarcely deferred to the playwright or to his intention (and next to a theatrical milieu that meaningfully acknowledged neither), from what conditions did a niche for literary celebrity arise, such that authors' names could eventually assume a prominence amid the network of figures on playbook title pages?

This endlessly complex—and here highly simplified—question has long since paid for itself in the illuminating studies it has sponsored of early modern book culture, printing practice, gender and political discourses, theatrical economics, and repertory. To the extent, however, that as a field of inquiry the "birth of the (dramatic) author" as a commercial and discursive formation has taken shape under the auspices of "the death of the author" as an integrating principle of textual immanence, it has also, as the reciprocal shorthands suggest, been handicapped by it: obituary frames biography. Eager to avoid the New Bibliographic optimism of preternaturally possessive playwrights concerned with the authoritativeness of their printed texts, or of stationers unduly attentive to fine discriminations in the lineage of relative ephemera like plays, many representative statements retreat into a new localism that merely reinstates authorial drives on a higher order. Jeffrey Masten, for example, tries to fix the impetus behind attribution wholly within book rather than theatrical production. As a class, playwrights buried themselves in the collectivity of their profession—in the case of the Beaumont-Fletcher-Massinger troika, literally—and, aloof to any posterity beyond the round of commission, performance, and payment, "were far less interested in keeping their hands, pages and conversation separate" than are the critics who have inherited them.[3] For proof that a vast gulf separated theatrical and book culture's attitudes toward dramatists, indeed, we need look no further than the piecemeal hacks who populate Henslowe's diary, or consider that a poet's name first appeared on a playbill in 1698, more than a century after it first appeared on a title page.[4] Clearly (and tellingly), what audiences expected from playhouses and playbooks came to be expressly different things.

It neither follows nor is sufficient, I would thus suggest, to conclude that individual attribution remained solely a publisher's gimmick capriciously concocted as a "selling point" for playbooks, "as a way to create desire" by associating them with "recognizable names"—such that Masten can answer the question, "*Where* is an author?" with "in the bookshop."[5] Like saying dramatic authorship's principal manifestation is on paper, this is trivially true; it is a description of how authors' names function rather than an explanation of how they came to function that way, the free-floating "desire" they supposedly manufactured more difficult to substantiate the further back we trace it. As James Marino and others have shown, early authorial attribution betrays no uniform rationale, spanning instead a spectrum of embryonic strategies that frequently involved industrial locutions less concerned with readers than with defining the text's relation to other commercial property. When in 1600 the byline "William Shakespeare" graced the first edition of *2 Henry IV,* for instance, it helped the Chamberlain's Men distinguish the play from theatrical competitors like *The Famous Victories* and *Sir John Oldcastle;* when William Jaggard set that same byline to a 1619 reprint of *Sir John Oldcastle,* he appropriated it on behalf of a stationer's logic that claimed rights not just to a text but to its cognates.[6] While the first approach still targets only playgoers, between these rival grammars there is little traction on which dramatic authorship could have founded a self-sustaining market.

And yet Masten is also correct in a way that Marino is not: extrapolated far enough forward, an extratextual "desire" does seem to enter the equation, qualitatively discontinuous with an arithmetic arms race over authorship's encrypted mercantile semantics. The context of Jaggard's retaliatory ascription of *Oldcastle* was a ten-quarto series consisting exclusively of Shakespeare, initially printed on continuous signatures to invite single-volume binding—a format superfluous to the property claims its constituent playbooks reiterated, and irrelevant to the Lord Chamberlain's edict that quashed it, which merely barred the printing of any King's Men plays without their consent. Its only conceivable purpose was sales. The players' goal in securing their check was certainly to assemble a collection of their own in whose profits they participated, and their naturalization of the author as a unitary site of labor would massively outstrip what Jaggard and his partner Thomas Pavier were attempting. But though the Folio compilers' aim in this monumental encasement of Shakespeare may have been to inoculate their property from trespass, in seizing the commercial *packaging* by which he could be used to do so, they were evidently the borrowers; Jaggard, after all, pressed into the players' cause, remained a principal architect. The Folio brilliantly consolidated its marketing concept, but it did not (and at £1 a volume, could not have afforded to) invent it. Indeed, the very thespian vein Marino discerns in Heminges and Condell's encomium—its elision of composition with an actorly "performance of composition," "happy" imitation and "easy" utterance—registers the anxiety of the project, beyond any reclamation of texts, to recover "Shakespeare" himself as a wayward commodity, a "brand" that had lost its association with the playhouse.[7]

The dramatic author as fetish, then—not just the gnomic code for a vendible ware, but more transparently subjectivized as the privileged origin of a unique literary artifact, and thus nominally invoked more for the benefit of readers than stationers—was never fully a creature of the theater, but it still will not do to say he was entirely of the bookshop, either. The cachet for "authorial versions" is a differential function, and cannot have been imposed unilaterally or conjured nonreferentially; at some point a more complex reality must extrude. To postulate a single, institutionally specific natal site for a figure who is *by definition* hybrid, who coalesces in the contact zone between two media of cultural production, is to mistake "birth" for parthenogenesis, and to hypothesize a fiat lux that, however un-anachronistic or unsentimental, in its discursive antisepsis merely surrogates authorship itself. If "anywhere," the dramatic author emerges in the germinative, interstitial space *between* the textual practices of playhouse and printing house.[8] A thicker description—one that incorporates avenues of cross-pollination—should confront the question of how writers all but ignored by playgoers could make the leap into a verisimilar commercial category when those same playgoers turned to buying playbooks. The disparity must be viewed within a larger circuit of consumption.

For stationers, the playwright's name delineated a proprietary relation among books; but for readers—whose perceptions would by 1623 overtake reality—it most readily denoted a relation with the counterpart market of the theater, and most saliently one of divergence. The Folio's repatriative putsch was preceded more distantly by a spate of early Jacobean quartos that had begun stressing Shakespeare typographically over, against, and occasionally at the direct expense of the company that staged his plays; in this respect they obliquely reflected a wider trend. Texts became marketable as extensions of authors (rather than vice versa) only insofar as authors seem to have often buttressed, and gradually supplanted, contradistinctive claims about a *state* of text being marketed. What separates Richard Jones's 1590 *Tamburlaine*—which exhaustively negotiates itself not only irrespective of the poet but by his negation, in the "frivolous jestures" it snootily removes—and Thomas Thorpe's 1607 *Volpone*—passed entirely through the poet, its title subordinate to him—is not any absolute difference in the cultural esteem for a Jonson over a Marlowe, or for the identity of dramatists in general, but rather the *textual* difference for which Jonson's name had by then come to stand. In its prior marquee appearances, it had been commodified in opposition to the theater: *Every Man Out of His Humour* (1600) is offered, sans company ascription, "AS IT WAS FIRST COMPOSED / by the Author B.I. / *Containing more than hath been Publickely Spoken or Acted*"; *Sejanus* (1605) severs itself from the past-tense notice "Acted, in the yeere 1603," and "The Author B.I." goes on to tell us that this play "is not the same with that which was acted on the publike Stage," because Jonson has jealously revised a collaborator out.[9] By 1607, then, his name had calcified into an inflection that marked a play text as disjunctive with the version previously available on stage—such that in the two title-page states of Bartholomew Sutton's *The Case is Altered* (1609), the "authorial" and "performance" formulas were adjudged mutually exclusive.[10] These vacillations remind us that stationers did not always know or care to verify the provenances of the texts they were selling, and their advertisements can be taken as infallible guides only to how they thought those texts would sell best. But the tectonic legibility with which emphasis fluctuates within these advertisements suggests that stationers expected readers to understand and believe them, and that stationers who heavily accented an "author" had some reason themselves to think that it corresponded to a material difference from playhouse fare.

In many instances (quite obviously with Jonson) this intuition came from where the texts themselves came from—the playhouse, and specifically from those playwrights enfranchised enough to initiate and oversee their own publication. They brought binocular perspective to the play's double life in performance and print and promoted the literary legitimation of dramatic poetry by further destabilizing the congruity of the two arenas. By the first decades of the seventeenth century, N. W. Bawcutt cautions, the generalization of institutionally fixed ciphers apathetic to the individuation, publicity, or finality of their work is highly contingent. For many playwrights, print supplemented if not challenged performance as the repository of a play's cultural value, a medium gradually worthy not only of signed prefaces (1602), patron dedications (1608), and commendatory verses (1610), but also of erratum appeals for readers to "correct" typographic faults—implying, presumably, an imaginary ideal.[11] When articulated, moreover, this ideal increasingly dissociated itself from performance: Douglas Brooks notes how theatrical failure was repeatedly capitalized as theatrical repudiation.[12] Audiences disliked Fletcher's *The Faithfull Shepheardesse* (1610) because they expected clowns, but in printing the play he has "redeem'd it from corruption," since on "this second publication" the ignorant public may yet "see the thing they scornd." Jonson's printing of *Catiline* (1611), lost in "these Iig-giuen times," lifts it "aboue such molestations now"; his *Alchemist* (1612), similarly, rejects the playhouse as a source of art because most poets capitulate to their fools, "presumers on their owne Naturalls." *The White Divel* (1612) "wanted . . . a full and understanding auditory," which—though most readers, like most playgoers, "inquire [not] for good bookes, but new bookes"—Webster nevertheless hopes "the generall view" can give it.[13] He is writing under a shifting paradigm: only years before, as with *Every Man Out* and *Sejanus,* the "authorial" text of a play might have been pitched as a "new" book superlative of its performed condition, the default original against which it would have been measured. Now, thanks to some resourceful self-fashioning, print is actively ascending as the primary or at least privileged mode of dramatic engagement, producing an *identical* artifact that can be recalibrated as inherently superior to the conditions of performance themselves, as "original": nonperformance has given way to antiperformance, material difference to ontological "authenticity."[14] And yet the effect has still been achieved due to how performance and print have interacted. No longer relying on self-revision or overlength composition to gain visibility in print, the ambitious playwright could, with the anticipation of readership in place, on some level actually write *for* theatrical failure—refusing to placate the appetite for clowns or otherwise to accommodate their play toward the instabilities of performance, resistances that not only complemented the aesthetic integrity its publication would extol, but also enabled that very publication itself. Poets did not retain rights in their plays, but a play that would not survive into repertory a company might be more content to let him publish. Performance and print are determining each other.

For a number of reasons, however, such methods seem to have been unavailable to playwrights like Shakespeare, and thus the riddle of his pre-Folio authorship persists. Like a handful of contemporaries—Thomas Heywood of the Worcester's/Queen's Men and (to a lesser extent) Thomas Dekker of the Admiral's/Prince's Men—he was not a freelancer but formally bound to his company as poet-in-ordinary; as a full sharer, indeed, Shakespeare was multiply invested in the playhouse system to a unique degree.[15] Even if revenue from the sale of a manuscript were a motivation to publish (and by 1597 he did not need it), his principal income lay in courting theatrical success rather than failure. Nor would the latter have in any case enlarged him to retail the play: company poets were customarily, even contractually, obligated to withhold all their commissioned output from the press for the duration of their tenure.[16] For Shakespeare that tenure, with all its allegiances and strictures, lasted almost the entire length of his career. Critical orthodoxy has thus managed to keep him quarantined not only from the culture of entitlement sprouting around him but from even the desire to participate in it: variously committed to the fluidity of performance and snobbishly partial to manuscript circulation, Shakespeare is ritually depicted as indifferent to whether and how his plays saw print.[17] This essay asks why, instead of alternatives to publication, such lateral disseminative pathways might not also have served under certain circumstances to vehiculate it.

The aversion to print may itself have been more circumstantial than categorical. To the prevailing wisdom can certainly be adduced Shakespeare's inscrutable silence in all the dramatic publications of his lifetime: no dedications, no epistles, no evidence of editorial involvement, no angry feedback (as with Heywood) about the resultant haphazard quality of his texts. And yet we must reconcile this silence to his obsession elsewhere, inordinate even as a topos of the age, with figurations of literary fame and textual paternity (again, the *Sonnets*); to his record as the most voluminously, widely, and attributively published dramatist of the period; and to the fact that by 1622, not 1623, a printer calls "the Authors name . . . sufficient to vent his worke." That Thomas Walkley here does not mean what he says—his *Othello* also lists company and theater on its title page— makes his gratuitous obeisance all the more indicative of a public mind-set that already accorded special status to plays to which his "name" adhered, "workes" to the extent that they were "his."[18] With the poet recused from the publication process, though, stationers were not privy to the textual history necessary to make such discriminations; and until they were, they had little motive to fabricate them. In a major new study, Lukas Erne argues that this barrier did not always exist. Embracing Peter Blayney's attack on the shibboleth of the players' opposition to print, Erne assembles the most cogent case yet for a coherence to the Chamberlain's Men's publication pattern that factored Shakespeare's literary aspirations. With a roughly two-year gap between theatrical debut and the appearance of playbooks until 1603, publication advertised revival; Shakespeare could write or revise overlength plays—especially in more dignified genres like history and tragedy—with print as a separate, parallel goal.[19]

Both the utility and the limits of this account reveal themselves, however, only when the strategy it exposes seems to break down. Erne is unable to explain why after 1603 the steady stream of new playbooks slows to a sporadic trickle. The function of recommending revived plays to theatergoers is no longer operative, since these playbooks not only observe no regular distance from initial performance (*Troilus and Cressida* is printed eight years later, *Pericles* barely one) but tend to exaggerate this distance, their aggrandizement of the author tied not to a freestanding literary reputation but to the same perceived pedigree of copy text that inspires phrases like "His *True* Chronicle Historie" and "the *true* relation."[20] Whatever the cause of their intermittence—among the stopgaps offered is a market "glut" for printed drama that is quite over by 1605, and contradictorily the company's shift toward manuscript presentation for aristocratic benefactors, which these editions would only devalue—clearly the King's Men no longer appear to be coordinating their release, or at least not according to the same scheme.[21] The texts are even more anomalous for a period when the King's Men *do* begin to exercise remarkable restraint over publication. The number of plays vaunting their performance between

1603 and 1613 is exceedingly small; by the time Fletcher joined them he had seen six plays in print, but would not see another until 1619.[22] The company's protectionism was both intensifying and simultaneously being circumvented—enough, at least, to elicit the Folio's charge of "stolne and surreptitious copies," a shortsighted sales tactic indeed if it impugned the very stationers with whom the players had just partnered. If we wish to imagine a Shakespeare who continued to care about seeing his name in print, then the means by which these later plays came to feature it might have changed as well.

This is not to resurrect conspiracy theories about authorial holographs underwriting printer's language, here smuggled out by the playwright in flagrant defiance of his company's and his own declared interests. If anything, this analysis presupposes his acute *removal* from the processes that constituted the authority of these texts. For Erne, until 1603 Shakespeare can be a "literary dramatist," compartmentalized activities that (so long as publication was as assured as performance) produced at any given moment *either* scripts to be acted or books to be read—one branching linearly out of the other through expansion or contraction, their respective identities materially dependent not on each other but on the playwright's decision of which to publish. In the absence of such adjudication, though, "authoriality" could not be an a priori value intrinsic to a text, its creative history inaccessible to those confined to only one side of the playhouse-printing house combine. Rather it had to be somehow collectively negotiated, out of the sequence of agencies and practices whose invasive interventions the life cycle of a play naturally comprehended but who themselves may not have comprehended what they were cumulatively doing. Luckily, we already have a name for this: "collaboration." Playwrights were not "interested in keeping their hands . . . separate" from each other, Masten reminds us, but from whom indeed *could* they keep them separate? Why should the fission of literary and theatrical "versions" end with the compositional moment of the play, when we cannot really say where that moment ends? The terminal articulations of stage and page were mediated by institutional machinery—adaptive, regulatory—made up of many moving parts, each capable of acting generatively and recursively on a play text and, as I will try to show, on occasion capable of dialectically interfering to improvise new discursive forms. Under such conditions, how one wrote a play "intended" for print and a play "intended" for performance might have become virtually indistinguishable; the *more* one wrote for performance, in fact, could one then let "textual intercourse" do the work of authorship itself.

In his 1997 essay "The Birth of the Author"—from which this essay takes both its evidentiary cues and its polemical animus—Richard Dutton advocates manuscript circulation as the extremity of Shakespeare's literary self-regard; explicating an apparent instance of its metastasis into print, however, catalyzes a narrative of potentially more systemic mediation than Dutton is prepared to consider. He includes a discussion of the double-state quarto of *Troilus and Cressida* (1609), the first (and canceled) title page reading "The Historie of Troylus and Cresseida. *As it was acted by the Kings Maiesties* seruants at the Globe. *Written by* William Shakespeare"; the second, more ornately, "The Famous Historie of Troylus *and* Cresseid. *Excellently expressing the beginning* of their loues, with the conceited wooing of *Pandarus* Prince of *Licia. Written by* William Shakespeare." Shedding its theatrical heraldry for decorous plot summary, the second state now also comes trailing an extraordinary epistle: "A neuer writer to an euer reader. Newes." The complex mechanics of this rebirth, shrouded by a metaphoric fog, are perhaps epitomized in the pronominal crux of the second period:

Eternall reader, you haue heere a new play, neuer stal'd with the Stage, neuer clapper-clawd with the palmes of the vulgar, and yet passing full of the palme comicall; for it is a birth of your braine, that neuer under-tooke any thing commicall, vainely: And were but the vaine names of commedies changde for the titles of Commodities, or of Playes for Pleas; you should see all those grand censors, that now stile them such vanities, flock to them for the maine grace of their grauities: especially this authors Commedies . . . And beleeue this, that when hee is gone, and his Commedies out of sale, you will scramble for them, and set up a new English Inquisition. Take this for a warning, and at the perril of your pleasures losse, and Iudgments, refuse not, nor like this the lesse, for not being sullied, with the smoaky breath of the multitude; but thanke fortune for the scape it hath made amongst you. Since by the grand possessors wills I beleeue you should haue prayd for them rather then beene prayd. (A1r–A1v)[23]

Assuming that the publishers meant "birth of *his* braine," Joseph Loewenstein reads the preface as a "shallow and illogical" appeal to the author, rhetorically prostituted to their wish to test the limits of stage rights; they are confident enough in the autonomy of print copyright, and have merely posed the scenario of a purloined play to make the point.[24] This dismissal resorts to post-New Bibliographic cynicism perhaps too far, since the invention of an *unperformed* play is unnecessary to such an experiment. "Your" is an unlikely misprint, and it is worth taking seriously as a wry index of the publisher's nagging sense that their rights are more tentative than the ensuing bravado suggests—that the commercial identity of their text is the product of a distributive calculus, in which their claims are determined as much by the structures of theatrical propriety as by stationers' monopoly. The author is here made to precede those claims instead of vice versa, but only insofar as he is the naturalized consequence of the stage (non)history on which the preface fundamentally and excessively insists. If there is a subconscious authority for this linchpin fiction, in turn, it lies in the one discourse with which its vision of economic scarcity is utterly riven: censorship. Inquisitors versus possessors: what compels the text's desirability may also be what prescribed its availability, changing "comedies" into "Commodities."

Dutton concurs that in the publishers' manic insistence on this issue, their disavowal of "vulgar" palms and "smoaky" multitudes does not imply performance solely at the private venue of the Blackfriars (highly unusual practice even if it did). Rather, he fruitfully reasons,

Surely the point of the epistle is that it is announcing a reading version of the play, new to a print readership and superior to what had doubtless been performed in a cut text by the King's Men at the Globe. Indeed, the difference may have been what got the publishers their licence.[25]

Though the modern confusion over regulatory terminology is inherited from the Stationers' own notational inconsistencies, the kind of "licence" Dutton here refers to was that acquired—for a fee dependent on the amount of perusal and emendation involved—from the Master of the Revels (sometimes called "authority" or "allowance") operating in his capacity as state censor, as opposed to that secured from the Wardens of the Stationers Company operating in its capacity as arbitrator of property claims among its members. Loosely speaking, the first certified the legal freedom to print a text, by virtue of its innocence of inflammatory matter; the second established the legal right to print it, by virtue of its commercial distinctiveness, and guaranteed satisfaction against any infringement. It was not always a strict division in practice, however. The supervisory criteria of the Revels Office overlapped and conflicted with those of the Stationers, since the Master (without putting his financial imperative aside) was embedded in a patronage network that made both his superiors and those of the players over which he presided the same. He answered directly to the Lord Chamberlain, to whom the companies could, and often did, sue for aid in safeguarding their plays not only from each other but from illicit publication. The players' hostility to print, albeit not as constitutional or unremitting as scholars once thought, is not altogether a delusion either: they merely wished to transact with the press on their terms, and, whether to ensure their profit participation or the viability of their presentation manuscripts, their efforts to perpetuate performance rights beyond the stage sometimes took the form of obstruction abetted by aristocratic influence. If the order suppressing the Jaggard/Pavier quartos was issued to the Stationers' Wardens—as was a 1637 injunction barring plays from entry in the Register without "some certificate in writing under the hands of . . . such persons as shall from time to time have direction of those companies"—then we can reasonably surmise that from early on, similar procedures obtained in the office of the Lord Chamberlain's client.[26] The Revels Master, as we will see, had more urgent priorities to prosecute, but he had his own interest in maintaining amicable relations with the players, and a tacit obligation to protect their property against obvious compromise.

The Revels Office could execute this unofficial double duty, of course, only while it licensed plays for the press, an arrangement that was not always the case. Until about 1606 that responsibility belonged to the Church Court of High Commission, under the direction of the Archbishop of Canterbury, which had been censoring all books for print since a royal proclamation had so invested it in 1586. These conditions would have been operative when a "Master [probably James] Robertes," so listed in the Register on February 7, 1603, may have brought "The booke of Troilus and Cresseda as yt is acted by my Lord Chamberlens men" before the clerical censors, since his Stationers' entry had been "stayed" until "he hath gotten sufficient authority for it."[27] For some reason, however, Robertes never got this allowance, and the play went unprinted; he may not have intended to publish, provisionally registering the copy as a block on behalf of the players, or (equally possibly) he may have been blocked by them.[28] All we know is that the first entry was considered irrelevant to the license granted to Richard Bonian and Henry Walley on January 28, 1609, which says nothing of Robertes or of any transfer of rights. By now censorial oversight had passed to Sir George Buc, who held the reversion to the

Revels post; here, so much closer to the players' power base, Bonian and Walley succeeded where Robertes seems to have failed, and the entry notes the authorization of William Segar, Buc's deputy. Dutton's certainty that Robertes's refusal implied a check by the players is perhaps unwarranted, but not his conclusion that their acquiescence—or at least the Revels Office's inference thereof—lay behind Bonian and Walley's result:

Is it possible that Bonian and Walley got a licence from Segar . . . because they had convinced him that what they were printing was different in kind from the acting version? That it was expressly not "as yt is acted by my Lord Chamberlens men" and so did not require their consent?[29]

Citing an analysis by Alan Nelson of Buc's annotations in playbooks (including one pregnant inscription—to which we shall return—on the title-page of a 1600 *Henry V, "much the same with that in Shakespeare"*), Dutton suggestively deduces Buc's belief that "playtexts might exist in different states—which could open up the possibility that different licences could apply to those different versions." Segar, he argues, faced a parallel situation with *Troilus and Cressida*—confronted not with an acting version of the play, but with an authorial one written for and previously available to him in private circulation, "foreshadowing . . . what Moseley describes in respect of the Beaumont and Fletcher texts, where . . . a particular cachet attached to what the authors had originally written." Thus, he concludes, "Bonian and Walley first advertised their text as something it was not, an acting version, and then haughtily changed their tune in trumpeting a text unsullied by the common stage."[30]

A subtle thread of non sequitur progressively warps this thinking, however. If Bonian and Walley possessed a manuscript already recognizable to them as "authorial" rather than acted, they would never have first advertised it as an acting version; their abortive strategy must be interpreted as a sign of misprision and correction. Furthermore, with Moseley's preface still forty years away, there was as yet no palpable market phenomenon of an "authorial cachet" to dictate Bonian and Walley's secondary choice of textual characterization. Rather, their sense of what kind of text they possessed seems to have been thoroughly guided by whatever reasoning informed the Revels officer's decision to let them print it, and the epistle to the second state can with less strain be read as an attempt to cajole its public into a taste for rarefied editions than as passively situated within a preexisting one. Because he presupposes the demand for dramatic authors whose very sources we are excavating, in sum, Dutton fails to grasp that his chain of scrutiny lands upon a mechanism by which "Shakespearean" texts—at least rhetoricized as such—could actually bootstrap themselves out of an institutional apparatus essentially oblivious to the concept. How did the Revels officer know what Bonian and Walley evidently did not, that their text was an authorial version and thus—a "thus" that will preoccupy the next section of this essay—did not require the overt accession of the King's Men? Weighing the analogous instance of Buc's note to *Henry V,* Dutton states the obvious only to brush past it:

So Buc was comparing the quarto either with a performance of the play or with what he had somehow read. Of all people, the Master of the Revels was the one man who would get to read a play in manuscript, so this has no bearing on that side of my argument.[31]

What here has "no bearing" on Dutton's argument would make it a far more elegant one. By invoking a pervasive traffic of coterie manuscripts to which the Revels Master had only probable social access, a new entity is introduced where none is required, forgetting the one manuscript to which the Revels Master already had *exclusive,* professional access: the allowed copy originally licensed for *performance,* not "what he had somehow read" but what he *had* to have read.[32] Dutton deftly retraces the construction of *Troilus and Cressida*'s textual identity to the Revels Office, only to hypostasize criteria extraneous to its administrative purview, at a moment when the redundancy of that purview made the allowed copy the most immediate and (as I will try to show) relevant "different state" against which its performance could be compared. While he was simultaneously licensing drama both for the stage and for the press, the Revels Master *was* the one man who would get to read a play in manuscript, see it staged, and then potentially see it in manuscript again, and was therefore in a unique position to discriminate between a play "as yt is acted" and an otherwise unadapted draft.[33] Because for him "unadapted" was all it would have seemed: the simplest answer to how the Revels officer "knew" what Bonian and Walley did not was that he also did not know. At the instant this press allowance was being granted for *Troilus and Cressida,* and possibly for other quarto playbooks like it during the same period, no one—not Buc, nor Buc's deputy Segar, nor the publishers who had brought it to them—would have been especially cognizant that what they were looking at was an "author's" edition. It was merely a relative of the allowed copy, which may have been the players' protected right to perform, but which their adaptive procedures in so doing made it not their prima facie right to publish. Indeed, the rationale for duplicating Revels censorship may have been bound up in preventing just this eventuality.

On November 21, 1606, the Stationer's Register records a license from Buc for a comedy by Edward Sharpham called *The Fleire.* The copy was then being transferred to John Busby and Arthur Johnson from John Trundell, who with Busby had entered it the previous May 13, "PROVIDED that they are not to printe yt tell they bring good aucthoritie and licence for the Doinge thereof."[34] The May entry speaks of no such license being subsequently furnished, but by the November transfer, the clerk notes that "[t]his book is aucthorised by Sir George Bucke." It is conceivable this was exactly the license that had been initially presented, but since no Revels officer had ever issued a license for the press, the precedent so puzzled the clerk that he rejected its validity—perhaps explaining the unusual specificity of "*good* aucthoritie and licence"—until by later that year Buc had established himself in this domain sufficient for his approval to be recognized. From this slightly fuzzy terminus a quo in 1606, and with only two exceptions until 1615, every play in the Stationer's Register carried either Buc's signature or his deputy Segar's.

By 1606, it turns out, there were sound reasons for collapsing the phases of theatrical censorship into a single regulatory agency.[35] The first was *An Act to Restrain the Abuses of Players,* passed by James's predominantly Puritan first Parliament. The statute imposed a ten-pound fine on "any person or persons . . . in any stage play, enterlude, shew, may-game or pageant, jestingly or profanely speak[ing] or us[ing] the holy name of God," and seems to have been readily interpreted as extending to printed plays as well.[36] Since the fine was only recoverable by private suit, however (with only a moiety going to the king), it quickly became routine for the Revels Master to filter oaths beforehand, to protect both players and the courts from the logjam of hearsay litigation this poorly conceived legislation seemingly invited. Assuming there were antitheatrical zealots intrepid enough to venture into the playhouse to record and entrap, censorship now took on the notary function not just of disallowing words to be uttered but of certifying those that were. The censor's traditional priority, slander, had also acquired new nebulosity in 1606. That year saw a Star Chamber verdict on *de Libellis Famosis* (of Scandalous Libels), in which one Lewis Pickering was tried for pinning to Archbishop Whitgift's hearse "a lewd writing." English jurisprudence had always treated the defamation of magnates as a crime against persons rather than sedition against the realm—just the sort of "personations" London playhouses trafficked in—but *de Libellis Famosis* now radically widened the scope of actionable offenses. Supplementing the medieval statutes known as *Scandalum Magnatum,* the case established several precedents: first, in the eyes of the law it was irrelevant whether the victim was living or dead; second, and especially problematic for fictive representation, in the eyes of the law it was irrelevant whether the allegation was true or false. *De Libellis Famosis* further menaced the theater to the extent that Pickering's public assault was both written and spoken: an infamous libel, Coke concluded, could be either "*in scriptis*" or "*sine scriptis.*"[37] Though usually interpreted as having a more tangible impact on press freedoms, the ruling turned up the legal heat on dramatic performance and publication more or less equally.[38]

The crucial obstacle of theatrical censorship, though, was that it could never enforce these standards of discourse in a truly preemptive manner. In a regulatory regime based on purely textual inspection, performances were effectively policeable only up to a point; the Revels Master could not be expected to attend every playhouse, every day, to ensure that no changes had been introduced on top of the copy he had previously allowed. The relative quiescence such a structural inequity was nevertheless able to inspire has led Andrew Gurr to stress the players' good faith and their regimented capacity for self-restraint:

The "allowed" book and its comprehensive text, the target of the most recent modern editors, was maximal. The conditions that determined the performed text always pushed it in the direction of the minimal. . . . For practical reasons, to protect themselves against the censor, the players needed their licensed playscripts to contain the fullest possible text that the company might perform. From such a maximal text the players could make any number of cuts, but they could not readily add anything new to what had been "allowed."[39]

My argument will come to partake slightly of Gurr's questionable bias here toward codified theatrical procedure, but this formulation, while explanatorily powerful, functions better as a rough guideline than as a fixed and absolute rule. Gurr imagines the players' strict obedience the product of a coercive, adversarial relationship with the Revels Office, when, as scholars have recently begun to point out (and as I have intimated thus far), it may be characterized more accurately as one of paternalistic insulation. The censor's license and the percolated royal authority behind it sheltered the players from civic obstruction and legal prosecution—and equally the censor himself and his superiors from political embarrassment. In a society that assumed an inherent danger in public speech, indeed, he protected the players from themselves. The prerogative thus always lay with the players to upset this fragile dynamic of mutual forbearance, and the dramatic record is replete with instances where they chose to spurn such protection in favor of more lucrative opportunities for sensationalism.

Against the minority of cases wherein a company sidestepped the Revels Master's authority outright and staged a play without license, Gurr's dictum must contend with the number of *approved* plays that somehow maneuvered themselves into transgression only in performance (without now appealing to the ineptitude of Jacobean censorship instead of its severity), and with the likelihood of a broad array of theatrical techniques not just for perverting already screened textual material but for introducing new material altogether.[40] Gurr cites the classic example of *A Game at Chesse,* wherein the King's Men took refuge behind the claim that they had staged nothing not already in the allowed text, but he considers the visual keys they used to render certain identities plain (previously unspecified properties, mannerisms, dress) the extreme limit of the players' willingness to exceed that text rather than simply its most elegantly deniable manifestation.[41] Eight years later, Henry Herbert—the same Revels Master who had disgracefully allowed Middleton's nine-day wonder—would threaten to ban further performances of Shirley's *The Ball,* again because "ther were divers personated so naturally, both of lords and others of the court, that I took it ill." He relented, however, on assurances from Christopher Beeston, then manager of the offending Queen's Men, that "many things which I found faulte withall should be left out, and that he would not suffer it to be done by the poett any more, who deserves to be punisht."[42] Whether the poet was really an instigator or a fall guy here matters less than that Herbert's "many things which I found fault withal" denotes not just interpretations of the script but material *additions* to it, unlicensed dialogue ascribable to "poett"s. That Herbert issued only a warning, moreover, reflects a resignation to the fact that performance inevitably entailed such liberties. This tolerance was abused again in 1632, when the Church Court grilled him over surreptitious additions to *The Magnetic Lady;* his "care to purge their play" was noted, but not before "[the players] would have excused themselves on mee and the poett."[43] After the King's Men's *The Tamer Tamed* was staged without relicensing for revival (another way of staging illicit matter without technically evading the censor), Herbert took the opportunity to reiterate default Revels Office procedures:

> The Master ought to have copies of their new playes left with him, that he may be able to shew what he hath allowed or disallowed. All ould plays ought to bee brought to the Master of the Revells . . . ye rather that in former time the poetts tooke greater liberty than is allowed them by mee. *The players ought not to study their parts till I have allowed of the booke.*[44]

The purpose of this last dictum is not to economize the players' effort; it embodies Herbert's clear unease, even by 1633 (in contrast to his recollection of even *greater* licentiousness), that the allowed text might be treated not as the premise of a performance but as an afterthought to it. The players not only "study their parts" independent of censorial approval but actively depart from it, for Herbert goes on to instruct the bookkeeper Knight to "purge their parts, as I have the book."[45] The prevalence of this attitude "in former time" is concisely attested to by the surviving manuscript of *The Second Maiden's Tragedy* (c. 1611), allowed by Buc "with the reformations to be acted publicly," but also bearing a trio of unscored passages alluding satirically to the conjugal privileges of Arbella Stuart and William Seymour while they were (ostensibly) being held in separate prisons. The scenes' gossipy titillations are unadulterated because, in all probability, they were not there when Buc read the original script—written as they appear to be, in a scribal hand, on pasted-in slips.[46] The players did not especially feel that what they could stage was rigidly delimited by what the censor allowed, such that they had to wait around for his corrections; they took only enough care that what they ultimately staged gave no offense to him or to anyone else watching. Herbert's office book documents merely those instances where they took not enough—infractions that so flagrantly flouted his authority or so trampled on sensitive affairs that they could not go without reprimand. As this essay will go on to suggest, surely there were other modes of interpolation into the allowed text which altogether escaped the censor's initial attention, not only because they were temporally beyond it but because they were also discursively beneath it.

Despite a hamstrung regulatory structure that always enabled the more extreme kinds of performative delinquency to be practiced on allowed texts, however, they were never the institutional norm; no Jacobean playwright or sharer, so far as we know, was ever criminally charged for a slander originating in the playhouse.[47] Without recourse to punitive diligence or even a transparent, enforceable means of prevention, the Revels Master superintended a censorial apparatus that kept the players' most rebellious instincts in check. What seems to us like a bark worse than its bite may simply have been biting somewhere out of view. If applied rigorously, the exclusive press licensing power extended to the Revels Office in 1606 and the redundancy it introduced may have given Buc an ex post facto leverage over performance, unattainable solely from his preliminary allowance—depending, crucially, on what version of a play text he might deem eligible or ineligible for publication. We get a glimpse into these criteria from a letter written by George Chapman in the spring of 1608, its concern to obtain a press license for his two-part play *The Conspiracy and Tragedy of Charles Duke of Byron* making it likely the unnamed censor to whom he addresses it is Buc.[48] The *Byron* plays, acted by the Blackfriars boys, incidentally comprise the most brazen, recidivist example of an "allowed" text superseded onstage. Buc had initially licensed its performance conditional on deletions, but perceiving its diplomatic flammability (a Marshal of France, lately executed by Henri IV for treasonous affiliations with Spain) referred it to the Privy Council, which granted it three shows. The company promptly restored the struck passages onstage, and upon complaint by the French ambassador De la Boderie, the play was banned. This prohibition must have created a more irresistible draw, because at the very next court vacation the players staged it in its entirety again, only this time with *new* scenes foregrounding the latent correspondences between Byron and Essex and between the French queen and Elizabeth.[49] Learning of this insolence upon his return, James charged Salisbury and Montgomery to imprison them and to hunt down the poet. Chapman took sanctuary with the Duke of Lennox, and was evidently at sufficient repose that—with what seems like stupefying gall—he began expediting the play's printing. Not surprisingly, Buc refused it. Chapman's rebuttal, though, intimates some unexpected factors:

Sr.—I have not deserv'd what I suffer by your austeritie; if the two or three lynes crost were spoken, my uttermost to suppresse them was enough for my discharge. . . . I see not myne owne Plaies; nor carrie the Actors tongues in my mouthe . . . if the thrice allowance of the Counsaile for the Presentment gave not weight enoughe to drawe yours after for the presse, my Breath is a hopeles adition;

if you say (for your Reason) you know not *if more then was spoken be now written,
no, no;* nor can you know that, if you had bothe the Copies, not seeing the first at
all: Or if you had seene it presented your Memorie could hardly confer with it so
strictly in the Revisall to discerne the Adition . . .[50]

Reconsider for a moment the intuition that "not surprisingly" Buc for-
bade the plays to be printed. If they had already received a license for
performance, then Chapman—or any playwright or playing company in
his position—had a ready text to whose confirmed acceptability they
could appeal. Couldn't an allowed copy be assumed, by definition, fit for
publication—especially that of *Byron,* where it had no foreseeable use
toward future performances that had been barred, by a company facing
disbandment?

Such an assumption underlies Chapman's reference to "the thrice allowance of the Counsaile for the Presentment" and the weight he hopes
it would carry with Buc. But what follows suggests the allowed copy
is decidedly *not* the text in question. The actors' utterance of (by his
doubtless conservative estimate) some "two or three lynes crost" does not
merely constitute a personal affront which Chapman's apology seeks to
redress; it seems to have precipitated a material disjunction in the kind of
text Chapman was forced to submit and which he must now attempt to
suture. Specifically, he must unfurl a train of circumlocution to persuade
Buc *not* that this is the allowed copy, but rather a transcript of *performance*
bearing no substantive deviation from the allowed copy; the opening
appeal he makes to Buc's (and the Privy Council's) prior approbation
must now, with obvious difficulty, be weaved through the genetic fidelity
of what was *staged* to the sanctioned original. The cavil Chapman thus
anticipates is not that "more than was written was spoken"; this much
he has already been forced to concede. Instead it is that "more than was
spoken be now written": his transcript, he claims, introduces nothing new
over and against the *performed* content, which *itself* (and this is where he
runs headlong into contradiction) introduced nothing new over and against
the content originally allowed.[51] The alleged surplus is the topical scenes
the "Revisal" had interpolated into the contraband performance, which
Chapman is here awkwardly obliged both to include and to defend, both
as "a matter so far from offence" and as paradoxically consistent with what
had been authorized—arguing that Buc does not have the allowed copy in
front of him for comparison, and that had he witnessed the performance, its

"adition" was so trifling that Buc's memory could hardly have distinguished the two. He could not seriously have expected such lame spin-doctoring to work, or the incendiary passages ever to see the press. But what seems here a blatant compounding of his offense may actually have been an effort to mitigate it: on some level, he knew that by submitting the play in its staged entirety he was coming clean, and that rather than being an insurmountable obstacle to its publication, his disclosure of the full performed text was, more basically, the play's only chance to be printed at all. Rather than use the allowed copy, Chapman chose to submit a complete transcript—and go through the futile contortions of excusing it—because he really had no choice.

On some level, that is, Chapman knew that a mere reproduction of the allowed copy would peremptorily *not* be reallowed for the press, and that Buc expected for publication only a performed version—an expectation with which, even at the risk of tendering written proof of his crime, he appears to have fully complied. Chapman may have thought better of the disingenuousness in which he tried to couch that compliance, since he ultimately never sent this letter (the only reason we still have it, in fact). But apparently he did not need to do so—and perhaps his hairsplitting equivocations would only have backfired—because *The Conspiracy and Tragedy of Charles Duke of Byron* was, sure enough, entered in the Stationers' Register, under Buc's allowance, on June 5, 1608. It is a highly corrected text (indeed, sheer delay may explain Buc's "austeritie"), and its internal irregularities confirm that it was based on a version of the illicit performance just as Chapman (mincingly) insists. Two major excisions are evident, one at act 4, scene 1 of *The Conspiracy* and the other at the beginning of act 2 of *The Tragedy.* In the first, what may have been a diplomatic exchange at the English court between Byron and Queen Elizabeth is crudely converted into a tedious reportage unlikely to have been staged, perhaps so that Elizabeth should not be depicted speaking in person. The second cut spans the division between the first and second acts, so that a council scene abruptly gives way to a masque celebrating the reconciliation of the French queen and one of her ladies-in-waiting, totally omitting the cause of their estrangement. This lacuna lines up with ambassador De la Boderie's account of how "those very actors whom I had barred from playing the history of the late Marshal de Biron, noting all the court to be away, did so nonetheless, and not only that but introduced into it the Queen and Mde. De Vermeuil, the former treating the lady very ill verbally, and giving her a slap on the face"—a scene which recalled Elizabeth's abuse of her own maids of honor for their trysts with Essex.[52] There may be other extant traces of censorship across the diptych, but the congruence between these and the circumstantial evidence around the plays' staging and publication indicates that they derive from a text closer to the performance than to the allowed copy.[53]

The *Byron* case gives us near-paradigmatic insight into not only censorship criteria but Revels Office procedure in authorizing dramatic publication, because the political firestorm it ignited makes Chapman's decision to submit the incriminating performed version dangerous enough to represent conformity to a mandated practice; his emphatic protest that the play contained "no more then was spoken"—when "what was spoken" was *precisely* the basis of the allegations against him—is intelligible in no other context. By 1608, an assumption that the allowed copy for performance was unrecyclable for publication makes perfect sense as a consequence of extending press allowance to the Master of the Revels in 1606. A standing policy of rejecting mere duplicates of the allowed copy closed a loophole by which one allowance might (as Chapman argues) propagate the other; it also rendered the Master's fee, predicated on reading labor rather than on the license itself, automatically applicable. More important, since the object was to gain access to the company's playhouse practice, such a policy imbricated into the censorial process a capacity for retroactive surveillance.

The essence of this strategy is expressed in a brief that Sir Henry Herbert drew up on July 25, 1663, while he was struggling to reassert his authority over the reopened theaters. In it he aims "to prove that the Master of his Maiesties Office of the Revells, hath not onely the power of Lycensing all playes . . . but of appointing them to the Press":

[I]t may bee concluded but rationall, that hee who hath the power of allowing and Lycensing (as the Master hath) should likewise bee authorized to appoint and order for the press, least after such examination and allowance, alterations should bee made, and the abuse prove a scandall and reflection vpon the Master.[54]

Even if he could not attend every performance to ensure that the parameters of his preliminary allowance were being met, tying the players' prospective profit chain to their provision of a stage transcript had the convenient effect of sooner or later bringing those performances to him. Such a structural redundancy would have worked backward to reinforce the authority of the preliminary allowance itself, since a company would know that the more salaciously they deviated from their allowed text to attract playgoers, the less likely they were to parlay that publicity into a sought-after quarto, which might fuel gate receipts in return; by insisting that print not only advertise but reflect performance to a clinical degree, Buc tried to attack the self-perpetuating business model at its choke point. Conversely, for players wishing to register their obedience of Revels Office dictates and their dutiful avoidance of scurrility or slander, publication might become an indirect means of documenting what they had staged, thus shielding them from any conniving informants—or, perhaps, from any *honest* informant who attended on a day when they elected to perform something different. Since the "transcript" policy of dramatic publication merely buttressed the primary perlocution of securing license to perform (the company promises to play no more than its allowed text prescribes) with a secondary perlocution (the company promises what it is publishing is the text it performed) no less vulnerable to prevarication or to the innate mutability of a play's day-to-day identity on the stage, this system was obviously far from watertight, and could be used to open more loopholes than it sealed. At best, it did not change the fact that live performances could still traduce their allowed text with impunity, but the redundancy could serve as a deterrent by guaranteeing eventual discovery and punishment: not just if the players tried to publish what they had staged, but also if they tried to publish anything *else*.[55]

With no other hard testimony to corroborate it, this inference of a logic of textual discrimination behind the Revels Office censorship of printed drama might strain credibility—at least no less than do the hypotheses that it followed no combinatoric logic (pace Dutton), or that there were no lapses in the observance of allowed copies for which such reduplicative perusal might have compensated (pace Gurr). My reading, however, attempts to reconcile the idiosyncrasies of what evidence we have (Chapman's performance transcript, Buc's redoubled dispensation) with the sustainable assumption that scripts were routinely permeable in their transition from authorial draft to stage production, and that the Master of the Revels would naturally have been responsive to this potentially subversive plasticity. So fully did he adapt to the expectation that his allowed copy would be transgressed in performance, indeed, that he began to *mandate* the existence of plays in at least two discrete states, so as retrospectively to monitor that performance. As a result, around 1606 Buc introduced a key

distinction in how textual identity might be constructed—a distinction
that facilitated the articulation of naturalized "authorial" play texts without
bibliographic access to authorship itself. He wanted to be able to equate
what was printed with what had been performed, but the corollary of
doing so meant installing the conditions of their commercial and rhetorical
divergence.

Though designed to elicit performance transcripts should a company
wish to print a play, the post-1606 Revels policy may have attained its most
far-reaching significance in the kind of text whose corporate publication
it thus had to resist: the "allowed copy"—surely a variegated species of
theatrical document, but in practice most readily conflatable (as we saw in
Bonian and Walley's 1609 *Troilus and Cressida*) with the authorial draft.
The Revels policy imposed on the players an "eligibility requirement" for
press license that was tantamount to circumscribing their print rights over
a play text in its unperformed state; such a slippage into proprietary dispossession would merely have been the flip side of the proprietary protection
the Master's scrutiny informally provided. He was not accountable to (or
perhaps even much aware of) the broader categories of literary property
that prevailed among the Stationers, or to how his policy might indirectly
prejudice the players' ability to print a different edition or, indeed, might
undercut their exorbitant sale of "unique" manuscripts.[56] As far as Buc was
concerned, he was still protecting the players' staging right and its extension into print; should the players elect to publish a play, he only asked in
exchange that he determine the version they published. If, however, the
version he was *not* interested in (the allowed copy or, more realistically,
some relatively proximate transcription of it) should happen to find its way
out of the playhouse and across his desk—the *same* play according to every
agenda but his own—an otherwise unprintable copy was an indefensible
copy, and thus one available to others.

An instance of these criteria in reverse action, in fact, may be preserved
in one of the two exceptions earlier noted in Buc's otherwise uninterrupted
string of press licenses until 1615—that issued instead by Master Wilson of
the Stationers' Company, on May 2, 1608, to Thomas Pavier for *A Yorkshire
Tragedy*. The spuriousness of Pavier's ascription to "Wylliam Shakespere"
(wrong at least by modern critical consensus) has long been thought to
underlie Buc's refusal to allow it; Buc, it is assumed, based his judgment
on a comparative familiarity with the playwright's individual corpus, leaving Pavier to call in favors at Stationers' Hall.[57] A Revels Master actively

impeding the players' right to print their unadapted scripts, however, would have also been disposed to uphold their eminent right to adapted ones—*A Yorkshire Tragedy* almost certainly being such a performance text, running to barely seven hundred lines and styled as "one of the four plaies in one . . . as it was plaid by the Kings Maiesties Plaiers," suggesting it had been stripped down for a medley format.[58] Buc needed no prescient reverence for the historical self-identity of an author's work to ascertain that Pavier had illegitimate claim to this play. The performance-derived state of the text, especially contrasted with the earlier version he would have allowed, made it clear to him that the company had propriety to print it. For Buc the Shakespearean byline was not factually false but discursively irrelevant; he would have denied the allowance *whosever* name was on the title page, simply because Pavier presumably could not show proof of purchase from the King's Men. A less condescending portrait would see Pavier not even bothering with such a smoke screen for Buc and adding it only later for Wilson, who had no access to the text's vicissitudes, and for whom the name of an author—*any* author, in this case the King's Men's generic one—might have sufficed as the Master's imprimatur of a vacated theatrical asset. That Wilson knowingly overstepped well-marked territory to "allow" it here, indeed, intimates a belief that this was precisely what authorial names on playbooks had by now come to connote.

The opaque referentiality of Buc's inscription on the 1600 *Henry V*—not necessarily made in 1600, of course—should now be apparent. The remark "much the same with that in Shakespeare" does not disclose an interrogation of anonymity consistent with a bibliographic interest in individual authorship; Buc is contrasting rather than collapsing different versions of the same play, and the author's name is here simply a metonym for the version he already knows, the allowed copy, from which this "bad" quarto is likely to have drifted measurably. They are "much the same"—but not quite, for the control text is given its own designation, applied purely for clerical convenience: one will be called "Shakespeare," the other will not. That Buc is here only casually rehearsing this mode of discrimination, on a playbook he had personally licensed neither for performance nor for print, makes it plausible to reconstruct how the identity of the text Bonian and Walley submitted for real allowance might similarly have been arbitrated. Seeing that their manuscript was substantively indistinct from the one the Revels Office had earlier allowed, Buc's deputy Segar could summarily deem it not the play the actors had staged, and thus not the play to which their honorary printing privileges adhered; this was *Troilus and Cressida* not "as yt is acted" by the King's Men but "by" William Shakespeare. The rest is salesmanship. Uncertain how to proceed, Bonian and Walley took the local claim of nonperformance for a global one; formerly one figure among the several constituting the sociology of the text, the author thus had to be elevated, by a process of subtraction, into a position of solitary self- sufficiency.[59] The remainder of the intersubjective operations by which the playbook had been left to them to print, the name "William Shakespeare" was now all they had left to market the playbook: and so that name became flesh, an artificial and monadic subjectivity on whose genius—in antithesis to the corruptive exteriority of the stage— its pristine value could be founded, such that "the most displeased with Playes, are pleasd with his Commedies." Yet it is exactly the play's multiple mediations—in performance, in censorship—that have engendered and gestated this claim of immediacy. Only *because* Bonian and Walley can inclusively misterm *Troilus and Cressida* "a birth of your braine," in a sense, can they ever *mean* to call it an exclusive "birth of *his* braine": the authorship that contingently conditioned the text as property has been transfigured into an essential property of the text.

What makes this particular naturalization of a placeholder for material interests new, however, is that the kind of text to which the placeholder would systematically attach *was* in fact reliably closer to the playwright's draft. Ignorant of its underlying dynamics, Bonian and Walley's claims complete a circuitous coincidence with something approaching bibliographic truth. And yet, the result of textual categories imposed with bureaucratic dispassion, it was a coincidence also methodical and predictably achieved. Using its administrative bottleneck to foreclose "irregular duplications" of authority, the Revels Office not only indirectly fostered just such a mitosis— the individuated poet (as opposed to a company, its theater, its patron) in whom textual identity inhered—but was furthermore capable of doing so with regularity.[60] For though the authorial tag itself might be only an emergent expedient, positing no creative origin, the criteria by which it was affixed—to bracket off an ensuing creative chronology—were stable and transparent, and thus as repeatable as interpolation was ubiquitous. Did the *Troilus and Cressida* scenario ever happen again? Had it already happened before? Under Buc's dispensation, the more dimorphic a play became with its "allowed" progenitor, the more available that progenitor became to stationers, whose publication might follow the same form; the "older" and the more exceeded by performance a text seemed, the likelier it was to be repackaged as "new," as "authorial." Attribution in print—for those playwrights unable to seek it privately—thus became a remote function not of synchronic composition on the page but of the play's diachronic life upon the stage. Authorship retroactively depended, in other words, *on other words,* on what verbal and dramatic accretions had already been introduced to invalidate the propriety of the allowed copy. This is not the same as writing overlength plays (though it does not preclude it) for theatrical cutting, which yielded only a strict subset of the first, exactly what the censor's activism was meant to reward. Rather, exploiting an inverse relation between performance and print would have involved theatrical instruments for the overt dilation of scripts—instruments with which, as it turns out, any playing company came standard equipped. We might thus tease one last question out of *Troilus and Cressida:* Why does the publishers' newfound confidence in its authorial status also leave them with the impression—contrary to their initial advertisement—that it is now a comedy?

Since we are exploring the exact obverse of the publication strategy he pioneered, we might do better to recall Jonson's jab at his contemporaries in *The Alchemist:* if Shakespearean "romance" is usually taken to be the target of his contempt for plays that "runne away from Nature, and be afraide of her," why did he lump Shakespeare among the "presumers on their owne Naturalls"—indulgent, that is, of his fools, who "mock at termes, when they understand not the thinges" merely to "tickle the Spectators"? This is the same Shakespeare, after all, who a decade earlier had Hamlet warn his clowns to "speak no more than is set down for them"—and yet in performance this moment actually seems to have been a spur to improvisation, for in the 1603 quarto Hamlet then launches into an otherwise unscripted parody of the clown's "cinkapase of jeasts." Q1 *Hamlet* is much shrunken to fit the exigencies of performance, but through performance it has obviously grown in places as well, in pockets that reflect (among other possible sources) the particulate interpolations of accident, whimsy, or private study—remember Herbert's anxiety that the actors' "parts" digress from the allowed book. Leaving aside the eccentricity that a "part"-based system already wove into the fabric of playing, Burbage, in this case, is not even one of those who specialized in extempore. Metatheatrical depictions of clowning technique—most of them, like *Hamlet's*, admonitory—are legion and require no catalog here; rarely noticed, however, and more difficult to reconcile with this tension, is the degree to which clowns were *expected* to augment or ad-lib their parts, beyond the logistics of the entr'acte. "*He playes and sings any odde toy*"; "*Jackie is led to whipping over the stage, speaking some word, but of no importance*"; "*Exit clown, speaking anything*"; "*speak anything, and exit*"; "*Here they two talk and rail what they list*": such "empty" stage directions seemingly have little to do with scene change, but rather illustrate a normative malleability to performance—wherein, the Caroline comedy *Lady Alimony* recollects, "the Actor could embellish his Author, and return a Pean to his Pen," perhaps belying Jonson's wishful generalization that English plays are, unlike the Italian, "all premeditated things."[61] Indeed, the aforementioned merely comprise the few (and extant) instances where improvisation was institutionalized within the text, given a finite outlet and frame. They are all written for playhouses where the anarchy of the jig was still to follow.

Those companies, however, that omitted this postlude—like the King's Men—might be less able to localize the assimilation of its energy in the body of the play. Eric Rasmussen has discovered how such disruption might have been more diffusely encoded, in his analysis of the manuscript revision of *Sir Thomas More* (a revision to which Shakespeare is thought to have contributed). Hand B's mislineated insertion of several "new" comic speeches represents not the addition of a clown's part but the marginal transcription of lines spoken by a character merely mute in the original— "Rafe," who often appears onstage but is mysteriously never given anything to say.[62] *Sir Thomas More* is early evidence of improvisation that not only encompassed an entire role but, more important, was subsequently *recorded,* integrated into an accumulating text whose growth spurts correspond to variations in performance as much as to the interventions of revising dramatists. Scripts, that is, were in this dimension perfectly capable of incrementally expanding on their own, and the more they did so, the more comic they got. Why else, as John Kerrigan notes, do plays revised for revival typically feature amplifications of jesting—the enlarged scenes of Robin/Dick, Horse-Courser, and Obtuse Knight in B *Doctor Faustus,* Strumbo in *Locrine,* Mouse in *Mucedorus,* the fool Passarello wholly invented for QC *The Malcontent?*[63] Given this pattern, why limit the adapters to playwrights? We cannot know where improvisation has infiltrated a play text, since—especially for those companies with no set regimen for it—it may similarly have occurred anywhere, needing no cue except the sheer onstage presence of a performer suitable to it. Q *Lear* (1608) does not even dictate a "manet Fool" for the division between scenes 2 and 3 of act 3 that, by the Folio text, now harbors his sixteen-line preposterous "prophecy." When we compare this irruption with the widespread convention of scripting such terminal audience addresses, we too may be looking at events preposterously, at least some of those "manets" merely serendipitous spontaneities grafted post hoc into later versions. The Folio *Lear* may be a case of mostly authorial self-revision, but its inclusion of the metrically crude prophecy intimates a debt to the play's performance history and to the potential range of material it deposited. Without suggesting that the Fool did not really disappear after act 3, scene 6—that, having outlined the role for Robert Armin, Shakespeare simply (as with "Rafe") stopped writing lines for him—the possibility remains that by 1608 *King Lear* had in performance become demonstrably distended from its cut, allowed original.

Could this be a difference for which the 1608 quarto's title page angles? Distancing it as literary property from the 1605 *Leir*, as has long been recognized, is surely a key task—but it is a task the publisher Nathaniel Butter already achieves by listing *Lear*'s distinctive plot points, by mentioning its court production, by noting its company affiliation. Yoking its overarching identity to a naturalized author, however, "M. William Shak-speare / HIS / True Chronicle Historie," is an overkill that here finds no natural place. Rather, as Douglas Brooks observes, in so configuring the title page (and in setting the verse continuously), Butter and his printer Nicholas Okes seem to be marketing *King Lear* like a Jonson play, an artifact transcendent of its theatrical incarnation— "not the play as it would have been performed at the playhouse" but instead, as the subsidiary equation announces, "*As it was played before the Kings Maiestie.*"[64] The author once again emerges to differentiate a play from itself, and the textual claim he subtends is once again calibrated to the single agency capable of supplying both. Having some months earlier supervised the play's rehearsal for court— having always *had* to do so, indeed, despite the fact that the "allowed" copy already implied suitability, since all licensed plays were technically "rehearsals" for court—when Buc authorized *Lear* for the press on or before November 26, 1607, he was ideally positioned to distinguish it from how it had been "usually" performed and might have permitted Butter to print it on just this basis. Because at more than three thousand lines, the quarto cannot really have been "as it was played," either. The claim of court performance functions in the same way as the claim of nonperformance in *Troilus and Cressida,* merely a back-formation of the last time Buc could verify conformity to the allowed book; the author, the allowed book's *nom de voyage,* remains their unlikely common denominator. If a second pass through the play had revealed fresh encrustations of interpolated matter to expunge, the irony may be that this *Lear* got published—for all its Jonsonian pretense—by virtue of its containing not just "more than hath been publickely spoken," but also less.

Discussing the creative autonomy habitually accorded the stage clown's extemporal wit, Tiffany Stern remarks that "authors are linked in this way with the very elements of their plays over which they have no control."[65] Here, however, is an institutional circuit—widened to include another traditional violator of literary integrity, the censor—in which that linkage becomes not just superficial but discursively generative, the radical multiplicity of authorship in one domain facilitating its radical singularity in another; the name of the playwright attains new regulatory and cultural value precisely *to the extent that* the distinction between actor and author has not yet solidified. As a result of the stereoscopic complexity that began in 1606 to interanimate the series of textual mediations separating composition and publication, having "no control" over a play in performance could paradoxically mean exercising remote control over its representation in print. A reduplicative system of perusal, improvising a license and a proprietary identity for the allowed copy, redoubled the playwright's incentive to license the improvisation that individuated it and—along for the ride—him: "the law of writ" and "the liberty" legislated and liberated each other, simultaneously, across different jurisdictions. The man of theater and the man in print can be one and the same: what turned a play written for the stage into one written for the page was just another copy of it, which private manuscript circulation could eventually be disposed to provide. Characteristic of the amphibious persona we are now coming to imagine, such self-interest converged with self-withdrawal. Whereas Jonson could erect his literary authority only by arresting the flux of theatrical adaptation, Shakespeare let his be produced by it, by successive interpretive communities indifferently implementing their own textual practices, each doing what came "naturally." His executors would commandeer this collaborative rhetoric of origin—in a folio that coincided, curiously, not with the death of the author but with the death of the Revels Master who formalized his estrangement. Yet in presenting his works "as he conceived them," Heminges and Condell must now overshoot the mark. Those works as much "conceived" him, an afterbirth of their promiscuities; Shakespeare's final intentions became a commodity because they were never intended to be final.

Notes

The author wishes to acknowledge the generous support of the Mellon Foundation and the Mabelle McLeod Lewis Memorial Fund for enabling revision of this essay.

1. *Shakespeare's Sonnets,* ed. Stephen Booth (New Haven, Conn.: Yale University Press, 1977), no. 111.

2. For succinct retrospectives, see Paul Werstine, "Narratives about Printed Shakespeare Texts: 'Foul Papers' and 'Bad' Quartos," *Shakespeare Quarterly* 41, no. 1 (1990): 65-86; and W. B. Worthen, *Shakespeare and the Authority of Performance* (Cambridge: Cambridge University Press, 1997), esp. chap. 4.

3. Jeffrey Masten, "Playwrighting: Authorship and Collaboration," in *A New History of Early English Drama,* ed. John D. Cox and David Scott Kastan (New York: Columbia University Press, 1997), 357-82; quotes from 367-71. See also his *Textual Intercourse: Collaboration, Authorship and Sexualities in Renaissance Drama* (Cambridge: Cambridge University Press, 1997).

4. Tiffany Stern, *Rehearsal from Shakespeare to Sheridan* (Oxford: Oxford University Press, 2000), 84.

5. Masten, "Playwrighting," 371 (his emphasis).

6. James J. Marino, "William Shakespeare's *Sir John Oldcastle,*" *Renaissance Drama* 30 (2001): 93-114, esp. 93-95, 102-7. Marino's argument is an incisive (and proleptic) application of Joseph Loewenstein's idea that authors emerge along "fault lines" between systems of property regulation, a fiction that "does duty for rights yet to be invented"; see Joseph Loewenstein, *Jonson and Possessive Authorship* (Cambridge: Cambridge University Press, 2002), esp. 15-68 and 35 for quote.

7. Marino, "Shakespeare's *Oldcastle,*" 110-11.

8. For Loewenstein the "borderland" in which the author emerges is "the competition between media" (*Jonson and Possessive Authorship,* 53), but it is a contest over rights rather than the consumers at the end of them; the author is thus always left "in figure, in fantasy" (*Jonson and Possessive Authorship,* 50), a fantasy everyone seems to be having except book buyers, who at some point must have been persuaded it had a descriptive bearing on the books they were being asked to buy.

9. *The Magnificent Entertainment* (1604) is also headed "B. JON: / HIS PART OF . . . " and includes "other additions." Jonson would reuse the formula of *Sejanus* in the F1 titles to *Catiline, Epicene, The Alchemist,* and *Volpone.* By F2 *Volpone,* interestingly, the task is taken over by the phrase "with the allowance of the Master of the Revels."

10. The first state begins, "BEN: JONSON, / HIS / CASE IS ALTERD"; when Sutton canceled it to include his partner William Barrenger, it was reset as "A Pleasant Comedy, / CALLED: / The Case is Altered. / As it hath beene sundry times acted by the children of the Black-friers." The

omission of Jonson (preserved in the Kemble copy), previously integral with the title, had to be deliberate: when the decision was overruled during printing, moreover, the name was replaced, in smaller type, *after* that of the company. Possibly the sales pitch shifted because, with the company's breakup in 1608, an item from its repertory rather than the writer's study became the rarer good; and so his case was altered. See W. W. Greg, *A Bibliography of the English Printed Drama,* vol. 1 (London: Bibliographical Society, 1939–59), 417–18; and *The Works of Ben Jonson,* vol. 3, ed. C. H. Herford and P. and E. Simpson (Oxford: Clarendon, 1925–52), 94–96.

   11. The dates correspond to Marston's *Antonio and Mellida,* Chapman's *Byron* plays, and Fletcher's *Faithfull Shepheardess.* For playbook errata, see N. W. Bawcutt, "Renaissance Dramatists and the Texts of Their Plays," *Research Opportunities in Renaissance Drama* 40 (2001): 1–24.

   12. Douglas Brooks, *From Playhouse to Printing House* (Cambridge: Cambridge University Press, 2000), 42–55; for other signals of this upmarket shift, such as continuous printing and Latin epigraphy, see also his "*King Lear* (1608) and the Typography of Literary Ambition," *Renaissance Drama* 30 (2001): 133–59; and Zachary Lesser, "Walter Burre's *The Knight of the Burning Pestle,*" *ELR* 29, no. 1 (1999): 22–43.

   13. John Fletcher, *The Faithfull Shepheardesse* (1610), Early English Books 1475–1640, 836:05, A1r and A3v; Ben Jonson, *Catiline His Conspiracy* (1611), 757:04, A2r and A3r; Ben Jonson, *The Alchemist* (1612), 757:01, A3r; John Webster, *The White Divel* (1612), 1296:01, A2r.

   14. The process is still in a schizophrenic state by Webster's *Duchess of Malfi:* both "*As it was Presented*" and "The perfect and exact Coppy, with diuerse *things printed, that the length of the Play* would not beare in the Presentment." Where exactly this text resides is complicated further by its inclusion of an actors' list.

   15. Though plays—particularly the sole copy bearing allowance—were company property, the company was owned by its sharers, into whose hands books passed upon defection or dissolution. In a very real (and provocative) sense, Shakespeare already partly "owned" the primal embodiments of his works, just not as their "author."

   16. For discussions and transcriptions of the Brome (1635) and Whitefriars (1607–1608) contracts, see G. E. Bentley, *The Profession of Dramatist in Shakespeare's Time, 1590–1642* (Princeton, N.J.: Princeton University Press, 1971), 264ff., and Loewenstein, *Jonson and Possessive Authorship,* 48, 53–54.

   17. Brooks concedes that "Shakespeare seems to have been reluctant to see his plays published" (*Playhouse,* 9); in Thomas L. Berger and Jesse M. Lander's more loaded phrasing, he "never showed the least bit of interest in being a dramatic author" ("Shakespeare in Print, 1593–1640," in *A Companion to Shakespeare,* ed. David Scott Kastan [London: Blackwell, 1999], 409). Kastan's position is more nuanced, but still sees textual and theatrical "logic" as hermetically sealed: see *Shakespeare and the Book* (Cambridge: Cambridge University Press, 2001), 9ff., and also his *Shakespeare after Theory* (New York and London: Routledge, 1999), 71–92.

   18. William Shakespeare, *Othello* (1622), Early English Books/STC 904:13, A2. Walkley's duplicity has only lately been noticed, to my knowledge, by Gary Taylor in a paper delivered at the Huntington Library, March 20, 2004.

19. Lukas Erne, *Shakespeare as Literary Dramatist* (Cambridge: Cambridge University Press, 2003), esp. chapters 3, 5, and 6.

20. Phrases preliminary to *King Lear* (1608) and *Pericles* (1609). The frequency of the modifier "true" in playbook titles is surprisingly low—only *Nobody and Somebody* (1606), *Tiberius* (1607), Heywood's *Rape of Lucrece* (1608), and *A Yorkshire Tragedy* (1609) carry it between 1603 and 1613, and these seem keyed to a representation of "non-fiction" rather than to the representation of that representation.

21. Erne, *Shakespeare as Literary Dramatist,* 101-9.

22. Bentley, *Dramatist,* 262; 275-79.

23. William Shakespeare, *Troylus and Cresseid* (1609), Early English Books 1475-1640, 904:15.

24. Loewenstein, *Jonson and Possessive Authorship,* 26-35.

25. Richard Dutton, "The Birth of the Author," in *Texts and Cultural Change in Early Modern England,* ed. Cedric C. Brown and Arthur F. Marotti (New York: St. Martin's, 1997), 153-79; quote on 167. The essay is reprinted in Richard Dutton, *Licensing, Censorship and Authorship* (London: Palgrave, 2000).

26. G. E. Bentley, *The Profession of Player in Shakespeare's Time, 1590-1642* (Princeton, N.J.: Princeton University Press, 1984), 163.

27. However conventional, the language of the Robertes entry, "as yt is acted," provides some indication of the play's prior performance on the public stage. It thus significantly bolsters the sincerity of Bonian and Walley's claims that this stock formula is absent from their entry.

28. Evidence for the former relies on the relationship Robertes had with the theater as a printer of playbills; Loewenstein (*Jonson and Possessive Authorship,* 38-45) inclines toward the latter, especially in light of the glaring clause in his July 22, 1598, entry for *Merchant of Venice,* "Provided that yt bee not prynted . . . without lycence first had from the Right honorable the Lord Chamberlen"—a still earlier precedent for the paternalistic intercessions the Revels Office was expected to make. Erne hypothesizes Robertes's habit of "flipping" preregistered properties to other stationers (*Shakespeare as Literary Dramatist,* 104-5)— but then why would Bonian and Walley choose to drop tenpence to register it again?

29. Dutton, "Birth of the Author," 168.

30. Ibid., 168-69. The Huntington copy of the *Henry V* quarto is viewable at Early English Books/STC 353:6.

31. Ibid., 168.

32. Two objections will instantly be raised: it was not Buc but his deputy Segar who authorized for the press here; *Troilus and Cressida* debuted c. 1601-1602, by any reckoning too early for either of them to have initially allowed it. Normative procedure upon licensing for the stage, however, seems to have been for copies to be left with the Revels Master, "that he may be able to shew what he hath allowed or disallowed"; Herbert's quotation is discussed subsequently. This trace objectified and perpetuated its commensurability with the copy allowed for the press. While the custom cannot have been too rigidly followed, and is not important where Buc's perusals were more adjacent, it is consistent with a Revels Office policy wary of interpolations in performance, and with the fact that as often as breaches still occurred, Herbert was invariably able to exonerate himself. The only dispositive instance,

indeed, of the Revels Master's *not* retaining a duplicate is Chapman's letter (as will be discussed), when Buc had sent his to the Privy Council. That Chapman even raises the issue implies conferral was routine.

33. This point eludes Dutton because he discounts that Buc was at this time clearing plays both for the stage and for the press, and in *Mastering the Revels: The Regulation and Censorship of English Renaissance Drama* (London: Macmillan, 1991), he quixotically attempts to disprove it despite the fact that it strengthens his overall thesis. I have omitted these arguments, but the evidence for Buc's having become de facto Master at least by 1606 in Edmund Tilney's stead is as follows: Tilney's semiretirement from court duties after 1603; Buc's financial stake in Revels Office affairs before his reversion took effect in 1610; a workload sufficient for Buc to hire a deputy; company patents that from 1606 onward refer to Tilney and Buc interchangeably; a patronage system designed (as Dutton shows) to defuse rather than sow factional discord. See Dutton, *Mastering the Revels*, 149ff.; for a life of Buc, see Mark Eccles, "Sir George Buc, Master of the Revels," in *Thomas Lodge and Other Elizabethans*, ed. C. J. Sisson (Cambridge, Mass.: Harvard University Press, 1933), 409–506.

34. Greg, *English Printed Drama*, vol. 1, 386–87.

35. How the Revels Office ultimately lost its exclusive press authority in 1615, in fact, may tell us who procured it in 1606—once again, the Lord Chamberlain (from 1603 through 1614 Thomas Howard, Earl of Suffolk). The headline Revels event of 1615 was the succession of Robert Carr, Earl of Somerset, by William Herbert, Earl of Pembroke, as Buc's manager. Pembroke was the most powerful ally the King's Men would ever have, and if Buc's policies ended up disadvantaging the players, his countermand makes sense as the force that put a stop to them. When his brother Henry Herbert reasserted the right after becoming Master of the Revels in 1623, he took care to apply it less circularly and vindictively, and he occasionally paid for it.

36. 3 Jac. I cap. 21, in *The Statutes at Large*, vol. 7 (Cambridge: Joseph Bentham, 1763), 194.

37. 5 Co. Rep. 125a; his digest is reprinted in *The Selected Writings of Sir Edward Coke*, vol. 1, ed. Steve Sheppard (Indianapolis: Liberty Fund, 2003), 145–48. My summary follows S. F. C. Milsom, *Historical Foundations of the Common Law*, 2d ed. (Toronto: Butterworths, 1981), 388–90; I am also indebted to correspondence with Debora Shuger and to an unpublished paper of hers on the topic.

38. See Frederick S. Siebert, *Freedom of the Press in England 1476–1776* (Urbana: University of Illinois Press, 1952), 116ff; Philip J. Finkelpearl, "'The Comedians' Liberty': Censorship of the Jacobean Stage Reconsidered," *ELR* 16, no. 1 (1986): 123–38; and Lindsay Kaplan, *The Culture of Slander in Early Modern England* (Cambridge: Cambridge University Press, 1997), 30–32.

39. Andrew Gurr, "Maximal and Minimal Texts: Shakespeare v. the Globe," *Shakespeare Survey* 52 (1999): 68–87; quotes from 70 and 76.

40. For a synopsis of this critical polarization of early Stuart licensing practice, see Finkelpearl, "'Comedians' Liberty,'" 124–30.

41. Gurr, "Maximal and Minimal Texts," 75.

42. Quoted in *The Dramatic Records of Henry Herbert*, ed. Joseph Quincy Adams (New Haven, Conn.: Yale University Press, 1917), 19, subscript for 18 November 1632. Bawcutt has

recently reedited the office-book transcripts; for their murky history, see *The Control and Censorship of Caroline Drama* (Oxford: Clarendon, 1996).

43. Ibid., 22, subscript for 24 October 1633.

44. Ibid., 20–21, subscript for 18 October 1633 (my emphasis).

45. Ibid., 21.

46. Dutton, *Mastering the Revels*, 194, 201–3.

47. To be sure, playwrights could be summoned, examined, incarcerated, and threatened with violence or destitution—the combined aftermaths of plays like *The Isle of Dogs, Eastward Ho,* and *Sejanus* furnishing these examples. But such rifts were reparable, and the consequences of a criminal trial were not.

48. Aware that because "it is universally assumed that this letter was addressed to Buc . . . it might seriously undermine my argument that Buc did not act as Tilney's deputy," Dutton spends several pages trying to squelch this opinion; see his *Mastering the Revels*, 152–56.

49. My reconstruction wholly follows Dutton's in his *Mastering the Revels*, 182–86.

50. MS Folger 420423, my emphasis. See Elias Schwartz, "The Dating of Chapman's *Byron* Plays," *Modern Philology* 58 (1961): 201; George Ray, ed., *Chapman's The Conspiracy and Tragedy of Charles, Duke of Byron,* vol. 1 (New York and London: Garland, 1979), 4; and Dutton, *Mastering the Revels*, 151–52.

51. Chapman makes this concatenation even more strenuous, indeed, by contradicting his premise that the text is a transcript (and that if he "had seene it presented" Buc would not have discerned it from the allowed copy) when he blames the actors for the "two or three lynes" restored, since "I see not myne owne Plaies." "See," however, might here mean only oversee through rehearsal.

52. The textual analysis is Dutton's, though my inspection of Ray concurs with it. See Dutton, *Mastering the Revels*, 182, 186–87.

53. Thus Chapman describes the plays in his dedication to Sir Thomas Walsingham as "poor dismembred poems." In "Sir George Buc's Authority as Licenser for the Press," *Shakespeare Quarterly* 12, no. 4 (1961): 467–68, Elias Schwarz asserts (with no support) that "the copy sent to Buc was clearly *not* the prompt-copy"—a claim that does not technically conflict with mine, but which amusingly forces him to insert a "[sic]" after Chapman's plea that "more than was spoken be now written," when it cannot be a metathesis.

54. *Dramatic Records*, 125.

55. The fact that the Byron plays were published at all evinces the Revels Master's need to show that he was doing his job, which was more preventive than penal. Such a policy did not preclude printing transgressive plays, but merely ensured that the Master be part of the circuit of redemptive authority; the price of this second allowance was the risk of punishment. Chapman, who clearly had important friends, gambled and won. Many of *Byron*'s counterparts, however—the Scottish Mines play, the *Second Maiden's Tragedy*— apparently declined it, and in most cases licenses for the press were either never obtained or never sought, corroborating what Finkelpearl calls "*ex post facto* censorship" ("'Comedians' Liberty,'" 125 n. 11). Licensing only performance transcripts for print explains this tiered inconsistency in permissibility.

56. The fabulous expense of presentation copies—Humphrey Moseley's estimate in the 1647 *Beaumont and Fletcher* Folio of "more then foure times the price you pay for [this]

whole Volume" is almost absurd, since the folio cost over £1—seems tied to their exclusivity. In an MS of *A Game at Chesse,* Middleton promises its dedicatee that no "Stationers Stall can showe" the play, or at least this version of it; see Erne, *Shakespeare as Literary Dramatist,* 90.

57. Dutton, *Mastering the Revels,* 149-50.

58. C. F. Tucker Brooke, *The Shakespeare Apocrypha* (Oxford: Clarendon, 1908), xxxiii-xxxiv.

59. See previous note 27.

60. "Irregular duplication" is the idiom of Christopher Barker, a stationer complaining of disorderly printing in the 1580s. Loewenstein treats it as a poetics of licensing: see *Ben Jonson and Possessive Authorship,* 17, and his *The Author's Due: Printing and the Prehistory of Copyright* (Chicago: University of Chicago Press, 2002), 27-51.

61. Robert Greene, *Orlando Furioso* (1594), Early English Books/STC 344:13 F4v; Thomas Heywood, *2 Edward IV* (1600) 323:8, L5r; Anon., *The Tryall of Chevalrie* (1605) 1191:11 G2 and E4; Jo(shua) Cooke, *Greenes Tu Quoque* (1614) 1169:05 J1r; Anon., *Lady Alimony* (1657) Wing 152:08, A1v; Ben Jonson, *The Case is Altered* 2.7.35, ed. Herford and Simpson. See Thornton S. Graves, "Some Aspects of Extemporal Acting," *Studies in Philology* 19 (1922): 429-56.

62. Eric Rasmussen, "Setting Down What the Clown Spoke: Improvisation, Hand B, and *The Book of Sir Thomas More,*" in *The Library: Transactions of the Bibliographical Society* 13 (1991): 126-36.

63. John Kerrigan, "Revision, Adaptation and the Fool in *King Lear,*" in *The Division of the Kingdoms: Shakespeare's Two Versions of "King Lear,*" ed. Gary Taylor and Michael Warren (Oxford: Clarendon, 1983), 195-245.

64. Brooks, *"King Lear* and Typography," 149.

65. Stern, *Rehearsal,* 102.

Reforming Shakespeare

RICHARD W. SCHOCH

I am a Reformer—a *Dramatic* Reformer! I would have *Shakspeare and the People* duly represented!

—"Philo-Dramaticus," 1830[1]

I N 1660, UPON the restoration of the British monarchy, Charles II awarded a monopoly on theatrical productions in London to William Davenant and Thomas Killigrew, establishing a royal precedent for the regulation of theater in the capital city. The patents, granted to successive generations of theater owners, remained in effect until the passage of the Theatres Regulation Act of 1843. The Licensing Act of 1737 prohibited the production of any play not previously licensed by the Lord Chamberlain and restricted authorized theaters to the city of Westminster. The combined effect of the royal patent and the licensing act was to confirm Covent Garden and Drury Lane (and, in the summer, the Haymarket) as the only theaters in London where Shakespeare could be performed legally for almost two hundred years.

On May 31, 1832, Parliament named Edward Bulwer-Lytton—novelist, playwright, and radical politician—chairman of its Select Committee on Dramatic Literature and charged him with the task of examining the chaotic state of theatrical licensing and censorship.[2] The Select Committee spent the next six weeks receiving testimony from a range of constituents in the theatrical world: the Lord Chamberlain's office, the patent theaters, the minor theaters, local magistrates, critics, playwrights, and actors. It was a particularly appropriate time to revisit the vexed issue of theatrical regulation. The patentees of Drury Lane and Covent Garden were continually bringing suits against London's minor theaters for the unlicensed performance of burletta and melodrama. Petitions were sent to King William IV urging fewer restrictions against the minor theaters. And treatises such as T. J. Thackeray's *Theatrical Emancipation* were being read in the coffeehouses and taverns of London.

By 1832, as Joseph Donohue has written, "the ability of the two major theatres to protect their domain against the encroachment of the 'minor' playhouses had dwindled into impotence," and the patent theaters had proved themselves "hopelessly inept . . . [at] preserving the monopoly originally granted a century and three-quarters before."[3] "The laws affecting Dramatic Literature," in the wry observation of the *British and Foreign Review* from 1836, are "flourishing in the full vigour of their incapacity." The publication further asserted that the "haughty dignity" of playhouse patents no longer stood for a benign Georgian paternalism, just as the rotten boroughs of the House of Commons no longer guaranteed the blessings of impartial aristocratic wisdom.[4] They both stood, shamefully, for "Old Corruption."

Although it would not become law for another eleven years, the Select Committee's major—and controversial—recommendation was that all licensed theaters in London "should be allowed to exhibit, at their option, the Legitimate Drama."[5] Reason alone dictated that the restrictions on the performance of "Legitimate Drama" had to be lifted. It was impossible for Parliament to define by "clear and legal distinctions" the difference between legitimate and illegitimate drama. And what Parliament could not define, it could not prohibit. To employ a phrase associated with early nineteenth-century political economy, Bulwer's committee advocated "free trade" in the drama. "Public interest is superior to any private considerations," the Shakespeare editor and theater historian John Payne Collier argued in his testimony; "if the minor theatres tend to make the drama a better school of morals and conduct, no private interest ought to stand in the way of that advantage" (*SC*, 25). "What just right can any government have," the *Westminster Review* similarly argued in 1834, "to make the pleasure or the good of a whole capital, nay indeed of a whole nation, bow to the private interests of a few?"[6] Here was unequivocal support for theatrical free trade, articulated in the language not of individual self-interest, but of the public good.

Of course, theatrical free trade meant the dissolution of the monopoly traditionally enjoyed by Drury Lane and Covent Garden in the production of legitimate drama—however the term "legitimate" might be defined.

Abolishing the letters patent of Charles II scarcely gave the Select Committee pause, however, since it concluded that the royal privileges bestowed upon the major houses "have neither preserved the dignity of the Drama, nor . . . been of much advantage to the Proprietors of the Theatres" (*SC,* 4). Indeed, during the nearly thirty years from the end of the Napoleonic Wars to the passage of the Theatres Regulation Act, box office receipts steadily declined, the patent theaters were continually on the verge of financial ruin, and Shakespeare gave way to spectacle and melodrama. If not even a monopoly could make Shakespeare "pay," then what rational objection could there be to allowing any licensed theater to perform Shakespeare? In the spirit of laissez-faire economics, the committee placed its trust not in political definitions of aesthetic practice (it knew better than that) but in the "ordinary consequences of Competition: convenience in the number and situation of Theatres, and cheap and good Entertainment in the Performances usually exhibited" (*SC,* 6).

The patentees, for their part, had no intention of swallowing the bitter pill of political economy. And as the financial outlook for their theaters grew increasingly bleak, the proprietors of Covent Garden and Drury Lane clung to their privileges more tenaciously still. But defending the patent system had become so ludicrously counterintuitive that the patentees, when testifying before Parliament in 1832, were often shamed into silence by the perverse logic of their own arguments. Charles Kemble, as the *British and Foreign Review* further reported, stood up "lustily" for a patent right which he "does not, because he cannot explain."[7] Kemble insisted that Shakespeare's plays needed to be staged in large theaters—that is, Covent Garden (which he partly owned) or Drury Lane. If the smaller, minor theaters staged Shakespeare, the resulting productions, he believed, would be inferior (*SC,* 44–45).

What Kemble deliberately overlooked was that nearly every minor theater in London that was outside the city of Westminster staged illegitimate productions of Shakespeare in the years leading up to the 1832 Select Committee. The *Theatrical Observer* reported in May 1831:

At the theatre royal, Drury Lane we have *Timour the Tartar* and the horses. At the theatre royal, Covent Garden we have the *Life and Death of Buonaparte,* as a mere spectacle accompanied by every kind of catch-shilling gew-gaw, and some horses; while, on the other hand, we find at Sadler's Wells, *Romeo and Juliet, Katharine and Petruchio;* at the Surrey, *Richard III,* several other of Shakespeare's plays and Cumberland's *Jew,* with [Robert] Elliston.[8]

To be sure, such productions frequently disguised themselves—disingen-
uously—through non-Shakespearean titles, such as *How to Die for Love*
instead of *Romeo and Juliet* and *Methinks I See my Father* instead of
Hamlet.[9] In one of his final performances, no less a star (though by then a
fading one) than Edmund Kean played Shylock and Othello at the Coburg
(now the Old Vic) and New City theaters.

As Bulwer's fellow committee members pointedly observed, Kemble's
argument lacked logic. If he honestly believed that minor theaters would
perform Shakespeare badly, then he should not object to giving them the
right to do so. Inept performances at minor theaters would not threaten
his position in the theatrical marketplace because audiences would not
attend inferior productions. Since market principles would ensure a flight
to quality, as it were, it was simply unreasonable to regard (conjecturally)
bad performances of Shakespeare at minor theaters as somehow both
threatening and irrelevant. Yet, as the committee surmised, Kemble se-
cretly feared that the minor theaters would perform Shakespeare with
considerable success and thus pose a direct threat to the patent theaters
(*SC*, 45). Parliament thus exposed the irrationality of Kemble's testimony:
that the minor theaters should be suppressed because their productions
of Shakespeare would be *inferior* to those mounted at the patent theaters.
Indeed, the opposite seemed true: that productions of Shakespeare at
the minor theaters did, in fact, attract audiences. And thus Drury Lane
prosecuted George Davidge, proprietor of the Coburg, for performing
Richard III (*SC*, 76). As Davidge testified, "I could produce tragedy . . .
as perfectly at the Coburg Theatre as it should be done at Covent Garden
or Drury Lane" (*SC*, 77).

James Winston, a stage manager at Haymarket and Drury Lane, generated
even more confusion on the question of legitimacy when he claimed that
a play was made legitimate not by its structure or content but by the
legal rights (or lack thereof) exercised by theater managers. Legitimacy,
in short, was a matter of property and not of poetics. A drama was
"legitimate" if a "legitimate" person staged it. As Winston triumphantly
concluded, if the Patent Houses "can play everything, then everything is
the regular drama" (*SC*, 20). The implications of that claim are astounding.
If "everything" performed at a patent house is legitimate by definition,
then the converse must also hold true: "everything" performed at a minor
house is illegitimate by definition. That was a crazy argument. It meant that
the elephants which graced the stage of Drury Lane in an 1827 pantomime

were warmed by the cloak of legitimacy, while Shakespeare was cast out into the frozen wasteland of the illegitimate when the Surrey Theatre, in 1809, had produced *Macbeth* as a ballet d'action—a performance which featured music, singing, and dancing to obscure its reliance upon a scripted text and thus evade charges of illegality. Yet Winston pleaded that he could make no *artistic* distinction between Shakespeare and pantomime, between the legitimate and the illegitimate. Between the elephant and the Thane of Glamis, one might add.

As Winston's audacious testimony reveals, the patentees were oligarchs of the first magnitude, for they sought to restrict the rights of everyone but themselves. Yet their claim to possess exclusive rights to the performance of Shakespeare was rejected out of hand by His Majesty's government. Thomas Mash, the comptroller of the Lord Chamberlain's office, turned the history of theatrical licensing on its head when he advised Parliament that the royal patents allowed Drury Lane and Covent Garden to perform legitimate drama but did *not* forbid other theaters from doing the same. Thus, when minor theaters performed scripted drama—as they did with alarming frequency—they violated their own patents but not the royal ones. The proprietors of the major houses may well deplore the activities of the minor houses, but they had no right to contest such activities. Nor could they seek any legal remedy if the Lord Chamberlain decided to license new legitimate theaters in the city of Westminster (*SC,* 14-15).

As legal documents, then, the patents had become worthless. If they possessed any value at all, it was their power to exclude and suppress. But as the Lord Chamberlain's office insisted, patent rights were not exclusionary—despite the best efforts of the patentees to make them so. If a patent did not bestow exclusive privileges upon its owners, then there was no point in owning it. When Bulwer's committee made its report to Parliament in August 1832, it merely confirmed what everyone in the theater—including Bulwer himself—had known all along: the patent system was a wreck. It was aesthetically bankrupt and offered neither economic benefit nor legal protection.

The absurdities of theatrical licensing in the early nineteenth century are only too obvious. What may be less obvious, however, is *why* the managers of Covent Garden and Drury Lane desperately defended a right that accorded them no financial reward but only the anxiety of unceasing—and unsuccessful—litigation. Why, in 1832, was a theatrical patent still worth fighting for? And what notion of cultural rights was behind that fight? One answer arises from the date itself: 1832, the year in which the Great Reform Bill extended the franchise to the urban middle class; the year in which Parliament was reconciled to the nation. That the British government set up an inquiry into theatrical licensing and passed the Reform Bill in the same year is hardly a coincidence, for the campaign to end the patent theaters' monopoly turned on the same rhetoric of property and ownership as the concurrent campaign for nationwide electoral reform. In July 1832, as the Select Committee concluded its hearings, the *New Monthly Magazine* conflated the events with its optimistic (though, as it turned out, premature) prediction that "the Reform Bill of our national drama is at hand."[10]

In the political sphere, the issue was whether the property and privilege of the landed gentry—the traditional basis of aristocratic government and Georgian constitutional monarchy—could be safely replaced by expanded suffrage and direct political representation. Many believed that enlarging the sphere of political participation would only enhance the power of an already violent and ignorant rabble at the expense of prudent aristocratic leadership. As the Whig historian—and future Examiner of Plays—John Mitchell Kemble (son of Charles, the oligarchic patentee) warned his sister, the actress Frances Anne ("Fanny") Kemble, in 1831,

the mass of the people, lawless and Godless, are let loose upon . . . all the venerable traditions and noble memorials of their ancestral ages . . . not to reform the accident and preserve the . . . old established creeds without which there is no nation, but to set up some new idol, . . . based on no firmer foundation than individual, miserable self-interest.[11]

Precisely equivalent issues were debated in the theatrical profession: Was the national drama best served by the long-standing aristocratic stewardship of the royal patents or by free trade? Should Shakespeare be circulated or, to misquote Macbeth, "cabin'd, cribbed, and confined"? Was the "miserable self-interest" of theatrical managers to be trusted more than the "old established creeds" of the royal patents? In short, could the middle class be trusted with both Shakespeare *and* the franchise? An affirmative answer was greatly in doubt.

The campaign for free trade gained a deeper significance when its proponents emphasized that Shakespeare himself was a free trader, whose "merits had been rewarded" by the theatrical marketplace of his own day.[12] In the "high and palmy state" of British theater during the reign of Elizabeth, all London theaters, Thomas Serle pointedly observed, "possess[ed] equal

rights." The decline of the British stage began with Charles II's establishment of the patent monopoly. To uphold Shakespeare as the national
poet is also to uphold the principle of theatrical free trade. You cannot
champion Shakespeare, so the logic of the argument proceeded, without
also championing "equal rights" for the long-oppressed minor theaters.

It is a cliché of theater historiography that the nineteenth-century stage
was depoliticized through a combination of state censorship and literary
infirmity. But that was manifestly not the case. T. P. Cooke, the popular star
of such nautical melodramas as Douglas Jerrold's *Black Ey'd Susan* (Surrey
1829), believed that "there is a tendency in the audience to force passages
never meant by the author into a political meaning" (*SC,* 219). In his essay
"The State of the Drama" (1832), Bulwer himself argued for the political
centrality of theatrical reform:

> Nor let it be said that Parliament is too much occupied to attend to what some per-
> sons may choose to denominate trifles: to relieve injustice, to remove oppression,
> ought at no time to be considered a trifle. It was during the busiest period of the
> Revolution, that the French legislature could find leisure to protect the interests of
> a favourite branch of their national literature. And, after all, is the Drama a trifle?
> — has it not exercised a mighty influence on the thoughts, the feelings, and the
> morals of the nation?[13]

The transcripts of the Select Committee's hearings amply demonstrate
that in the 1830s, political and theatrical reform were spoken of in the
same breath. The dramatist George Colman affirmed the political acuity of
the theater when he explained that the Lord Chamberlain's office always
deleted political allusions from new plays: that is, they censored anything
"applied to the existing moment, and which is likely to be inflammatory"
(*SC,* 66). In an even more pointed remark, Colman revealed that "it was
but the other day the word 'reform' was mentioned [during a perfor-
mance], and I understand there was a hubbub . . . at all the theatres." He
recommended that the word "reform" be stricken from that offending
drama. And with unquestioned obedience to precedent and tradition—the
cornerstone of conservative philosophy—he declared that "if the minor
theaters be wise, they would wish for no further latitude than they now
enjoy" (*SC,* 68). Those words, which smacked of Tory paternalism, so
deeply outraged Bulwer that he advised Colman not to hazard "any opinion
as to the interests of the minor theatres, as they are the best judges of their
own affairs" (*SC,* 68).

Colman's desire to expunge the word "reform" and to prevent the minor theaters from entering pleas of equal rights enacts the mutuality between late Georgian theatrical and electoral reform: that is, they were the same kind of political processes, yet each was necessarily executed within its own sphere of influence. Theatrical and electoral concepts of reform were inseparable, for the debates on cultural and political power both centered on questions of inclusion and access to nationhood, whether through the ballot box or the benches of the pit.[14] By successfully challenging the long-standing dominance of a culture of exclusion, nineteenth-century theatrical reform legislation broadened the base of British national identity. In the theater, emancipation was discussed largely in terms of access to Shakespeare—whether that access be desired, denied, or even, as we shall see, compelled.

The status of Shakespeare as either a right or an obligation lies at the center of nineteenth-century theatrical reform, much more so than the threat of burletta and melodrama. In the slow transition from theatrical oligarchy to theatrical democracy, Shakespeare was the cultural equivalent of the franchise, the ticket of admission to nationhood itself. Even Thomas Carlyle, a disconsolate man of letters if ever there was one, enthused in his third lecture on heroes and hero worship that "Shakespeare is ours; we produced him, we speak and think by him; we are of one blood and kind with him."[15] That Englishmen "speak and think" by Shakespeare, that he is the substance of national identity—the "noblest, gentlest, yet strongest of the rallying-signs"—and the progenitor of the English race are not simply the armchair conceits of Victorian critics who may never have purchased a seat in the stalls. Anticipating, as it were, Carlyle's conviction that Britons "speak and think" by Shakespeare, Bulwer focused his inquiry not on infringements of the royal patents but on the oppression of the minor theaters. That is, he investigated prohibitions against performing Shakespeare—and thereby framed the issue of theatrical reform as one of extending the right to Shakespeare. Although the Select Committee failed to persuade Parliament to emancipate the minor theaters, Bulwer and his colleagues nonetheless defined that emancipation in Shakespearean terms.[16]

The patentees, realizing that their privileges could be statutorily withdrawn, filed a claim for their exclusive rights to Shakespeare. The treasurer of Drury Lane, William Dunn, conceded that the managers who leased his theater failed to turn a profit from performing Shakespeare, but he argued nevertheless for the preservation of the monopoly on the speculative grounds that performing Shakespeare at the minor houses would "ruin the national drama entirely" (*SC,* 74). Thomas Morton, a script reader at Drury Lane, fervently declared that it was "a command upon his [i.e., Shakespeare's] countrymen that his pieces should be produced only in the noblest temples of the Muses. . . . I never witnessed a representation of any of Shakespeare's plays at the minor theatres without sorrow or disappointment" (*SC,* 216, 217). The poet's secret desires were not withheld from yet another beneficiary of theatrical protectionism, and so Samuel Arnold, the proprietor of Covent Garden, confidently informed his learned and noble questioners that if Shakespeare were alive in 1832, he would prefer to see *Hamlet, Julius Caesar,* and *Coriolanus* acted at "Drury Lane or Covent Garden, no doubt," because only those establishments could provide the "perfect costume and good scenery" that Shakespearean drama demanded (*SC,* 57).

After the Select Committee's hearings, it was no longer possible to credit any theater's claim to exclusive rights to perform Shakespeare. Such a claim, however much it was rooted in legal precedents and royal patents, made no sense in the theatrical marketplace of the 1830s. And yet the desire to restrict access to Shakespeare remained. One of most improbable sites of this residual theatrical oppression was not a patent house, but a minor theater: the St. James's Theatre, in the heart of the fashionable West End.

As a minor theater, the St. James's was permitted by law to stage burletta but not the legitimate drama. That privilege was reserved for the patent houses, one of which—the Haymarket (which had a patent only for the summer season)—was a few hundred yards away. When John Braham opened the St. James's in December 1835, theatrical legitimacy was very much on his mind. Although he hailed from Whitechapel, in London's impoverished East End, Braham sought to win the patronage of the "nobility" and the "gentry" (as he identified them in newspaper advertisements) who lived in the environs of St. James's Square.[17] He failed. The gentry were hardly inclined to forsake Italian opera only to embrace English burletta. Despite its enviable location, the St. James's still carried the stain of illegitimacy. Facing financial ruin, Braham relinquished control in 1838.

During Braham's brief management, the house dramatist was Gilbert Abbott A'Beckett. One of the plays he wrote for the St. James's was *King John (with the Benefit of the Act),* a burlesque of Shakespeare's history play. Although written in 1835, the burlesque was not performed until

1837. When writing his parody of *King John,* A'Beckett could not have failed to recognize the implausibility of Braham's bid for social prestige. After all, the audience that the St. James's sought to attract had not been captivated by the increasingly spectacular productions of legitimate Shakespeare at the patent houses. Yet it was precisely this sort of production that the burlesque ridiculed. Indeed, *King John (with the Benefit of the Act)* blatantly travestied Covent Garden's production of *King John,* which starred Charles Kemble as Faulconbridge, W. C. Macready as the eponymous tyrant, and the nineteen-year-old Helen Faucit as Lady Constance.[18] But the parody didn't matter very much, at least in terms of enticing the "nobility" and the "gentry" to patronize a minor theater. Since Braham's target audience showed no great enthusiasm for legitimate Shakespeare performed at Covent Garden, we can hardly be surprised that it showed a similar disregard for a Shakespeare burlesque produced in a minor West End theater by an East End Jew.

In its blatant appeal to a patrician audience—which never, in fact, materialized—the St. James's occupied an anomalous position among London's minor theaters. With the exception of the patentees themselves, most London theatrer managers in the 1830s believed that the road to prosperity lay not in acquiring aristocratic patronage but in performing the legitimate drama—above all, Shakespeare—to their existing middle-class and lower middle-class audiences. From the perspective of most minor theaters, "free trade" meant giving legitimate Shakespeare to a more popular audience, not giving illegitimate Shakespeare to aristocrats.

As the manager of a minor house licensed to produce burlettas, Braham found himself in an untenable position. His desire to attract an aristocratic audience was entirely at odds with the insistence of his fellow managers that the aristocracy was to blame for the long-standing oppression of the minor theaters. Indeed, under the Licensing Act of 1737, Braham could not present Shakespeare's *King John* and remain within the law. Indeed, the burlesque's subtitle—*(with the Benefit of the Act)*—comically alludes to the regulatory statutes that circumscribed theatrical production. Moreover, it was only too easy to read the historical narrative of King John as an allegory of theatrical liberty. That is, just as the sturdy barons forced the tyrant king to recognize their rights by signing Magna Carta, the minor theaters would force the tyrannical patent houses to countenance the right of all theaters to produce scripted drama. In producing *King John (with the Benefit of the Act),* the St. James's was well poised to exploit the suggestiveness of Shakespeare's original play to advocate the politics of theatrical emancipation. A burlesque *King John* could comment ironically on the oppression of minor theaters and the highly publicized campaign for theatrical reform. Indeed, the production could have drawn inspiration from the Old Price Riots of 1809, when *King John* was the Shakespearean touchstone for the inviolable "dramatic rights" of Britons threatened by the theatrical tyranny of the insolent "King John" Kemble.[19]

But none of that happened. Nobody talked about *King John (with the Benefit of the Act)* as an allegory of theatrical emancipation—as the sequel, if you will, to the Old Price Riots. In fact, the burlesque (which lasted only nine performances) received largely negative notices, none of which interpreted the performance in light of debates about theatrical regulation. The *Spectator* pronounced the play an abject "failure"; *John Bull* dismissed it as a "stupid travestie of Shakespeare's play"; and the *Times* deemed it "hardly bearable."[20] In short, the political possibilities of a *King John* burlesque staged at the exact moment when London theater managers were fighting for their "dramatic rights" were foreclosed by the very circumstances of the play's production. For under Braham's management, the St. James's Theatre championed not theatrical emancipation but theatrical exclusion. The potentially progressive uses of Shakespearean burlesque were forestalled by an institution whose management was curiously conservative. "Reform" was not a word defiantly pronounced on the stage of the St. James's Theatre.

In 1843, when Parliament finally passed a theatrical reform bill, Shakespeare was still uppermost in the minds of the legislators; and, indeed, the final obstacle to the bill's passage was the much-revised "Shakespeare clause." In the bill's earliest version, only the patent theaters would be allowed to perform Shakespeare. The Earl of Glengall defended the continued prohibition by arguing that since it was "impossible to give proper scenic effect to Shakespeare in a small theatre," it was clearly in the "interest of the theatrical profession that the plays of Shakespeare should be confined to the patent theatres."[21] That clause failed, and it was rewritten to include the moderately protectionist stipulation that while the minor theaters *may* perform Shakespeare, the patent theaters *must* do so— no matter how unprofitable that enterprise might be and no matter how much (or how little) competition they faced from the minor theaters. It, too, failed. (Had it succeeded, the clause would have established Britain's first *national* theater by virtue of the patent houses' legal obligation to perform Shakespeare.)[22] An additional clause prohibited the performance of Shakespeare at any theater within a five-mile radius of a patent house.[23] That clause lasted until the bill's second reading on August 11, 1843, in the House of Lords. At the end of the day, Shakespeare—like Ariel—was set free to the elements, as both houses of Parliament concurred with Lord Monteagle that it was a "disgrace to the times in which they lived—a disgrace to literature, and to common sense, to prohibit the representation of the plays of that dramatic author, who, by all consent, was the greatest author the world had ever produced."[24]

This full measure of cultural liberation became law only in 1843. Political liberation—even if only on the symbolic level—had been achieved somewhat earlier, in 1832. That the middle class won the right to vote a full decade before it won the right to Shakespeare suggests just how destabilizing cultural emancipation could be. Discussions of Shakespeare, patents, censorship, and legitimacy in the first half of the nineteenth century were caught in a double bind. For the sake of political economy—free trade and individual self-interest—Shakespeare ought to be deregulated. Culture, as well as politics, needed reforming. Yet for the sake of moral economy—the expression of national identity through the national drama—Shakespeare ought to be protected. Britain's greatest poet needed to be insulated from the dangers of the marketplace. Yet that kind of intervention represented the worst of Georgian patrician politics. On the question of the franchise, the visionary politicians in the 1830s knew what they had to do; on the more vexed question of the theater, however, they did not know whether to grant mobility or impose constraint. Reform-minded Whig governments could tolerate free trade in everything, it seemed, *except* Shakespeare.

Following the Great Reform Bill of 1832, there was no going back. Political emancipation was irrevocable. Yet in the theater it was still touch and go. A mere five years after London theaters were granted unrestricted freedom to produce Shakespeare, a new call for censorship was heard in the halls of Westminster. This time censorship came not through an exclusive patent but through a proposed government subsidy. In 1848, Effingham Wilson published the first serious manifesto for a British national theater, entitled *A House for Shakespeare: A Proposition for the Nation.* Yet again, the date is resonant. The revolutions of 1848, a series of uprisings in France, Germany, the Austrian Empire, and parts of Italy, sought either to establish constitutional governments or to secure independence for particular nationalities. In Britain, the principal threat came from Chartism, the grassroots workers' movement committed to such democratic reforms as universal male suffrage, annual parliaments, and the elimination of property requirements for members of Parliament. Prince Albert dismissed the radical protestors as "evil-disposed people" destined to fail in their campaign against "the force of the law, the Government, and the good sense of the country."[25]

As a paralyzing fear of domestic anarchy and continental-style revolution gripped the British Isles, the nationalistic—indeed, counterrevolutionary—face of the theater grew strikingly visible. "The spirit of faction is detrimental to society," the *Theatrical Times* cautioned in late September 1848; "it is a link disjoining itself from the great chain."[26] In that single year, an irate and xenophobic audience hissed a visiting French troupe off the Drury Lane stage during a performance of Alexandre Dumas's *The Count of Monte Cristo.* "It was profanation for the foreigner to set his profane foot upon the sacred boards of 'Old Drury,' " one patriotic theatrical veteran recalled many years later. The "home of SHAKESPEARE must not be desecrated by actors and actresses who could not speak SHAKESPEARE'S mother tongue."[27] The *Theatrical Journal,* whose subscribers included Victoria and Albert, had incited the Drury Lane riot by urging its readers to "set their faces against this new attempt to un-Anglicize our public amusements."[28] In this anxious climate, Shakespeare was pressed into the service of counterrevolutionary sentiments—showing, once more, that the stage was far too significant to be left to the people. The popular and commercial theater that had been celebrated as the "people's house" during the Old Price Riots of 1809 was now repossessed as "Shakespeare's" house. Eviction notices to be posted shortly.

Notes

1. *Age,* December 19, 1830; cited in Jane Moody, *Illegitimate Theatre in London, 1770–1840* (Cambridge: Cambridge University Press, 2000), 45.

2. An earlier, unsuccessful attempt at theatrical reform was the presentation of the Interludes Bill in 1788, which was followed by a deluge of petitions from the "minor" theatrical houses to produce legitimate drama. But just as British political reform could not be countenanced during a period of revolution on the Continent, so, too, theatrical reform would have to wait.

3. Joseph Donohue, *Theatre in the Age of Kean* (Oxford: Basil Blackwell, 1975), 3, 10.

4. *British and Foreign Review* 2 (1836): 526, 576.

5. House of Commons, "Report from the Select Committee on Dramatic Literature: with

Minutes of Evidence," *Sessional Papers*, 2 August 1832, vol. 7, p. 3 (hereafter cited in text as *SC*).

6. *Westminster Review* 20 (1834): 154–55.

7. *British and Foreign Review* 2 (1836): 570.

8. *Theatrical Observer*, May 26, 1831.

9. William Pitt Lennox, *Plays, Players, and Playgoers at Home and Abroad*, 2 vols (London: Hurst and Blakcett, 1881), 1:131. "I myself have seen *Macbeth* acted as a burletta at the Royal Circus, with a pianoforte accompaniment, and it was said that the name of some celebrated play was altered to one not likely to catch the ear of the Licenser. Thus, according to the wags of the day, *Othello* was performed under the title of *Is He Jealous?* . . . *Macbeth* as *Murder Will Out*, *The Comedy of Errors* as *Who is Who, or As Like as Two Peas*, *The Merchant of Venice* was [*sic*] *Diamond Cut Diamond*, [and] *Taming of the Shrew* as *A Conjugal Lesson*."

10. *New Monthly Magazine* 36 (July 1832): 303.

11. John Mitchell Kemble to Frances Anne Kemble, 16 January 1831, W.b. 596, Folger Shakespeare Library, Washington, D.C.

12. Thomas Serle, quoted in the *Morning Chronicle*, March 23, 1832. See also Jacky Bratton, *New Readings in Theatre History* (Cambridge: Cambridge University Press, 2003), 83–88.

13. Edward Bulwer-Lytton, "The State of the Drama," *New Monthly Magazine* 34 (1832): 133.

14. See also Clive Barker, "A Theatre for the People," in *Nineteenth-Century British Theatres*, ed. Kenneth Richards and Peter Thompson (London: Methuen, 1971), 3–24.

15. Thomas Carlyle, *On Heroes, Hero-Worship and the Heroic in History* (1840; Boston: Ginn and Co., 1901), 130–31.

16. The committee's respondents, largely from the theatrical profession, frequently invoked Shakespearean characters and taglines in their replies. See Julia Swindells, "Behold the Swelling Scene! Shakespeare and the 1832 Select Committee," in *Victorian Shakespeare: Theatre, Drama and Performance*, 2 vols., ed. Gail Marshall and Adrian Poole (Basingstoke: Palgrave Macmillan, 2003), 1:29–46.

17. Quoted in *Chronicle of the St. James's Theatre*, 2.

18. *Morning Post*, October 17, 1837.

19. J. J. Stockdale, ed., *Covent Garden Journal* (London: J. J. Stockdale, 1810), 198. The riots, which lasted sixty-seven nights, were instigated by Kemble's attempt to raise ticket prices and reduce the number of cheap seats at the rebuilt Covent Garden. On the Old Price Riots, see Marc Baer's impressive study, *Theatre and Disorder in Late Georgian London* (Oxford: Clarendon Press, 1992).

20. *Spectator*, October 21, 1837; *John Bull*, October 22, 1837; *Times* [London], October 17, 1837. In one of the lone favorable notices, the *Literary Gazette* (October 21, 1837) observed that the "well attended" comedy was "drawing laughter."

21. *Hansard Parliamentary Debates*, 3d ser., vol. 71 (1843), col. 544.

22. See Tracy C. Davis, *The Economics of the British Stage 1800–1914* (Cambridge: Cambridge University Press, 2000), 39.

23. House of Commons, "A Bill for Regulating Theatres," *Sessional Papers,* 14 March 1843, vol. 4, p. 479.

24. *Hansard,* 3d ser., vol. 71 (1843), col. 544. Following the passage of the 1843 act, the number of London theatrers where Shakespeare could be performed legally increased by 800 percent. This increase was not the result of new theaters being built but rather the result of the Lord Chamberlain granting licenses for the performance of legitimate drama to the former "minor" theaters. (Before 1843, the minor theaters received their licenses from the Middlesex magistrates.) Additionally, the Haymarket's summer patent was effectively converted into a year-round patent; Her Majesty's Theatre, a ballet and opera house, was also licensed to produce scripted drama. The newly emancipated playhouses were the Adelphi, the Albert Saloon, the Albion, the Apollo, Astley's Amphitheatre, the Bower Saloon, the Britannia Saloon, the City of London Theatre, the Effingham Saloon, the Garrick, the Grecian Saloon, the Haymarket, Her Majesty's, the Lyceum, the Marylebone, the Olympic, the Pavilion, the Princess's, the Queen's Theatre, Sadler's Wells, the St. James's, the Standard, the Strand, the Surrey, and the Victoria (formerly known as the Coburg). See House of Commons, "Memorandum on Theatres," in *Report from the Select Committee on Theatrical Licenses and Regulations, Sessional Papers,* 12 March 1866, vol. 11, p. 281.

25. Prince Albert to Lord John Russell, 10 April 1848, cited in Arthur Christopher Benson and Viscount Esher, *The Letters of Queen Victoria,* 1st ser., 3 vols (London: John Murray, 1908), 2:168.

26. *Theatrical Times,* September 21, 1848.

27. Unattributed clipping, 15 January 1871, Theatrical Miscellany Scrapbook 11, Folger Shakespeare Library, Washington, D.C.

28. *Theatrical Journal,* June 8, 1848.

Dancing in a (Cyber) Net: "Renaissance Women," Systems Theory, and the War of the Cinemas

COURTNEY LEHMANN

F OUR HUNDRED YEARS after the curious skirmish known as the War of the Theaters, a markedly similar phenomenon has taken hold of the cinema, emerging in films that purport to represent the Renaissance and, particularly, its bankside beacon, Shakespeare. Revolving around a fundamental division, as Richard Helgerson has persuasively argued, between a "players' theater" and an "authors' theater," the war was really a bid for social preferment and economic survival in a culture making an uneven transition from patronage to market forces.[1] On one side, the proponents of the authors' theater strove to distinguish the singularity of their poetry from its debased embodiment on stage, catering to a privileged clientele through learned plays performed by elite children's companies, whose combined objective was to disparage the unsophisticated audiences and common players associated with the public amphitheaters. On the other side, the players' theater remained the "caviar" of "the general."[2] Refusing the lure of more privatized venues such as Blackfriars and St. Paul's, as well as the social division of labor between players and "authors" which, for figures like Shakespeare, proved a paradox, advocates of the players' theater continued to rely on collaborative authorship, adult actors, and popular themes for their plays—but not without leaving scathing rejoinders in their wake.[3] Nevertheless, what distinguished the war as a bizarre interlude in the English theater's ongoing struggle for respectability was the way in which *children* came to mediate this debate. As the most

121

"impressionable" members of society (a fact that Renaissance child-rearing manuals anxiously certify), children were used and, often, abused by both sides as mouthpieces for cultural changes they were poised to inherit but not benefit from—since, with any luck, they would live to become the adults who were the very subject of their spite.[4] Although the War of the Theaters was a small-scale, short-lived contest of wits enacted on both page and stage, it had a lasting impact on the repertories, venues, and reputation through which Renaissance theater culture was understood and experienced.

I am interested in exploring the ways in which children are currently being linked to Renaissance power plays in the *cinema*, wherein, I will argue, the terms of the war have been reinvented along the axis of gender. Whether present as implied audiences, conspicuous absences, or actual performers, children have emerged in recent years as an unlikely hermeneutic for articulating the rival claims of the "authors' cinema" and what I will call the "cybercinema." Representing the authors' cinema, films such as John Madden's *Shakespeare in Love* (1998), Marshall Herscovitz's *Dangerous Beauty* (1998), and Adrian Noble's *A Midsummer Night's Dream* (1996) offer highly romantic and unabashedly anachronistic takes on the Renaissance by re-creating it as an author's paradise. Literalizing the Renaissance trope that conflates supple writing surfaces with the female body, these films represent authorship as an erotic and, ultimately, male prerogative, often performed for the prurient gaze of young boys eager to learn how to become men.[5] By contrast, films from *Shakespeare: The Animated Tales* series,[6] as well as Julie Taymor's *Titus* (2000) and Christine Edzard's *The Children's Midsummer Night's Dream* (2001), adapt Shakespeare's cautionary tales of political tyranny and patriarchal absolutism as allegories of authorship which, provocatively, employ children in ways that return us to the contested terrain of female authorship in the Renaissance. Indeed, children figured centrally in the complex nexus of filiation, encryption, and self-abnegation that precipitated Renaissance women's entry into print—a precarious process that Wendy Wall describes, appropriately, as "dancing in a net."[7] In keeping with this precedent, recent Shakespeare films by the feminist vanguard resist situating children as the offspring of a unilateral and frequently violent process of "impressment," locating them instead within a *systems* environment that privileges flows across and between boundaries. In light of important recent work focusing on plural authorship and textual economies in which women function only as metaphors for collateral or even homoerotic exchanges between men,[8] these films invite us to imagine both early modern and postmodern authorship in a more dynamic, cybernetic context in which optimization supplants eroticization and collaboration is understood not as reciprocity but as complex circuitry, born of fluid combinations of "the organic, the technical, and the textual."[9]

Although systems theory is a relatively recent invention of the computer age, systems themselves are as old as the universe, accounting for how complex biologic, mechanical, and conceptual "organisms" become self-regulating. Cybernetics, which is a critical subfield of systems theory, is concerned with how mechanisms of communication and control—foremost among them, feedback—use information to produce homeostasis or, alternatively, entropy. In social systems such as families, children play a central role as channels through which information passes and is fed back into the system as a means of achieving equilibrium. Yet, within the sex-gender system of the English Renaissance, children were considered to be dangerously capable of altering the feedback loop, particularly during the formative years in which boys and girls were in the care of women who, as we shall see, did not necessarily enforce cultural codes pertaining to gender distinction. As critical sites for the inculcation of authority, children also became the locus of competing ideas of authorship. Aspiring women writers, for example, used children to circumvent protocols against female speech while communicating legacies that were legally denied to them by their culture. As Wall explains of the emergent discourse of the maternal legacy, pregnant women leveraged the presumption of their death in childbirth against the stigma of print, publishing advice to their unborn children and, in so doing, achieving immortality for themselves. What is fascinating about this authorial dynamic is not only the way in which children come to be positioned, paradoxically, as "midwives" but also the fact that, long before the advent of poststructuralism, Renaissance women acknowledged the "death of the author" as constitutive of the birth of the text. The filmmakers I align with the cybercinema remarkably reproduce this dynamic by employing children as the birthing agents of their cinematic narratives and, more important, as the repository of subversive codes of conduct in a system which, like cinema itself, cannot function without such collaboration. By contrast, the films of the authors' cinema appear bent on decoupling their portraits of authorship from the contingencies of collaboration and, to this end, either eliminate children altogether or position them as guardians of a resolutely patriarchal status quo. A variation on the Renaissance theme of primogeniture, children in the authors' cinema are charged with maintaining system equilibrium at all costs. What I will theorize here, then, is the point at which children become the site of convergence between cultural assumptions about gender and authorship, and what happens to the equation—indeed, the system— when these terms do not comply with each other.

Cybernetic theory offers a particularly useful bridge between the early modern and postmodern concerns of this essay because it explores the gap that separates a potentially democratizing implementation of com- munication technology from what Donna Haraway calls the "informatics of domination" or the militaristic deployment of C^{3}I (command-control- communication-intelligence). Akin to Haraway's socialist-feminist objec- tive of "recoding communication and intelligence to subvert command and control,"[10] I will consider how the *cinematics* of domination may be undermined by an oppositional approach to authorship—one that derives from the communication technology of Renaissance child-rearing practices. To import the terms of cybernetics into what I am calling the War of the Cinemas, then, whereas the authors' cinema situates children as mechanisms of *control* operating within a "closed" or autonomous system, the cybercinema positions children as mechanisms of *commu- nication* across an "open" system, which depends on interaction with its surrounding environment to evolve. I should clarify that throughout this essay, I do not use the term "war" as lightly as it was deployed in Renaissance theatrical discourse, for in tracing the widening arc from theater to film and from authorship to authority, it is critical to recognize that what most distinguishes early modern from postmodern culture is not a change in social attitudes toward the prevailing sex-gender system but the technologies used to enforce them. Hence, just as women's authorship in the Renaissance was often a dangerous endgame, so, too, is a culture—as the films of the cybercinema remind us—poised on the brink of displacing unprecedented opportunities for communication with fantasies of remote control.

Introduction: The Illusion of Life
and the Tremor of the Author

The principle of poetry is to transform, to convert.
In comedy, this "principle" becomes action.
In Shakespeare's tragedies, people change.
In Shakespeare's comedies, the characters are transformed constantly . . .
In Disney—they turn into each other.

—Sergei Eisenstein[11]

Before exploring how these systems collide directly in films such as Adrian
Noble's *A Midsummer Night's Dream* and Julie Taymor's *Titus,* I will
introduce the ways in which selected films from the children's series
Shakespeare: The Animated Tales propose a systems-based approach to
authorship and identity that is remarkably attuned to the contingent conception of "character" in the Renaissance, providing an antidote to the
anachronistic portraits purveyed by "period" films such as *Dangerous
Beauty* and *Shakespeare in Love.* Significantly, in *The Illusion of Life,* Alan
Cholodenko describes the animated film as sharing a certain ontological
kinship with children—specifically, as the site of disputed paternity. For
example, animation is regarded by film theorists "as either the 'step-child'
of cinema or as not belonging to cinema at all," despite the fact that
"animated film not only preceded the advent of cinema but engendered
it."[12] Similarly, in the context of theatrical performance, animation is often
classified as aesthetically immature, dismissed as "a child [compared] to
live action's adult form."[13] But as Sergei Eisenstein discovered in his study
of Disney, what is childlike about the animatic process is also what makes it
potentially subversive, for animation exists at the threshold of "prelogical"
modes of thought which, he explains, are free from "prescribed norms of
nomenclature, form and behavior."[14] Indeed, for Eisenstein, the undulating
borders of Disney's sketched characters represent a distinctly "lyrical"
revolt against the "partitioning and legislating" that is the basis of capitalistic society.[15] Hence, as a cow becomes a radio and a radio becomes
a milk pump, we can't help but marvel at the residue of their *likeness*—
the remainder that ruptures the self-identity of each object while leaving
something more powerful in its wake—a transformative connection that
Eisenstein deems worthy of the neologism: "*a*ffectiveness," or, "*formal
ecstasy.*"[16] By contrast, Shakespeare's characters, though capable of individ-

ual transformation, are incapable of such liberating fusion. For what makes Shakespeare great, according to Eisenstein, is the teleological process in the plays whereby personality determines action and, through a steady process of accretion, action shapes personality. This is the quintessential difference between (Disneyan) animation and (Shakespearean) personification and, in turn, what distinguishes the ideology of the authors' cinema from that of the cybercinema: whereas personification leads to a monadic concept of identity, based on a differential calculus that is inseparable from socio-economic values, animation operates according to a nomadic principle of affinity, materializing what Eisenstein exuberantly describes as "the dream of a flowing diversity of forms" (24).[17]

Had he lived to see *Shakespeare: The Animated Tales,* Eisenstein might have had to revise his assumptions about the fundamental differences between Shakespeare and Disney. In fact, more than half a century after Eisenstein's death, the tables have turned, and it is Disney who has become associated with the tailorized cult of personality—from Mickey Mouse to the Little Mermaid—against which all other animated films are evaluated. Consequently, when producer Christopher Grace took on the *Animated Tales* project, he made it clear that the series was "actively seeking a style and flavor of animation which would *not* smack of Saturday morning cartoons or the relentlessly commercial, thoroughly controlled Disney animating machine."[18] Nevertheless, a rapprochement between Disney and Shakespeare might prove more productive than yet another reversal of terms, for as Laurie Osborne contends, the *Animated Tales* "subtly underscore how Shakespeare," contrary to Eisenstein's assertions, "presented character development and motivation from *outside the outlines* of his supposedly organic characters."[19] Indeed, what Eisenstein failed to acknowledge in his analysis of the disparities between Disney-style animation and Shakespearean drama is the fact that Shakespeare himself was a character who, as an "author," undermined the very ontological momentum ascribed to his protagonists. This is precisely the point of connection I wish to highlight in exploring the relationship between Shakespeare, animation, and the cybercinema. For what Eisenstein identifies as the "tremor of the author"—the force that flows between the lifeless and the animated[20]—is a particularly apt metonymy for articulating the ways in which Shakespeare, Renaissance women, and the feminist filmmaking vanguard challenge us to read "outside the outlines" of periodizing schemes that relegate authorship to a false choice between life and death, originality and plurality, without considering all the animating forces in between.

I focus on the films of the female directors of the *Animated Tales* not only because they have received considerably less attention than the work of their male counterparts (even though Natalia Orlova's *Hamlet* was the only film to receive an Emmy), but also because they consistently employ techniques that resist re-creating the "illusion of life" so central to the more traditional art of cel animation deployed by the majority of the male directors in both the 1992 and 1996 series. It would be difficult to claim, however, that *any* film in either the 1992 or the 1996 series is overtly "feminist" in content. Quite the contrary, the *Tales* tend to eliminate even the most casual suggestions of nonnormative desire from their plots and manage to subdue some of Shakespeare's strongest female characters. The animated films by women—*Hamlet* (1992), *Twelfth Night* (1992), *Richard III* (1996), and *The Taming of the Shrew* (1996)—are no exception. For example, in comedies such as Mariya Muat's *Twelfth Night* and Aida Ziablikova's *Shrew*, Viola and Olivia are remarkably passive, while Kate appears tame from the beginning, and, consequently, her final speech is delivered without a hint of irony. Similarly, in the tragedies, which are typically dominated by male characters, the already diminished female roles suffer disproportionate abridgment, as Osborne observes of *Richard III* in particular: "Elizabeth—as well as the other women including Anne—are radically cut and appear in the tale only on parapets and beyond the castle walls, barely visible or only at the margins of the painted images of Richard."[21] It is almost as if the women become part of the architecture itself. And this, it seems to me, is precisely the point of the highly unorthodox techniques unique to these films. For while Muat and Ziablikova employ nine-inch, hand-painted and hand-manipulated puppets, Orlova turns to the even more painstaking process of painting on and scraping off images applied to a single pane of glass; both animation strategies draw attention to the *constructedness*—rather than the organic fluidity—of the forms they generate.[22] Moreover, when viewed within the Soviet context of the *Animated Tales*'s creation, these "tremors of the author" acquire a political dimension that materializes their distinctly feminist intervention in the War of the Cinemas.

While Gorbachev's policies of glasnost and perestroika produced progressive trends in Soviet cinema, they also led to a conservative and, specifically, antifeminist backlash, evidenced by the sudden popularity of films dramatizing the failure of Soviet women to reconcile their professional and personal lives. As Francoise Navailh observes, the genre of *Zhenskie fil'my,* or, "films about women," emerged in the 1980s as a reaction against female accomplishments in the public sphere: "Forty years ago, women had been revered because public interest had prevailed over private life. Nowadays, the emancipated woman is punished for the same choice."[23] According to the dominant themes of *Zhenskie fil'my,* which, not coincidentally, resurface in films such as *Dangerous Beauty* and *Shakespeare in Love,* women are entitled to minor victories, but "when important things are at stake—Revolution, Motherland or Economy—man is there, and he stands alone."[24] At first glance, the *Animated Tales* directed by Soviet women appear to reinforce this conservative logic, subscribing to a formula whereby weak men and strong women undergo a reversal of fortunes—a theme that has been rendered familiar to audiences through Shakespeare and repackaged, Navailh explains, as "the Soviet version of *The Taming of the Shrew.*"[25] Upon closer examination, however, these films, while conforming to the genre of *Zhenskie fil'my* at the level of content, utterly undermine this vision of strong men "standing alone" at the level of form. In Orlova's work, for example, Hamlet and Richard are brought into being only as by-products of the negative space that surrounds and, often, threatens to envelop them. Indeed, Orlova's animation style, which is based on the repeated use of a single pane of glass, not only makes the audience "always aware that each image is a revision of the previous one"[26] but also suggests a cynical gloss on Gorbachev's "innovations," underscoring their palimpsestic status as an insufficiently revised sequence of familiar Kremlin dictates. Similarly subversive are the puppets employed in *Twelfth Night* and *Shrew.* For despite their closing validation of a patriarchal order consolidated by marriage, both films, by virtue of their reliance on stop-motion puppetry, represent men as *literally* incapable of standing alone. By revealing strong men to be mere functionaries of the animators who manipulate their "articulation points" or joints, Muat and Ziablikova expose the ways in which "women's work"—uniquely defined in terms of their double duty to both domestic and party imperatives—has historically propped up the Soviet regime, while also implying a more sinister connection between puppetry and realpolitik. Embodying the frustrating fits and starts of Soviet feminism, Orlova's stained glass technique and Muat and Ziablikova's stop-motion puppetry envision life outside the lines of an oppressive regime, reinventing Shakespeare's characters through the lens of alternative or, in Haraway's words, "partial, contradictory, permanently unclosed constructions of personal and collective selves."[27]

Quite remarkably, then, the *Animated Tales* reproduce the posthuman and distinctly cybernetic quality of the premodern texts they adapt, materializing the capacity of Shakespeare's characters to morph before our very eyes. Indeed, the fact that the majority of the plays published in the First Folio lack dramatis personae lists—and those that do contain such lists situate them at the end of the text—renders the very concept of "character" a contingent effect rather than a cause of the dramatic action. As Margreta De Grazia and Peter Stallybrass explain, "quite literally without a program and therefore not programmed to encounter a group of unified characters," Renaissance readers "had to arbitrate for themselves the boundaries of identity . . . negotiating an array of positionalities relating to rank, family, gender, age, and even the specific personnel of the theatrical company."[28] Such arbitrations offer a surprising window onto a delicate fossil record of transitional forms—human hands attached to movable type, paper derived from discarded foreign linens, and ink infused with household items such as juniper gum, linseed oil, lampblack, and even "the residual traces of the urine of the printshop workers"—all of which contribute to making the Shakespearean text, as De Grazia and Stallybrass conclude, "a provisional state in the circulation of matter."[29] Hence, had Eisenstein derived his analysis of the differences between Shakespeare and Disney from textual practice rather than stage presence, he might have found in Shakespeare an equally compelling point of entry into the "prelogical" processes that he ascribes to Disney's lyrically unprogrammed characters. For just as Disney's figures flow into unpredictable combinations of the animate and the inanimate, Shakespeare's texts emerge from similar, undifferentiating collisions of human and machine, presenting us with an unlikely blueprint—realized in the work of the female directors of the *Animated Tales*—of a cybernetic system wherein, as Haraway concludes, "no objects, spaces, or bodies are sacred in themselves; any component can be interfaced with any other if the proper standard, the proper code, can be constructed for processing signals in a common language."[30]

That children are the intended recipients of this common language is significant, for like the readers of the Shakespearean text, the child viewers of the *Animated Tales* are also potentially resistant to programming, representing a gateway to the prelogical processes that enable a "departure from one's self" and, more important, "from once and forever prescribed norms of nomenclature, form and behavior."[31] This emphasis on the *dual* temporality of the prelogical as that which provides access not only to the past of prememory but also to a potentially deprogrammed future is critical. Indeed, far from invoking a nostalgic return to the lost golden age of childhood, Eisenstein appropriates child perception as a preemptive strike against an overdetermined future, hoping to suspend the impulse toward differentiation that has been naturalized within capitalistic culture. The fact that the *Animated Tales* were created for distribution on television rather than in the movie house makes them a particularly potent vehicle for disrupting this differential principle. For these films not only challenge the conventions of realism and continuity central to classical narrative cinema but also, as self-contained, thirty-minute, commercial-free programs, resist the discontinuous and serial quality of televisual reception. The home theater environment of the *Animated Tales* thus situates children at the threshold of a new space-time altogether—the "future anterior"—a "tense of open potentiality" which, in Althusser's words, is comprised of the "backwardness, forwardness, survivals and unevenesses of development which *co-exist* in the structure of the real historical present: the present of the *conjuncture*."[32] This conjunctural space-time, for which children provide the perceptual access code, is the conjectural site of what I am calling the cybercinema. The authors' cinema, by contrast, presents us with an approach to conjuncture that serves only to reinstate a teleological vision of the sovereign author "standing alone." Herein, children serve not as participants in but as the unacknowledged consequences of or secret witnesses to creative—but distinctly not procreative—acts of sexual conjuncture disguised as textual collaboration. Hence, in the authors' cinema, children are positioned as decoys for the *women* who embody the ontological differences between animation and personification: rather than serving as animating agents in the provisional circulation of matter, women circulate as sexual objects between men and, in timely—that is, timeless—fashion become screens for projecting the "once and forever" personification of the author.

The Author Strikes Back: A Return to
Our Regularly Scheduled Programming

"You're Veronica Franco, you're a poet, and you're my lady."
                                        —Marco Venier, *Dangerous Beauty*

"By me, William Shakespeare."
                                        —Will Shakespeare, *Shakespeare in Love*

Whereas the *Animated Tales* undermine the viewing conventions of both film and television, *Dangerous Beauty* and *Shakespeare in Love* epitomize the regularly scheduled programs broadcast on basic cable channels such as Oxygen and WE, which replay films from the romance genre as a staple of their evening "cinematherapy" offerings. The purpose of the WE network in particular is to generate a viewing space wherein women are not necessarily on display for an objectifying gaze—from the television screen to the TV viewing couch. However, despite the pretense of collaboration announced by the promotional slogan "I am WE," the programs offered by this network ostensibly of and for women are not substantially different from those broadcast in the normative space of what I'll call "ME," or, Men's Entertainment. *Dangerous Beauty* and *Shakespeare in Love* usher us into this common ground where WE and ME meet, holding out the prospect of female collaboration only to leave their heroines, quite literally, in the hands of powerful men. Rather than acknowledging the ways in which Renaissance women used collaboration to subvert the monopoly on publication that excluded them, these films exalt the reversal of fortunes whereby men became authors by positing women as the "unauthorized ground on which [their] authority could be established."[33]

"If," as Wendy Wall asks, "women were tropes necessary to the process of writing, if they were constructed within genres as figures for male desire, with what authority could they publish? How could a woman become an author if she was the 'other' against whom 'authors' differentiated themselves?"[34] At first glance, *Dangerous Beauty* sets out to answer as well as to intervene in this predicament by dramatizing the life of Veronica Franco, one of the most famous members of Venice's elite courtesan caste and a figure central to the literary successes of *Ca' Venier,* the central meeting ground for writers and intellectuals in mid-seventeenth-century Venice. Indeed, Veronica Franco not only published impressive volumes of poetry and personal correspondence but also served as an editor and anthologizer in Domenico Venier's prestigious literary *ridotto,* or salon. Franco's professional relationship to *Ca' Venier* was intertwined with the two key players in the Venier family—Domenico's nephews, Marco and Maffio—who vied for discursive authority with each other by appropriating the polarizing figure of the courtesan as a foil for their displays of poetic prowess, offering a perfect demonstration of the ways in which women's bodies served as the "unauthorized ground" for the inscription of male authority.[35] The event that crystallized the complex relationship between Marco, Maffio, and Franco was the literary duel that evolved under the cover of polite intellectual exchange at *Ca' Venier.* Taking shape as a series of published attacks and counterattacks, the duel began with Maffio's scathing assault on Franco, followed by Marco's exalted defense of her, and finally culminated in Franco's attempt to vindicate herself as a woman, poet, lover, and intellectual equal.[36] As if to say "I am WE," Franco's reply to the men who desired and despised her took shape as a rejection of the fixed roles for women implied by the discourses of Petrarchan adulation and papal abomination, generating a pluralistic view of the Renaissance woman that expressly challenged the social programming that constituted the early modern network of men's entertainment.

By contrast, Marshall Herskovitz's 1998 film, *Dangerous Beauty,* replaces this interactive ethos of social and literary production with a sexual teleology of authorship. If, as Jyotsna Singh explains, Renaissance culture imagined female sexuality as simultaneously "dangerous," "vulnerable," and "marketable,"[37] then the duel scene that is the centerpiece of *Dangerous Beauty* brings all three of these assumptions into alignment. In this scene, Veronica Franco is first and foremost represented as "marketable," for Herscovitz converts her published verse dialogue into a sexually charged spectacle at *Ca' Venier,* a place that is represented as less of an intellectual gathering point than an upscale brothel. That Franco appears to be more interested in cheap sexual transactions than rich textual commerce is also what makes her come across as "dangerous" in this film. Retaliating against Maffio's bawdy sword blow to her volume of verse—a move that violently slices her book in half—Franco seizes a sword herself and, to the delight of the male patrons who depend on her to rouse them from the cold beds of their chilly wives, she proceeds to remove her skirt to reveal pants, replete with a codpiece. But Franco's delightfully dangerous personification of authorship as a distinctly male prerogative goes too far, for her masquerade exposes the thinly veiled homoeroticism that shores up the textual and sexual commerce of Renaissance authorship and therefore proves threatening to the men who rely on her femininity as the source of their differentiation. Hence, having defeated Maffio not only with her tongue but also with her sword, she must now be represented as "vulnerable." As if on cue, Maffio lands a cheap blow on her jaw that causes her to bleed and stumble back into her proper place. The bookend scene to this misogynistic display is *Marco* Venier's belated entry into the duel with Maffio as the man who can put Franco in the place where, at least according to the film, she wants to be: his bed. Storming into her chamber after she has publicly refused his help in the duel, Marco makes up for his passive spectatorship by literally manhandling her—seizing Franco and forcefully kissing her on her badly bruised mouth. Significantly, not a single word is exchanged during this scene, but as Marco tosses Franco's limp body onto the bed and she melts into his embrace, the message is clear: vulnerability is for women, pants are for men—especially when they're off.

What *Dangerous Beauty*'s capitulation to the romance topos crucially ignores is that the real Veronica Franco collaborated with Marco Venier in a way that challenged traditional citational and erotic practices. Although Marco was, in fact, her part-time lover, he was more importantly positioned as the full-time interlocutor in her published volume of verse, *Terza Rime,* demonstrating Franco's dexterous use of alliances as a means of circumnavigating barriers to female authorship. *Dangerous Beauty*'s focus on Franco's role as Marco's mistress also obscures the fact that her collaboration with him was more politically advantageous than sexually opportunistic—particularly when Marco's status as a distinguished Venetian senator bolstered Franco in her battle against the Roman Inquisition in 1580, when she was charged with practicing "heretical incantations." Remarkably, in the midst of a historical epidemic wherein all female speech was considered potentially heretical, Franco exploited her rapport with influential men to create a network for *women,* entreating the Venetian government in 1577 to build a halfway home for women who were unable to support themselves but sexually ineligible to enter a House of Convertites. Hence, despite being "caught in legal, social, and economic nets," Franco's poems, which explore strategic partnerships as a locus of strength, exemplify how women writers in the Renaissance learned "to dance within them quite visibly, to piece together discursive forms that circumvented restrictions on their public appearances."[38] Importantly, Franco also used publication as an opportunity to "piece together" a future for her children. Capitalizing on her role as elite courtesan and respected citizen, Franco aligned herself with powerful, wealthy men such as Jacomo di Baballi and Ludovico Remberti, with whom she had acknowledged children and whom, consequently, she charged with financial and familial responsibilities in her will. Rather than revealing this markedly open system of sexual, textual, and legal communication or, for that matter, the children who were its direct beneficiaries, *Dangerous Beauty* ends with a vision that reduces the constitutive complexity of Franco's legacy to a story of one man's noblesse oblige. The film's final scene shows Marco coming to Franco's rescue once again, liberating her from prison and whisking her away on a gondola that sails into the Venetian sunset, as Franco's all but inanimate body becomes a pliant surface for the inscription of a Hollywood ending.

At a time when one quarter of women died in the early years of marriage from complications due to childbirth, the "sudden and prolific production of female-authored tracts couched in the language of will-making," as Wall observes, "provided the ground from which women publicly challenged cultural demands for their silence."[39] At least indirectly, then, children played a far more significant role in the articulation of female authorship than their conspicuous absence in *Dangerous Beauty* would have us believe. For in an environment wherein the act of publishing is predicated on both a literal and imagined exchange between mother and child at the threshold of life and death, it is the child—unborn or just born—who quite literally becomes the *midwife* of the mother's nascent text.[40] In the authors' cinema, however, this critical role reserved for children is either eliminated, as in *Dangerous Beauty,* or perverted, as in *Shakespeare in Love,* where a young John Webster witnesses the simultaneous creation of the "seminal work" and the sovereign male author over the prone body of Viola de Lesseps. *Shakespeare in Love*'s variation on the burgeoning theme of the maternal legacy distorts the reciprocity whereby the presumed death of the mother leads, paradoxically, to the birth of the author, as newborn child and text enter the world in tandem. For what the authors' cinema takes for its theme are the ways in which this "self-constituting gesture based on self-annihilation" fractures along the axis of gender, as men and boys derive their authority—and texts—from an act of conjuncture that demands the erasure of the female body from this equation.[41]

In a culture wherein both sex and gender were believed to be in large part determined outside the clutches of the womb, children—and their proper education—were a particular source of anxiety. According to the emergent evangelical discourse of seventeenth-century England, children were a source of parental distress because they were innately willful and naturally sinful. Using the Bible as a child-rearing manual, Puritan ex-patriot John Robinson explains in his 1628 treatise on education that children must therefore be subject to the discipline of the rod, as ordained by the ultimate parent, God the Father: "the wisdom of God is best; and that saith, that 'foolishness is bound up in the heart of a child which the rod of correction must drive out:' and that 'he, who spares his rod, hurts his son.' "[42] Another reason why children, like women, were deemed potentially dangerous was because the establishment of male identity was predicated on performative *separation* from the female. According to both the "two-seed theory," which assumed a struggle for primacy between male and female seed, and the "topological theory," which posited homologous sex organs in men and women, gender complied with sex only on the basis of an often violent assertion of difference—either through the "defeat" of the female seed vying for prominence within the male body or, alternatively, as Stephen Greenblatt observes, through "the selective forcing out through heat of the original internal organ" in order to manifest the male genitalia.[43] What is fascinating about *Shakespeare in Love* is the way in which the child John Webster witnesses this act of differentiation between Will and Viola and, hence, becomes a party, if not a kind of midwife, to the "birth" of Shakespeare the author.

This act of witnessing is critical in *Shakespeare in Love* since, at the beginning of the film, it is all too clear that Will is not sufficiently distinguishing himself from the female, for he is in the throes of impotence. The film's first full scene involving the young Will Shakespeare shows him lying prone on a couch, complaining to his analyst-apothecary about his writer's block: "It's as if my quill is broken," Will exclaims. "As if the organ of the imagination has dried up. As if the proud tower of my genius has collapsed. . . . Nothing comes." In a film allegedly about authorship, this shift of emphasis from the textual to the sexual is a brilliant gambit on the part of the film's creators, since the real "mystery" at stake in *Shakespeare in Love* has less to do with the queen's wager concerning whether or not a play can represent "the very truth and nature of love" than it does with an "author" whose own body is missing in action at the scene of textual production. By rendering this fundamental dismemberment between textual corpus and authorial body as a *sexual* deficiency, however, *Shakespeare in Love* masterfully locates the missing link between them in the insertion of another body— the virginal Viola De Lesseps—whose flesh becomes word and, therefore, compelling evidence of the fantasy that authorship, like masculinity, is the natural product of differentiation from the female. But it is not until the young John Webster, future playwright and, in *Shakespeare in Love,* man-midwife par excellence, bears witness to this process of differentiation that the film's vision of authorship as an exclusively male prerogative is secure. In fact, Webster's presence as a witness in *Shakespeare in Love* suggests a variation on the theme and practice of midwifery in Renaissance England, wherein midwives were called upon "to examine the bodies of the accused and decide whether they have 'witches' marks.' "[44] This role, broadly speaking, is John Webster's purpose in *Shakespeare in Love* as he bears witness to the marks of gender difference that are inscribed on Will's hard body as he labors over the bewitching feminine curvature of Viola's reclining figure. The importance of this brief scene to the overall logic of the film cannot be underestimated, for Webster's voyeurism succeeds in straightening out the sexual uncertainty that inheres in the historical representation of William Shakespeare, in the performance exigencies of Renaissance stage practices, and, potentially, in the film audience itself.

Indeed, *Shakespeare in Love* flirts rather dangerously with the failure to distinguish male from female, author from text, not only in the form of Will's impotence but also in the specter of homoerotic desire. Though this confusion is easily overshadowed by the film's romantic teleology of authorship, there can be no mistake that Will is initially fascinated with Viola in the likeness of her male stage persona, Thomas Kent. Playing upon this sexual ambiguity, the filmmakers go so far as to have Will make love to Viola backstage—in the midst of rehearsal—when "she" is still dressed as Thomas/Romeo. That this is the *last* time Will and Viola are shown making love and the *first* time that John Webster is present as a witness is particularly significant; for Webster's gaze is implicitly aligned with ours, and it is his testimony that clarifies once and for all the fact that Shakespeare has a "will" of his own. Watching curiously as Thomas becomes a woman and Will becomes a man, Webster, according to screenwriters Marc Norman and Tom Stoppard, "takes his eye away from the peephole, and frowns, thinking it out."[45] As Webster "thinks it out," so do we—and the learning curve is not terribly steep; in fact, it is not long before the prodigious boy announces to the master of the revels that there is a woman in their midst, proudly exclaiming, "I saw her bubbies!" According to the punitive logic of *Shakespeare in Love,* the problem that this scenario presents is not so much that Will has, until now, struggled to become a man but that *Viola* may continue to succeed in this very endeavor. Hence, this scene inscribes a vision of authorship that stems not merely from the act of separation from the female but, more important, from the utter rejection of women in favor of male parthenogenesis. For just as Shakespeare the star is born from the mediating gaze and testimony of the young John Webster, so, too, it would seem as though Will's "rod" has left an indelible impression on Webster the playwright, whose Jacobean revenge tragedies will hinge on the misogynistic treatment of upstart women like Viola. Appropriately, Webster's last words in the film, in response to the queen's question as to whether or not he liked the play, reveal how successfully this legacy has been inscribed: "I liked it when she stabbed herself, your Majesty."

Quite unlike the collaborative energies that animate the cybercinema, then, the authors' cinema operates according to the principle of personification through differentiation, which, in turn, shores up the boundaries that maintain the closed system of patriarchal authority. That the title of Will's masterpiece changes from *Romeo and Ethyl* to *Romeo and Rosaline* and, finally, to *Romeo and Juliet* underscores the fact that *men* are the "constant" or standard against which Renaissance conceptions of gender emerge, even as it signals the exchangeability of women as goods to be consumed and, if necessary, discarded in the process of both identity formation and play production. Moreover, if the increasingly romantic construction of authorship toward which the film gravitates requires the expulsion of all other agents in the creative process, then in order for Will to become the author he never was, Viola must become the feminized object of exchange she has always already been. As in *Dangerous Beauty,* then, in *Shakespeare in Love,* the WE is systematically sacrificed on the altar of the ME; Viola devolves from collaborator and player to mere spectator in her own tragedy and the Renaissance returns with a vengeance to validate her devolution as the divine right of history to repeat itself. Adding insult to this injury, the fact that the queen herself requests a sequel from Will implicitly blames women for exacerbating their own powerlessness even as they extend the scope of their entertainment value in a culture wherein beauties must be dangerous to each other to survive. Now with a television network devoted to men—the phallic prowess of which is announced by the name "Spike"—*Shakespeare in Love* should have a long afterlife in syndication, for the treatment this film prescribes for viewers in need of cinematherapy is nothing less than the cathartic benefits of channel surfing. Ending with an image of Will's handwriting superimposed on a vision of Viola, whose destiny is now literally in his hands, the film recuperates Shakespeare's invisible authorial hand as the ultimate exercise of remote control—the perfect cure for women who threaten to steal the show.

Osheen-en-abyme

> Look what kinde of words or behaviour thou wouldst
> dislike from thy servant or childe, those must thou
> not give to thine husband, for thou art equally
> commanded to be subiect.
> —William Whately, *A Bride-Bush: or a direction for married persons* (1619)[46]

It is a striking coincidence that Adrian Noble's 1996 version of *A Midsummer Night's Dream* and Julie Taymor's 1999 film, *Titus,* position a child at the threshold of entry into their respective cinemascapes. Noble's addition of an anonymous boy observer and Taymor's considerable augmentation of the role of Young Lucius lead to uncanny similarities between these two very different films: both situate the boy as a semi-interactive witness linking the filmic frame to the play; both employ a "rabbit hole" effect through which the boy falls from the frame into the world of the film proper; and both contain a somewhat ominous, leather-clad, goggles-sporting motorcyclist who transports the boy at a critical juncture in each film. Yet what is even more remarkable is that the role of the child is played by the *same* actor: Osheen Jones. Whether or not Taymor consciously intended *Titus* to be a remake of Noble's *Dream,* Jones's presence in both films produces a mise-en-abyme effect that leads to an unexpected feedback loop between them, particularly when we realize that Jones plays a character whose age, in terms of Renaissance child-rearing practices, would place him at the threshold of passage from maternal to paternal care. Hence, although in Noble's film the boy's ultimate rejection of the mother appears to seal his education in and perpetuation of phallocratic tyranny, we cannot help but recognize this same boy as the slightly older and wiser Young Lucius who, in Taymor's *Titus,* actually becomes a mother himself. As Young Lucius, Jones causes an unbearable surge of entropy in the otherwise self-contained system that characterizes Adrian Noble's *A*

Midsummer Night's Dream, demonstrating how—in the open system of the cybercinema—characters not only maintain the Disneyesque capacity to "turn into each other" but also the potential to nourish a new order.[47]

Fears about the adverse effects of prolonged exposure to female nurture were particularly high in late sixteenth- and early seventeenth-century England, which witnessed a Puritan revival of the doctrine of original sin. The ensuing cultural hysteria surrounding children and their "proper" education was based on the "deadly fear of the liability of children to corruption and sin, particularly those cardinal sins of pride and disobedience," to which women were considered exceptionally prone.[48] Hence, John Robinson warns that although "children, in their first days, have the greater benefit of good mothers, not only because they suck their milk, but in a sort, their manners also, by being continually with them, and receiving their first impressions from them," when "they come to their riper years, good fathers are more behoveful for their forming in virtue and good manners, by their greater wisdom and authority: and ofetimes also, by correcting the fruits of their mother's indulgence, by their severity."[49] Robinson's invocation of a gender-segregated system of child rearing, presided over by biological mother and father, respectively, is an extremely efficient rendering of the elaborate network of surrogate parenting to which children in the Renaissance were subject. This bifurcated system of nurture began with wet nurses, serving women, and sundry other female domestics who, in the case of male preadolescents, were abruptly replaced by all-male "households," constituted by the authoritarian environment of schools, apprenticeships, and universities. A boy's first encounter with these more "severe" sites of nurture would likely be the Latin classroom, which, as Wall explains, "was designed to correct the faults inculcated in the female and vernacular world of early childhood. Hyperdetermined against a gender- and class-based commonality, Latin enabled the production of the 'closed male environment' of academia, as well as the professional and courtly institutions it fed."[50] Yet the violence of this learning process, which often entailed beatings with a rod, ferule, or other suitably phallic object, betrays the extent to which gender education in the Renaissance was not the product of a "closed male environment" but rather a dangerously open system wherein biologic sex and gender did not always agree with each other. Under such circumstances, then, might the male child be prone toward emulating *either* end of the spectrum of parental surrogation to which he had been exposed?[51] In other words, in a cultural milieu wherein gender is an ongoing performance rather than a fixed destination, *could* the maternal legacy exert a pull beyond the household—or, indeed, the grave—coaxing the male child back into the more fluid "social alliances" and "common" citational practices he enjoyed while still in the company of women?[52]

By framing his adaptation of Shakespeare's play with a preadolescent boy who becomes a site of the competing gender impressions that Robinson anxiously invokes, Noble's version of *Dream* implicitly begs this question. The film begins in the boy's bedroom, which, significantly, is not marked as distinctly feminine or masculine. In fact, the only prevailing sign of the child's interests is the puppet theater that the camera momentarily lingers over, suggesting the performative, provisional relationship between identity formation and play production that the boy—if he is to become a man, let alone an author—must come to reject. Nevertheless, the fear that he has not yet made the necessary transition from maternal nurture to paternal emulation and therefore is susceptible to "corruption" by the twin sins of pride and disobedience born of bad (female) example is broached in the very first scene. Here, the boy is represented as a sympathetic witness to Hermia's defiance of her father's will and to Hippolyta's decision to slap Theseus as she exits the room, an interpolated expression of her disgust with his threat to subject Hermia to the strict Athenian law that polices female sexuality with death. That the plight of these women has made an impression on the boy is implied by his ensuing fascination with Helena, whose plan to pursue Demetrius into the woods causes the boy to run after her and, in his excitement, accidentally propel himself out of a second-story window. The clash of child-rearing systems thus begins when he falls down a uterine-like shoot out of the comforts of his home and into the film proper, shrieking "Mummy!" only to find himself deposited in the all-male "household" of Oberon and Puck's fairy kingdom. As in the Athenian world he left behind, the boy soon learns that the specter of female insubordination also haunts the green world, for Titania is denying Oberon's bed and refusing to hand over the Indian child (also played by Osheen Jones), who is the subject of their custodial dispute. In representing Jones's boy as an outsider looking into Titania's system, while presenting his alter ego as a figure trapped within this system, Noble cleverly materializes the crisis of the male child's riven subjectivity at the "breeching" age, that is, the point at which a boy must abandon the company of women and, quite literally, learn to "wear the pants."[53] But

Noble goes one step further to dramatize the rejection of *all* bonds—including those between men—that might corrupt the feedback loop which perpetuates the dynastic chain between fathers and sons.

Consequently, although we might expect the film to valorize Oberon and Puck's surrogate parenting of the boy as an alternative to the "common" and "indulgent" system of maternal nurture to which he has evidently grown accustomed, Noble proceeds to render the relationship between Oberon and Puck as one that revolves around deviance and even sodomy. For example, the first time the boy encounters Oberon and Puck, he sees them engage in a passionate kiss after a series of flirtatious verbal and physical exchanges. Later, when Oberon discovers that his script has miscarried due to Puck's improvisations, Noble glosses this moment of textual deviation as evidence of Puck's sexual aberration; begging Oberon's forgiveness on all fours, Puck pulls down his pants and invites Oberon to spank him—a form of punishment that both parties clearly enjoy. By presenting the commerce between Puck and Oberon through the lens of nonprocreative sexual relations and thus as a threat to the autonomous reproduction of the system, Noble's film unwittingly recapitulates the editorial tradition that considers collaboration to be synonymous with "corruption."[54] And what could be more corrupt than Noble's implication that the perfect complement to Oberon's sodomitical relationship with Puck would be the boy's entry into this perverse partnership as an apt pupil for pederasty? It is little wonder that the boy appears to be utterly terrified of Oberon, whose authority he must nevertheless learn to emulate. Thus, it is Noble who, as an extension of Oberon, takes it upon himself to break the boy to the rod by demonstrating its proper function in the realm of "normative," that is, reproductive sexual and textual, relations, wherein the boy will come to recognize that becoming a man involves schooling *women.*

If the fundamental goal of cybernetic systems is to maximize the capacity to communicate and therefore replicate, then the greatest threat to this self-sustaining equilibrium is the potential for "noise" or disorganization that increases with the repeated transmission of information, raising the level of entropy to potentially unsustainable levels. As Lisa Trahair explains, entropy is defined "algorithmically" as "the maximum amount of disorganization permitted before what is perceived as a system is transformed into another system."[55] In an effort to prevent such transformation, systems develop an "algorithm for redundancy," a built-in maintenance program

that (1) detects external influences; (2) monitors corresponding internal changes; and (3) performs adjustments to regulate operations. This
maintenance function is precisely the role assigned to the boy in Noble's
film, for in the context of the patriarchal sex-gender system at stake in
Dream, children are critical components of this cultural hardware as literal
repositories of the code for system redundancy. Our first indication that
Jones's boy is aiding rather than aggravating system maintenance is the
fact that, like Shakespeare's Oberon, he becomes increasingly associated
with an omnipotent, "god's eye" perspective, looking down on the drama
from the oculus of his puppet theater. Even more striking is the boy's
shift from observer to participant when Noble suddenly reveals him to be
literally pulling Oberon and Puck's strings, lifting them out of the playing
space to set the stage for Titania's roll in the hay with Bottom. Unlike
Shakespeare's play, as well as other cinematic adaptations of *Dream*, in
Noble's film, the boy actually accompanies Bottom and Titania on their
tryst, as Bottom takes his diminutive dominatrix and the boy on an *E.T.*-
style (motorcycle) ride across the moon to the fairy queen's bower.[56] Yet
not even this striking allusion to the topos of children's cinema can bridge
the gap between Bottom's grotesque appearance and the boy's apparent
innocence. Indeed, against the cinematic tradition of rendering Bottom
as a sympathetic and essentially likable figure, Noble envisions Bottom
as hairy and obese, replete with filthy, protruding teeth and, we are led
to believe, a donkey-size "rod."[57] Since this is the point at which Titania
must learn to revere the rod and, in keeping with Puritan pedagogy, have
her childlike "stubbornness, and stoutness of mind . . . broken and beaten
down,"[58] it is perhaps not surprising to find that phallic objects dominate
the mise-en-scene. What *is* troubling, however, is that the most prominent
of them is an obscenely long, strapped-on carrot nose worn by a member
of Titania's fairy train—an unmistakable allusion to Stanley Kubrick's *A
Clockwork Orange*—which, in turn, casts the ensuing "love scene" in
terms of rape.[59] Worse, in positioning the boy as the surrogate puppeteer
of Oberon's production, Noble begs the question as to who the author of
this perverse sexual encounter really is.

    After the boy and Titania's fairy train wish the odd couple good night,
the camera steadily retreats from his anxious gaze, suddenly cutting away
to a close-up of Oberon, who exclaims: "This falls out better than I could
devise." As Oberon nods over his shoulder to reveal Puck by his side, our
attention is drawn to the offscreen space where, even before the camera

lights on Bottom and Titania, we hear hard, rhythmic pounding followed by groans that suggest more pain than pleasure. Clinging to her inverted umbrella as though it were a stripper's pole, Titania arches her back and braces for the impact as Bottom stands and thrusts violently into her, emitting a crude "hee-haw" with each effort. Noble's decision to represent this potentially subversive exchange between Bottom and Titania as an encounter more akin to rape is disturbing on multiple levels. In the context of cybernetic communications, wherein boundaries are constantly traversed and strange bedfellows are born of unexpected acts of interfacing, Bottom's aggressive violation of boundaries suggests a brutal burlesque of Titania's open system. For unlike Theseus and Oberon, Titania is a character who continually shifts the investment strategies around which her system is configured, first by moving away from Oberon to "gossi[p] by [the] side" of the Indian votress (2.1.125)—an image evocative of the "female and vernacular world of early childhood"[60]—and later, by building her system around the child who proved mortal to this configuration. Bottom's violent subjugation of Titania thus turns her capacity for embracing entropy against her; for this scene is intended to teach Titania a lesson by placing her on the same level as the child she nurtures—a particularly sinister application of the Puritan commonplace that a child must be made as "serviceable" as a horse, "being never to be left to his own government, but always to have his rider on his back, and the bit in his mouth."[61] Yet what is most troubling about the bridling of Titania's will is the possibility that the boy *himself* devised this misogynistic spectacle. Although Noble is careful not to position Jones's character as a direct observer of Bottom and Titania's "violent delights," it is his gaze that marks the vanishing point from which this scene springs. And what better way to get back at "mummy" for refusing his cry for help than to imagine having his way with a mother substitute? Ultimately, though, whether the boy is a bystander in or an instigator of this fantasy, the upshot remains the same. For if the goal of the closed patriarchal system toward which Shakespeare's play and Noble's film slouches is to control the investment strategies of its component parts and, in so doing, maximize its capacity for reproduction, then this mission is accomplished when Titania relinquishes control of both her body *and* her Indian boy to Oberon—a clear indication that opportunistic domination has replaced her ethos of radical connection.

But in Noble's film, there is still one child to be accounted for in order to insure that disruptions to the system have been sealed off and autonomy has been achieved. The sign that Oberon's system no longer requires the boy's monitoring and maintenance is the emergence of the unidentifiable hand that suddenly takes over for the boy's puppetry. As an extension of Oberon or, perhaps, Noble himself, this mysterious force that now pulls the strings alludes to the invisible hand that polices the closed system of the authors' cinema. All that is required to complete this vision of order restored, then, is the sought-after "algorithm for redundancy" that perpetuates system homeostasis, healing the breach in Oberon's authority once and for all. This algorithm is, of course, the heterosexual imperative of marriage, which, as in Shakespeare's play, is articulated by Puck as follows: "And the country proverb known / Every man should take his own." Spoken in voice-over to accentuate its disembodied ubiquity, this algorithm is reinforced by a visual gloss from the boy, who spins giddily in circles as the scenery is lifted high over his head, becoming an emblem of the restoration of the unimpeded feedback loop between father and son. Fittingly, at this threshold moment, Puck repeats the algorithm in the form of an easily memorized nursery rhyme: "Jack shall have Jill; / Nought shall go ill; / The man shall have his mare again, and all shall be well." In keeping with the self-determining logic of the authors' cinema, the boy now willingly takes hold of Puck's hand and walks with him into a larger-than-life moonrise, smiling for the first time without hesitation because, we are led to believe, his place in the system is at last secure. After a final dance in which he is lifted high into the air and spun around by the fairy cohort beneath him, the boy is carefully placed between Oberon and Titania, as the film ends, appropriately, with a tableau of a family portrait.

Perhaps it is just a coincidence that Julie Taymor's *Titus* culminates in a vision of the very same actor, Osheen Jones, cradling a baby in his arms and walking toward an imposing, artificial sunrise, but Taymor's tragedy contains many more scenes that suggest parallels with Noble's comedy. Indeed, *Titus* similarly begins with establishing shots that take us into the boy's world, beginning not in his bedroom but in the kitchen. This time, however, rather than venturing down the hallway and peering through a keyhole onto a play that will eventually be performed in his puppet theater, the boy peers out from the eyeholes of a crude paper bag mask, as the camera pulls back to reveal that he has converted his kitchen table into a stage for a dramatic clash of action figures. Uncannily, the boy's "fall" from this filmic frame into the world of Shakespeare's play is brought about by a gruff-appearing man who sports motorcycle goggles but no motorcycle—a figure who looks so out of place that it's hard not to recall the only slightly less bizarre figure of Bottom in Noble's film. Finally, in a shot that dovetails with the end of *Dream*, *Titus* begins officially when the boy is raised up over the head of his rescuer/abductor, a gesture of triumph that results in cheers from a crowd that is, rather disturbingly, nowhere to be found. *Titus* thus takes shape as a film which, like Noble's, positions the audience as an observer of an observer; that the latter observer is Osheen Jones is significant because his presence ruptures the homeostasis achieved by Noble's *Dream*, prying open this closed system as if to retroactively inject entropy—and transformation—into it.

Although Jones's boy is central to the monitoring, maintenance, and marring of the feedback loop in *Titus*, the film refuses to align our gaze exclusively with that of Young Lucius from its opening frames. Rather, Taymor enters the war of the cinemas by relentlessly drawing our attention to—while seeking to revise the relationship between—observation and violence that is the very basis of cybernetic theory. Born of Norbert Wiener's work on antiaircraft tracking devices during World War II, cybernetic theory crystallized in Wiener's discovery of the feedback loop as a regulatory mechanism for insuring communication and control across a system's constituent subsystems, a discovery that enabled antiaircraft guns to adjust their trajectories continuously in order to strike moving targets. It is no coincidence, then, that Taymor evinces this association with World War II by choosing the remains of Mussolini's government center for one of her two on-location shooting sites for *Titus;* the other site is a Roman coliseum in Croatia, the circular form of which becomes, in this film, an emblem of the inexorable feedback loop that sustains the relationship between spectatorship and violence. Even before we enter the film proper, however, Taymor similarly implicates the film audience in a complex observational dynamic that skews our attention between Young Lucius's perspective and a menacing offscreen space. In the opening shot, for example, an unseen television bathes Lucius's drama of toy carnage in intermittent blue glow; as the noise and flicker of light subsumes the room, it becomes increasingly difficult to determine whether the boy is watching TV or the TV is watching *him*. This unsettling milieu sets the stage for the ensuing collapse of boundaries between the boy and his toys, for the more he mimics the unguided rage of battery-operated, remote-control machines, the more his plastic action figures assume human qualities, appearing to writhe in agony under his unrelenting blows. Yet when this disturbingly real, escalating mock battle transports the viewer into the Roman coliseum, the audience experiences another reversal of terms, as squadrons of stiff-legged gladiators march toward the boy like so many toy soldiers seeking revenge against his child's play—only now their gaze is trained on us. Posing stark contrast to these robotic warriors, nimble Roman "chariots" comprised of high-tech combinations of Hummers, horses, and humans amble across the coliseum floor, linking the military prowess of ancient Rome to the cyborg technology of postmodern warfare, wherein remote-control, "smart" weaponry demonstrates the extent to which "our machines are disturbingly lively, and we ourselves frighteningly inert."[62] The opening sequence of *Titus* thus entrenches the film audience in a frighteningly familiar mise-en-scene that marks the threshold where violence and entertainment meet. By dispersing our gaze across a spectrum of real and virtual points of identification that originate in the seemingly innocent world of child's play, Taymor seduces us into entering a far more sinister space, wherein we have the sneaking suspicion that although the fun and games are over, the toys are *us*.[63]

In his complex assessment of *Titus,* Richard Burt contends that Taymor's film becomes complicit in the violence it sets out to critique, by relentlessly "romanticizing" the figure of the "innocent child" who, "dead or alive, . . . often legitimates violence against the Other in German and Italian Fascist cinema."[64] Such a claim, while highly provocative, ignores the fact that Young Lucius is patently *not* innocent, a point that is underscored from the very beginning of *Titus* as well as throughout the film. Moreover, in contending that Taymor's "attempt to critique violence via Fascism and the Holocaust are inevitably in tension with her reinscription of the horror genre,"[65] Burt does not acknowledge Taymor's revisionary approach to horror as yet another genre that employs the topos of child development (or lack thereof) as its preferred mode of legitimating violence against the Other—in this case, the female body. While Fascist cinema positions the child as an agent that mediates or incites violence between men, horror—particularly the slasher subgenre often associated with *Titus*—revolves around a male character who, still in the throes of boyhood, brutally inscribes his psychosexual confusion on the bodies of women only to be vanquished by a female survivor, or the "Final Girl."[66] Taymor's

Titus presents us with a series of disturbing variations on these combined themes. Despite the powerful lead played by Anthony Hopkins, the focus of Taymor's film is the violence that women perpetrate against other women, reflected not only in the elaborate, highly sophisticated production values Taymor employs to represent Tamora and Lavinia but also in the comments revealing her directorial fascination with Tamora and her barely concealed disdain for Lavinia as "Daddy's little girl, all ready for defilement."[67] If this shift of emphasis suggests a reversal of the gendered violence of Fascist cinema, then it also has a transformative impact on the perverse child psychology adumbrated by the horror film. Rather than representing childhood as inherently pathological, while depicting the female adolescent survivor as the boyish, Final Girl left to negotiate an uncertain future, *Titus* represents childhood from an Eisensteinian perspective—as the locus of a potentially progressive reversion—in the form of a male adolescent whose contradictory coding renders him Other, mother, and, as Lisa Starks argues, "Final *Boy*."[68]

If we are to view *Titus* through the combined lens of Fascist cinema and the horror film, then we cannot ignore the ways in which this structure of allusion retroactively glosses Noble's *A Midsummer Night's Dream*. Although *Titus* cannot be classified as a remake of *Dream*, the relationship between these two films forged by Osheen Jones forever undermines their self-identity, inserting, in the gap that separates them, a series of virtual films that are left for the spectator to imagine.[69] Hence, as this gap becomes a site of contention between the authors' cinema and the cybercinema, Taymor radicalizes the act of observation, rendering it a form of filmmaking in its own right. But which virtual film will prevail? On the one hand, as Titus's grandson, Young Lucius certainly contains the code for perpetuating the phallocratic tyranny featured in Noble's *Dream*, as well as in *Titus*'s own ongoing flirtation with the specter of Fascism that inheres in Roman military orthodoxy. This potential for system redundancy is implied not only by Young Lucius's initial kitchen table brutality but also by his dinner table "murder" of a fly which, he explains to Titus, he mistook for "a coal black moor." In assigning this role to the boy rather than, as in Shakespeare's play, his uncle Marcus, Taymor does in fact underscore the function of the child in Fascist cinema as an excuse for and, in this case, an agent of violence against the Other. On the other hand, Young Lucius's encounters with the castrating specter of Lavinia's raped and mutilated body do *not* precipitate the "dread of difference" that is the raison d'être of violence against women in the horror film but instead lead to a profound assertion of kinship with her.[70] In an interpolated scene, Young Lucius confronts Lavinia with a pair of wooden hands from a nearby doll shop, a gesture that recalls his destructive role in the film's opening frames as an agent of interanimation between people and playthings, as girls and dolls—like boys and their toys—merge unexpectedly and, indeed, horrifically. Yet Lavinia's prosthetic hands, while evincing a sense of revulsion at the absence they cannot ultimately conceal, also suggest a subversion of horror, for as Lisa Trahair asserts, "Horror opens the door . . . to a history of philosophy whose basic method is to differentiate and distinguish, to attribute value to, to set parameters and boundaries so as to make inclusion and exclusion, truth and fiction, subject and object—all the polarities that make meaning—possible."[71] Hence, as Young Lucius presents Lavinia with a pair of wooden hands that elide the gap between the animate and the inanimate, organic and synthetic, Taymor opens the door to a virtual film wherein, as Donna Haraway might conclude, "our bodies and our tools" are not sacrosanct but rather mutually imbricated in a system of transformative conjuncture, wherein authorship—like maternity—offers a liber⁓   from certainty.[72]

        at the end of *Titus* it is uncertain at best as to what virtual   will prevail, for this act of filmmaking is assigned not to Jones's boy but to the spectators who now occupy the coliseum. As Taymor explains, in contrast to the image of the empty coliseum with which the film begins, "this time the bleachers are filled with spectators. Watching. They are silent. They are we."[73] *Titus* concludes with a vision of Young Lucius's back to the camera, as he walks out of the film bearing Aaron and Tamora's mulatto child in his arms. Whether the boy will kill the child as he did the fly or nurture it as he has Lavinia remains to be seen and, perhaps, screened. Nevertheless, in deliberately *exiting* the theater of cruelty, Jones's character avenges his earlier role in Noble's film. For in representing Young Lucius as simultaneously mother, Other, and Final Boy, this tableau scrambles the vision of the discrete nuclear family with which Noble's *Dream* ends, replacing the algorithm for redundancy with entropy, born of "the interpenetration of boundaries between problematic selves and unexpected others."[74] Unlike the spectators whose silence encircles and, in effect, protects the genocidal violence of the film's conclusion, Young Lucius now recognizes that our machines and our screens *are* us:

their codes reflect our drives, their programs our processes, their networks our destinies. Neither vanquisher nor victim, he stands at the threshold of a cybernetic system wherein violence and healing are privileges that are actuated through observation—and feedback—and, in turning his back on us, it is only *our* gaze that can lead toward, or away from, the sequel.

Conclusion: Skeuomorphs and Unruly Replicants; Or, How Shakespeare Became Posthuman

In her recent book, *How We Became Posthuman: Virtual Bodies in Cybernetics, Literature, and Informatics,* N. Katherine Hayles explores the perils and possibilities of a systems-based approach to subjectivity, taking for her point of departure cybernetic theory and its originary act of severing information from embodiment. During its early articulation in the 1940s, cybernetics was concerned, as Hayles notes of Norbert Weiner's work in particular, with "extend[ing] liberal humanism, not subvert[ing] it."[75] "Seduced by fantasies of unlimited power and disembodied immortality," first-wave cybernetics was concerned "less to show that man was a machine than to demonstrate that a machine could function like a man" and, in the process, learn the tactics of domination and oppression.[76] This encounter between the Enlightenment subject and cybernetics led to the notion that humans are not merely information-processing entities but also self-regulating—if not self-creating—mechanisms, an assumption that has been hypostatized as an exclusively male privilege within the authors' cinema. Second-wave cybernetic theory, which reached its zenith in 1980 in conjunction with the work of figures like Niklas Luhmann, dealt a resounding blow to this logic of self-determinism by focusing on the reflexivity of systems, recognizing—as we have seen in several of the *Animated Tales*—that systems are comprised of mutually constitutive components in a continuous feedback loop.[77] Julie Taymor's *Titus* goes one step further to demonstrate how new systems, born of differential replication, can be generated by extending the feedback loop from the observed to the observer. Christine Edzard's *The Children's Midsummer Night's Dream* offers a coda to *Titus* by aligning her filmmaking enterprise with third-wave cybernetic theory—the intent of which, in the age of virtual reality and artificial life, is "to evolve the capacity to evolve" by recasting replication as "the springboard to emergence."[78]

HAMLET: What, are they children? Who maintains 'em? How are they escoted? Will they pursue the quality no longer than they can sing? Will they not say afterwards, if they should grow themselves to common players—as it is like most will, if their means are not better—their writers do them wrong to make them exclaim against their own succession?

—Shakespeare, *Hamlet* 2.2.345–51

In the original War of the Theaters, much was made of the fact that children were being employed as puppets of the so-called authors' theater playwrights, who, as Thomas Heywood lamented in his *Apology for Actors,* took advantage of the children's "juniority," supposing it "to be a privilege for any rayling" against their adult rivals in the bankside theaters.[79] But in so doing, the children were dealing a preemptive strike to their own future; they were, as Hamlet observes, being made to "exclaim against their own succession." Four hundred years later, Christine Edzard revised this scenario for the War of the Cinemas, releasing a film version of *Dream* in which the adults are puppets and the children follow their own cues. Beginning with a vision of schoolchildren gathered in a small theater, the film opens onto a life-size, puppet-show version of Shakespeare's *Dream* in which the parts of the principal players, Theseus and Hippolyta, are spoken by Derek Jacobi and Samantha Bond, respectively—two paragons of the British theatrical tradition whose voices instantly command reverence. The children auditors, however, are not so easily impressed, taking exception not only to the puppets' stiff appearance and stuffy delivery but also to Theseus and Egeus's abuse of Hermia. Hence, in a moment of childlike spontaneity, a girl springs up from the audience and usurps the puppet-Hermia's line—"I would my father looked with my eyes"—and a complete coup de théâtre ensues. As the children proceed to displace their adult counterparts by taking over the performance, the rarefied milieu of the small theater is replaced with the more naturalistic settings associated with cinematic realism. Significantly, this change of venue is represented by Edzard as a kind of rebirth, as the children's gradual shedding of their school uniforms enables them to negotiate a new relationship to their identities and bodies, having escaped from British educational orthodoxy and their "wooden" adult mentors.

When explored from the perspective of the War of the Cinemas, this sequence encapsulates the challenge that third-wave cybernetics poses to the concepts of homeostasis and redundancy adumbrated by the authors' cinema. For example, in re-creating the adult authority figures in

Shakespeare's play as puppets, Edzard implies the crisis of accountability incited by "the leap from embodied reality to abstract information," as Theseus and Egeus wield their power with machinelike compulsion, unable to accommodate any deviation from their phallocratic program.[80] Here Theseus's notorious rebuke of Hermia—"To you your father should be as a God . . . / To whom you are but as a form in wax / By him imprinted, and within his power, / To leave the figure or disfigure it"—sounds uncannily similar to the warning issued to the "mechas" in Spielberg's *AI* and the "replicants" in Ridley Scott's *Blade Runner,* who are informed that any malfunction or deviation will lead to their destruction.[81] Like these intentionally futuristic films, Edzard's *Dream* dramatizes what happens when replicants prove to be more human than their creators. Consequently, in their rush to enforce system equilibrium through Athenian law, Theseus and Egeus neglect the tension building within the recursive loop between programmer and progeny until, "like a spring compressed and suddenly released," the children "break out of the pattern of circular self-organization and leap outward into the new."[82] Indeed, in seeking to *embody* rather than merely succumb to their prosthetic extensions on stage, the children attempt to establish a new, more interactive relationship between identity formation and information. Insisting on the ways in which the technology of performance can forge meaningful connections between the simulated and real bodies and therefore "evolve spontaneously in directions the programmer may not have anticipated," the children of Edzard's film succeed—at least temporarily—in replacing patriarchal structures of succession with skeuomorphs of emergence.[83]

Central to the history of cybernetics, skeuomorphs demarcate the path of seriation, indicating how systems develop their capacity to evolve from a continual feedback loop between replication and innovation.[84] With one eye fixed on the past and one eye focused on the future, skeuomorphs, as Hayles points out, are "threshold devices" that simultaneously undermine both temporalities.[85] Children are, in a sense, the ultimate skeuomorphs, selectively reflecting "their parents and original" (*Dream* 2.1.117) in the very act of displacing them with their own performance of adulthood. In Edzard's film, the children's status as threshold figures is underscored by their ages, for Edzard chooses to feature 360 eight- to thirteen-year-olds from London-area schools—boys and girls poised not only on the brink of adulthood but also of gender definition.[86] Critics have taken great exception to Edzard's casting of amateurs, describing the film as "some horribly over-extended school play, in which you know none of the children."[87] Another typical objection is aimed at the performers' often awkward pronunciation which, uttered in their native Southwark dialects, sounds to some like a "search and destroy work on Shakespeare's poetry,"[88] suggesting the extent to which the Renaissance disdain for the local or "female" vernacular remains a powerful code for perpetuating dominant views of social entitlement today. Such criticisms imply an ongoing concern with paternity in a culture that places a pathological premium on individuality. For to "know" the children—based on their bankable faces or well-trained accents—is to recognize them as products of a biologic, institutional, or national pedigree that halts the sliding of the faceless, raceless signifiers that mingle promiscuously amid Edzard's stunningly multiracial cast which, in and of itself, generates a visual pun that equates the children's undisciplined language with the specter of loose-tongued and therefore sexually available mothers. That the children's relative anonymity, unpolished accents, and cultural diversity also reflect the environs of Edzard's own production company, Sands Films, is particularly significant. Located in two abandoned warehouses with views of the dilapidated Rotherhithe dockyards—signifiers of the postindustrial fallout from Thatcherite neglect—Sands Films is itself a kind of skeuomorph, indeed, a graveyard of unfulfilled promises. Hence, Edzard's film is positioned similarly to the unborn children whom Renaissance women writers charged with the future performance of their will. With one foot in the neglected past of their parents and one foot in the prospect of a more just future, the children of Edzard's *Dream* embody the democratizing dream of what I will call the feminist filmmaking "vernacular" which, hardwired with the code for emergence rather than succession, leads to the literal renaissance of "an alternative idea of community and nation."[89]

But according to the logic of this film, once their midsummer night's dream meets the morning after, these same children will be subject to a countereducation which, if the opening scene is any indication, will take shape as an oppressive hardening process that converts them into adults and, therefore, "puppets" of the dominant social order. When, at the end of the film, the child performers of the roles of Hermia, Helena, Demetrius, and Lysander are replaced on stage by their puppet counterparts, it is hard not to read this act of disembodiment as the victory of precisely this order. Yet I would argue that what the children have arrived at is something more powerful than what their bodies alone could achieve—

something that Renaissance women writers imagined long ago as an *embodied* virtuality.[90] Having abandoned the limits of their given identities, the "real" Hermia, Helena, Demetrius, and Lysander have, by the end of the performance, not only morphed into the puppets onstage but also remain, at least in spirit, with the anonymous children now viewing the play, who evince the feistiness of their precursors by reprimanding the "adults" for interrupting the rude mechanicals. In this final incarnation, the child protagonists of Edzard's film signal their intervention in the War of the Cinemas by replacing the concept of the authorial holograph—so essential to the eponymous replication of the authors' cinema—with a *hologram* of the interactive performances that had to be suppressed in order for Shakespeare to lose his body to a fantasy of male parthenogenesis in the first place, credited with the supreme authorial honor of "inventing the human" before he even became one.[91]

In positioning children as a veritable seriation chart of the ways in which Shakespeare has emerged as the "original" unruly replicant, the adaptations by the feminist filmmaking vanguard I have examined here forge a provocative kinship between Shakespeare's posthuman status as the signifier of disembodied information par excellence and the prehuman status of women writers in the Renaissance. Hence, if "the posthuman view thinks of the body as the original prosthesis we all learn to manipulate,"[92] then we might think of "embodied virtuality" as the sequel to the ways in which Renaissance women converted their own bodies into microcosmic versions of cybernetic systems, according to the subjective technology of the "matrix." In Renaissance midwifery and medical manuals, the womb was commonly called the matrix, and its constituent parts were thought to function or "agree" with each other by entering into relationships of empathy in the act of exchanging information.[93] In a culture wherein authors are pronounced virtually dead but are, in reality, alive and well in the apocalyptic paternalism of U.S.-led preemptive strikes and the disembodied promptings of terrorist leaders, might we consider embracing a model of communication more akin to this early modern one, which can teach us how to handle the very prospect of the future—indeed, of virtual life—with care, so we don't all wind up exclaiming against our own succession? If, as Bruno Latour claims, "we were never modern," and, as Hayles replies, "we have always been posthuman," then does it follow that we might yet become *early* modern?[94] Renaissance women past and present suggest that this could be a step in the right direction. For in a global culture whose

authorities increasingly value acting alone, the cybercinema's vision of a
system wherein "individuality," in Donna Haraway's memorable phrasing,
is "a strategic defense problem," may suggest nothing less than the code
for our collective survival.[95] We might call it the matrix: revolutions.

Notes

I wish to thank Skip Willman, Cynthia Dobbs, and Jim Hetrick, as well as Wendy Wall, W. B.
Worthen, and Jeffrey Masten.

1. See Richard Helgerson, *Forms of Nationhood: The Elizabethan Writing of England*
(Chicago, University of Chicago Press: 1992), esp. "Staging Exclusion," 193–245.

2. I appropriate this phrase from Shakespeare's *Hamlet* (2.2.438–39) in *The Oxford
Shakespeare: Tragedies*, ed. Stanley Wells et al., 4 vols. (Oxford: Oxford University Press,
1987), 3:1123–1163. Subsequent references to *Hamlet* are from this edition, hereafter cited
in the text.

3. I am oversimplifying the relations between the playwrights involved in the War of
the Theaters. For example, the company for which Shakespeare wrote at the time (the Lord
Chamberlain's Men) virtually initiated the fashion for satiric railing by staging Ben Jonson's
Every Man in His Humour (1598), following the success of which the boys' companies ran
with the new fashion. However, when Jonson abandoned the Lord Chamberlain's Men to
join the boys' companies, Shakespeare's company responded by staging Thomas Dekker's
attack on Jonson, *Satiromastix* (1601), a response to Jonson's attack on adult players in
Poetaster (1601). Similarly, although Dekker was something of a commercial hack associated
with the players' theater, he teamed-up with John Marston to write *Histriomastix* (1601)
and eventually wrote for the Children of St. Paul's. Marston, meanwhile, decided that rather
than trading blows with the players' theater, he would make Jonson the chief target of his
satire, considering him to be his primary competition for the more refined audiences that
both playwrights sought to attract in the smaller, semiprivate venues associated with the
boys' companies. For a more thorough exploration of the War of the Theaters, see Rosalyn
Knutson, "Falconer to the Little Eyases: A New Date and Commercial Agenda for the 'Little
Eyases' Passage in *Hamlet*," *Shakespeare Quarterly* 46, no. 1 (1995): 1–31; James P. Bednarz,
"Marston's Subversion of Shakespeare and Jonson: *Histriomastix* and the War of the Theaters,"
*Medieval and Renaissance Drama in England: An Annual Gathering of Research, Criticism
and Reviews* 6 (1993): 103–28; and Andrew Gurr, *Playgoing in Shakespeare's London*
(Cambridge: Cambridge University Press, 1987).

4. Particularly in the wake of Puritanism, children became a literal and literary source
of impression-making activities—through physical, sexual, and rhetorical violence. I will
be exploring the anxiety incited by children in the context of the Puritan thinking that
shaped the grammar school experience of seventeenth-century English boys in particular.
For primary materials from this era, see D. W. Sylvester, comp., *Educational Documents:
800–1816* (London: Methuen 1970), esp. "The Puritan Revolution and Education,"156–62.
See also John Robinson's 1628 treatise "Of Children and Their Education" in *Child-Rearing
Concepts, 1628–1861: Historical Sources*, ed. Philip J. Greven Jr. (Itasca, Ill.: F. E. Peacock,

1973), 9-18. For extremely useful secondary readings, see Lawrence Stone, *The Family, Sex and Marriage in England: 1500-1800* (New York: Harper and Row, 1979); and Wendy Wall, "'Household Stuff': The Sexual Politics of Domesticity and the Advent of English Comedy," *ELH* 65, no. 1 (1998): 1-45.

5. *Shakespeare in Love,* videocassette, directed by John Madden (1998; Burbank, Calif.: Buena Vista Home Entertainment, 1998); *Dangerous Beauty,* videocassette, directed by Marshall Herskovitz (1998; Burbank, Calif.: Warner Home Video, 1999); and *A Midsummer Night's Dream,* videocassette, directed by Adrian Noble (1996; Burbank, Calif.: Buena Vista Home Entertainment, 2002). The assertion that a film such as *Dangerous Beauty,* which is the story of the Venetian courtesan and poet Veronica Franco, renders authorship a "male prerogative" may sound like a paradox. However, I will demonstrate that this film, like others I have included under the rubric of the "authors' cinema," reinforces a sexual teleology of authorship that accords the privilege of inscription exclusively to men. The trope equating the female body with impressionable parchment or wax is a commonplace in the Renaissance. For a concise exploration of this act of appropriation, see Wendy Wall, "To Be 'A Man in Print,'" in *The Imprint of Gender: Authorship and Publication in the Renaissance* (Ithaca, N.Y.: Cornell University Press, 1993), 1-22. For an account of a slightly different phenomenon, whereby the male poet appropriates womb imagery as an example of "pregnancy without impregnation," see Katherine Eisaman Maus, "A Womb of His Own: Male Poets in the Female Body," in *Sexuality and Gender in Early Modern Europe: Institutions, Texts, Images,* ed. James Grantham Turner (Cambridge: Cambridge University Press, 1993), 266-88, quotation at 275.

6. I will be focusing on Mariya Muat's *Twelfth Night,* videocassette (1992; Cardiff, Wales: SC4 International, 1999); Aida Ziablikova's *Taming of the Shrew* (Christmas Films with S4C, 1996); Natalya Orlova's *Hamlet,* videocassette (1992; Cardiff, Wales: SC4 International, 1999); and *Richard III,* directed by Natalya Orlova (Christmas Films with S4C, 1996). See also *Titus,* DVD, directed by Julie Taymor (2000; Beverly Hills, Calif.: 20th Century Fox Home Entertainment, 2001); and *The Children's Midsummer Night's Dream,* videocassette, directed by Christine Edzard (2001; North Harrow, England: DD Video, 2001).

7. See Wall, *Imprint of Gender,* esp. "Dancing in a Net: The Problems of Female Authorship," 279-340. For a complementary argument about the relationship between mother and child as a means of authorizing the female voice, see Pamela Hammons's "Despised Creatures: The Illusion of Maternal Self-Effacement in Seventeenth-Century Child Loss Poetry," *ELH* 66, no. 1 (1999): 25-49.

8. I am thinking particularly of Jeffrey Masten's pathbreaking work on plural authorship, especially *Textual Intercourse: Collaboration, Authorship, and Sexualities in Renaissance Drama* (Cambridge: Cambridge University Press, 1997).

9. Donna Haraway, *Simians, Cyborgs, and Women: The Reinvention of Nature* (New York: Routledge, 1991), 212.

10. Ibid., 175. In employing cybernetic discourse, I mean to invoke its socialist-feminist application in works such as Haraway's *Simians, Cyborgs, and Women* and N. Katherine Hayles's *How We Became Posthuman: Virtual Bodies in Cybernetics, Literature, and Informatics* (Chicago: University of Chicago Press, 1999). Both appropriate the terminology and technology of cybernetics to explore various means of handling the information age,

the environment, and the human subject with greater care, calling for situated knowledges, vulnerable bodies and, above all, the recognition that subjectivity is not given but rather the product of strategic assemblages.

11. Sergei Eisenstein, *Eisenstein on Disney*, ed. Jay Leyda, trans. Alan Upchurch (New York: Methuen, 1988), 39.

12. Alan Cholodenko, introduction to *The Illusion of Life: Essays on Animation*, ed. Cholodenko (Sydney: Power Publications, 1991), 9.

13. Ibid.

14. Eisenstein, *Eisenstein on Disney*, 10.

15. Ibid., 4.

16. Ibid., 42.

17. This distinction is implied by Eisenstein when he observes that "such is the stage where the 'animalization' (the opposite process of the 'personification' of an ape, moving forward) of man, with the effect of the reconstruction of the sensuous system of thought, occurs not through identification . . . but through likening" (ibid., 51).

18. Laurie Osborne, "Poetry in Motion: Animating Shakespeare," in *Shakespeare, the Movie: Popularizing the Plays on Film, TV, and Video*, ed. Lynda Boose and Richard Burt (New York: Routledge, 1997), 105.

19. Laurie Osborne, "Mixing Media in Shakespeare: Animating Tales and Colliding Modes of Production," *Post Script* 17, no. 2 (1998): 76.

20. Eisenstein, *Eisenstein on Disney*, 47.

21. Osborne, "Mixing Media," 84.

22. It strikes me as significant that not one of the women directors of the series opts to employ the traditional cel animation technique. In terms of the gender breakdown of the films that rely on alternative techniques, two of the four films that use puppetry are directed by women, and two of the three that rely on the extremely rare "stained glass" technique are directed by women.

23. Francoise Navailh, "The Image of Women in Contemporary Soviet Cinema," in *The Red Screen: Politics, Society, Art in Soviet Cinema*, ed. Anna Lawton (London: Routledge, 1992), 215.

24. Ibid., 216.

25. Ibid., 217.

26. Osborne, "Poetry in Motion," 117.

27. Haraway, *Simians, Cyborgs, and Women*, 157.

28. Margreta De Grazia and Peter Stallybrass, "The Materiality of the Shakespearean Text," *Shakespeare Quarterly* 44, no. 3 (1993): 267.

29. Ibid., 282, 280.

30. Haraway, *Simians, Cyborgs, and Women*, 163.

31. Eisenstein, *Eisenstein on Disney*, 10.

32. For the description of this "tense of open potentiality," see Elsbeth Probyn, "Technologizing the Self: A Future Anterior for Cultural Studies," in *Cultural Studies*, ed. Lawrence Grossberg et al. (New York: Routledge, 1992), 511; for the citation from Louis Althusser, see *Reading Capital*, ed. Louis Althusser and Etienne Balibar, trans. B. Brewster (London: NLB, 1970), 108.

33. Wall, *Imprint of Gender,* 7.

34. Ibid., 282.

35. For the most comprehensive account of Veronica Franco's life and literary merits, see Margaret Rosenthal, *The Honest Courtesan: Veronica Franco, Citizen and Writer in Sixteenth-Century Venice* (Chicago: University of Chicago Press, 1992). Marco Venier was a distinguished Venetian senator, a part-time Petrarchan poet who praised Franco in his verse and, at one point, Franco's lover. Maffio Venier was, by contrast, a patronage-seeking poet who grew increasingly frustrated with his lack of preferment. After publishing a series of vitriolic verses against Franco and her courtesan compatriots, he turned to an ecclesiastical career as the last hope of the unsuccessful and, eventually, succumbed to syphilis—an ironic coda to a life dedicated to rooting out the corruption posed by the "dangerous beauty" of Venice's famous courtesan community.

36. Published in the form of *capitoli,* a genre governed by the codes of "proposta/riposta," Franco's *Terza Rime* was the centerpiece of the duel, implicitly challenging the male performance of courtiership by engaging in both soldierly and scholarly sparring. For example, Franco cleverly confuses her critics' sense of masculine decorum by warning them to consider all the implications of how they use their weapons: "I warn you," she writes, "that if on the one hand it is unseemly for a strong man to joust with a woman, on the other hand, it is considered a highly important event" (quoted in ibid., 192).

37. Jyotsna Singh, "The Interventions of History: Narratives of Sexuality," in *The Weyard Sisters: Shakespeare and Feminist Politics,* ed. Dympna Callaghan, et al. (Oxford: Blackwell, 1994), 33.

38. Wall, *Imprint of Gender,* 283.

39. Ibid., 297.

40. There are, of course, notable exceptions to the idea that Renaissance women entered into print through the "medium" of pregnancy and childbirth. Nevertheless, the idea that female publication required a kind of midwife to coax it into existence persists in the work of figures such as Margaret More Roper, who used her father Sir Thomas More in this manner, and Mary Sidney, whose literary efforts sprung to life from the dead body of her brother Phillip. See also Hammons, "Despised Creatures," for an account of how women used *dead children* to authorize their entry into print.

41. Wall, *Imprint of Gender,* 289. *Shakespeare in Love* is a particularly interesting candidate for alignment with the authors' cinema, since its director, John Madden, is rarely ever mentioned in discussions of the film's merits. Also, Tom Stoppard (known for his cultivated sense of irony) and cowriter Marc Norman are clearly intent on parodying the romantic construction of Shakespeare the author in their screenplay. An added layer of intrigue concerning the authorial dynamics of *Shakespeare in Love* emerged when a plagiarism scandal—not unlike the episodes of generous "borrowing" Will himself undertakes in the film—followed the film's release, claiming that Norman and Stoppard's Oscar-winning best "original" screenplay mirrored the plot of the 1941 novel *No Bed for Bacon,* by Carol Brahms and S. J. Simon (Akadine Press, 2001). Nevertheless, despite the fact that this film is less director driven and more playful than both *Dangerous Beauty* and Noble's *Midsummer Night's Dream,* I maintain that the use of women and children in *Shakespeare in Love* betrays an ultimately conservative cultural agenda associated with the authors' cinema.

42. Robinson, "Children and Education," 13.

43. Stephen Greenblatt offers a particularly lucid discussion of these early modern medical theories in *Shakespearean Negotiations: The Circulation of Social Energy in Renaissance England* (Berkeley and Los Angeles: University of California Press, 1988), esp. 66–93.

44. See Elaine Hobby, introduction to *The Midwives Book; Or, the Whole Art of Midwifery Discovered*, by Jane Sharp (New York: Oxford University Press, 1999), xii.

45. Marc Norman and Tom Stoppard, *Shakespeare in Love: A Screenplay* (New York: Hyperion, 1998), 117.

46. William Whately's *A Bride-Bush: or a direction for married persons* (1619) is quoted from Lisa Jardine, *Still Harping on Daughters: Women and Drama in the Age of Shakespeare* (New York: Columbia University Press, 1989), 106.

47. For a reading of how "Noise destroys and horrifies. . . . Noise nourishes a new order," see Michael Serres, *The Parasite*, trans. Laurence R. Schehr (Baltimore: Johns Hopkins University Press, 1982), 127. For a discussion of "noise" in a new-media context, see p. 141 above.

48. Stone, *Family, Sex, and Marriage*, 125.

49. Robinson, "Children and Education," 11.

50. Wall, " 'Household Stuff,' " 5.

51. By describing Renaissance child rearing as a system conceived around "surrogation," I mean to invoke W. B. Worthen's coining of the term to describe cultural practices that derive their meaning from citation and, more important, repetition. See Worthen, "Drama, Performance, Performativity," *PMLA* (October 1998): 1093–1107. As both "an act of memory and an act of creation," surrogation, Worthen explains, represents an alternative and, indeed, performative mode of meaning production that is inseparable from the contingencies of its citational context (1101). Moreover, in refusing to reconstruct, telelogically, "an authorizing text, a grounding origin" invariably allied with the imperatives of patriarchal culture, surrogation maintains the potential to subvert and, in fact, invert this foundation by "construct[ing] that origin as a rhetorically powerful effect of performance" (1101).

52. As Jeffrey Masten observes, wills are, above all, not legal but social practices that "seek to preserve affiliations beyond the grave" and, in so doing, "to reproduce social alliances" (4). In this context, then, the maternal legacy not only suggests a powerful attempt to leave an impression on the unborn child but also a preemptive strike against the other forces that will inevitably stake a claim to its moral upbringing. In fact, I would suggest that the paradoxical status of the mother's will, which demands "the erasure of the subject at the very moment of powerful self-assertion" (Wall, *Imprint of Gender*, 286), resonates with the "riven subjectivity" of the male child in particular, whose own passage to adulthood is contingent upon killing off the remnants of female influence for fear of a gender "relapse." For analyses of this cultural fear of lapsing from male to female, see Wall, " 'Household Stuff' "; and Stephen Orgel, "Nobody's Perfect; Or, Why Did the English Stage Take Boys for Women?" in *Displacing Homophobia: Gay Male Perspectives in Literature and Culture*, ed. Ronald R. Butters et al. (Durham, N.C.: Duke University Press, 1989), 7–29.

53. See Stephen Orgel's discussion of the Renaissance practice of breeching in "Nobody's Perfect."

54. Masten offers a rigorous exploration of negative attitudes toward collaboration in *Textual Intercourse*.

55. See Lisa Trahair, "For the Noise of a Fly," in *The Illusion of Life*, ed. Alan Cholodenko (Sydney: Power Publications, 1991), 198.

56. Steven Spielberg's *E.T. The Extra-Terrestrial*, videocassette (1982; Universal City, Calif.: MCA Home Video, 1988) contains the famous image of the boy and E.T. riding a bicycle across an enormous moonscape. Noble's most obvious allusions to other children's or family films include *Mary Poppins*, DVD, directed by Robert Stevenson (1964; Burbank, Calif.: Buena Vista Home Entertainment, 2000); and *Home Alone*, DVD, directed by Chris Columbus (1990; Beverly Hills, Calif.: 20th Century Fox Home Entertainment, 1999).

57. Consider, among the most popular versions of *Dream*, James Cagney's lovable impersonation of Bottom in Max Reinhardt and William Dieterle's *A Midsummer Night's Dream*, videocassette (1935; Burbank, Calif.: Warner Home Video, 1993) and Kevin Kline's more pathetic Bottom in Michael Hoffman's *William Shakespeare's A Midsummer Night's Dream*, DVD (1999; Beverly Hills, Calif.: 20th Century Fox Home Entertainment, 1999).

58. Robinson, "Children and Education," 13.

59. *A Clockwork Orange*, videocassette, directed by Stanley Kubrick (1971; Burbank, Calif.: Warner Home Video, 1986).

60. Wall, " 'Household Stuff,' " 5.

61. Robinson, "Children and Education," 14.

62. Haraway, *Simians, Cyborgs, and Women*, 152.

63. An extensive analysis of the dynamics of spectatorship in *Titus* may be found by consulting Lehmann, Bryan Reynolds, and Lisa S. Starks, " 'For such a sight will blind a father's eye': The Spectacle of Suffering in Taymor's *Titus*," in *Shakespeare and Transversal Theory* (New York: Palgrave/MacMillan, 2003), 215–43.

64. Richard Burt, "Shakespeare and the Holocaust: Julie Taymor's *Titus* Is Beautiful, or Shakesploi Meets (the) Camp," *Colby Quarterly* 37, no. 1 (2001): 95.

65. Ibid., 92.

66. For a discussion of *Titus* and the slasher subgenre of horror film, see Lisa S. Starks, "Cinema of Cruelty: Powers of Horror in Julie Taymor's *Titus*," in *The Reel Shakespeare*, ed. Lisa S. Starks and Courtney Lehmann (Madison, N.J.: Fairleigh Dickinson University Press, 2002), 121–42. See also Carol J. Clover's foundational essay on horror and the Final Girl phenomenon in "Her Body, Himself: Gender in the Slasher Film," in *The Dread of Difference: Gender and the Horror Film*, ed. Barry Keith Grant (Austin: University of Texas Press, 1996), 66–113.

67. Taymor makes this remark in *Titus: The Illustrated Screenplay, Adapted from the Play by William Shakespeare* (New York: Newmarket Press, 2000), 181.

68. Starks, "Cinema of Cruelty," esp. 134–36.

69. Lisa Trahair explores the capacity of the remake genre to generate "virtual films" in "For the Noise of a Fly."

70. I invoke Barry Keith Grant's collection of essays on the sexual politics of the horror genre, titled *The Dread of Difference: Gender and the Horror Film* (Austin: University of Texas Press, 1996). More specifically, as the essays throughout this collection demonstrate, it is the encounter with the female body's disturbing "lack" that gives rise to the "dread of difference" and instigates male violence against women.

71. Trahair, "Noise of Fly," 205.

72. Haraway, *Simians, Cyborgs, and Women,* 181.

73. Taymor, *Titus: Illustrated Screenplay,* 185.

74. Donna Haraway, "The Actors Are Cyborg, Nature Is Coyote, and the Geography Is Elsewhere: Postscript to 'Cyborgs at Large,'" in *Technoculture,* ed. Constance Penley and Andrew Ross (Minneapolis: University of Minnesota Press, 1991), 24.

75. Hayles, *How We Became Posthuman,* 7. Hayles provides an excellent introduction to cybernetic theory in her first chapter, "Toward Embodied Virtuality," 1–24. Likewise, Haraway's *Simians, Cyborgs, and Women* contains a brilliant chapter on cybernetics titled "The Biological Enterprise: Sex, Mind, and Profit from Human Engineering to Sociobiology," 43–70. For examples of Weiner's work, see *Cybernetics; or, Control and Communication in the Animal and the Machine* (Cambridge, Mass.: MIT Press, 1948); and *The Human Use of Human Beings: Cybernetics and Society,* 2d ed. (New York: Doubleday, 1954).

76. Hayles, *How We Became Posthuman,* 5, 7.

77. For a collection of Niklas Luhmann's reflections on reflexivity, see Niklas Luhmann, *Essays on Self-Reference* (New York: Columbia University Press, 1990).

78. Hayles, *How We Became Posthuman,* 11.

79. The exact date of Heywood's pamphlet is unknown, though it is conjectured to have been written about 1607–1608. This excerpt is quoted from Gurr, *Playgoing in Shakespeare's London,* 155.

80. Hayles, *How We Became Posthuman,* 13.

81. *Blade Runner,* DVD, directed by Ridley Scott (1982; Burbank, Calif.: Warner Home Video, 1999); *AI,* DVD, directed by Stephen Spielberg (2001; Glendale, Calif.: Dreamworks Home Entertainment, 2002).

82. Hayles, *How We Became Posthuman,* 222.

83. Ibid., 11.

84. Hayles observes that a skeuomorph is akin to a Janus figure, for it is "a design feature that is no longer functional in and of itself" but is nevertheless retained in the form of "a gesture or an allusion used to authenticate new elements in the emerging constellation of reflexivity" (ibid., 17).

85. Ibid. Again, in her introductory chapter of *How We Became Posthuman,* Hayles presents an extremely useful seriation chart documenting the history of cybernetic theory (16).

86. Updating the Renaissance practice of clothing girls and unbreeched boys in dresses, the age-group Edzard employs in her film is particularly prone to gender ambiguity, since the boys' high-pitched voices are virtually indistinguishable from the girls' and, if anything, the girls' bodies are taller and stronger than the boys' physiques. Accentuating the anxiety that Shakespeare's play seeks to dispel, namely, that female dominance may spread from throne to household, Edzard highlights the disproportionate maturity of the girls. In the exchanges between Oberon and Titania, for example, the camera consistently looks down on Oberon, emphasizing his height disadvantage and subtly entering into league with the defiant Titania. But it is Edzard's vision of Titania's beloved Indian "boy"—with his hair mounted in two high ponytails and his body clad in a sarilike combination of pants and dress—that most powerfully engages Renaissance anxieties about emerging from the "common gender" of childhood and excessive exposure to female nurture.

87. Christopher Tookey, review of *The Children's Midsummer Night's Dream,* directed by Christine Edzard, *Daily Mail,* June 22, 2001, p. 7.

88. Nigel Andrews, review of *The Children's Midsummer Night's Dream,* directed by Christine Edzard, *Financial Times,* June 21, 2001, p. 12.

89. Wall, " 'Household Stuff,' " 29.

90. I borrow the concept of "embodied virtuality" from Hayles, who uses this phrase in her introductory chapter of *How We Became Posthuman* in an effort to intervene in the crisis of subjectivity posed by posthuman disembodiment. While Hayles explains that she does not "mourn the passing" of the liberal humanist subject into the posthuman subject, she explains that she is wary of the prospect of disembodiment "being rewritten, once again, into prevailing concepts of subjectivity." Nevertheless, Hayles is equally interested in determining how "certain characteristics, especially agency and choice, *can* be articulated within a posthuman context" (5, emphasis mine). Hence, her project is to "show what had to be elided, suppressed, and forgotten to make information lose its body" (13).

91. I am invoking Harold Bloom's ambitious tome *Shakespeare: The Invention of the Human* (New York: Riverhead Books, 1998).

92. Hayles, *How We Became Posthuman,* 3.

93. See Hobby, "Note on Humoral Theory," in *Midwives Book,* xxxiii.

94. Bruno Latour, *We Have Never Been Modern,* trans. Catherine Porter (Cambridge, Mass.: Harvard University Press, 1993); Hayles, *How We Became Posthuman,* 291.

95. Haraway, *Simians, Cyborgs, and Women,* 212.

Taymor's Titus *in Time and Space:*
Surrogation and Interpolation

THOMAS CARTELLI

I N THE PROCESS of explaining her penchant for superimposing the architectural excesses of Mussolini's Italy on imperial Rome in her film version of Shakespeare's *Titus Andronicus,* Julie Taymor claims that she "wanted to blend and collide time, to create a singular period that juxtaposed elements of ancient barbaric ritual with familiar, contemporary attitude and style."[1] Taymor elsewhere remarks that "the time of [her] film is from 1 to 2000 AD" and observes that "the film represents the last 2000 years of man's inhumanity to man."[2] Taken together, these comments effectively conflate the conceptual postmodernity Taymor brings to bear on her filmic "iteration" of Shakespeare's *Titus Andronicus* with an approach to the play's content that is avowedly humanistic, if less pointedly political, in its aims and applications.[3] In so doing, they help bring into focus one of the many apparent contradictions—and defining features—of a project which combines the affectless attitude and sleekly ironized stylings of the contemporary cinematic, visual art, and theatrical avant-garde with the visual and auditory excess of the Hollywood blockbuster and horror-film genre, all the while seeking to moralize on an ethos of institutionalized violence and predatory behavior which it more often seems to celebrate than revile.[4]

Like Fellini (who arguably exerts more influence on Taymor's cinematic imagination than does Shakespeare), Taymor has a quintessentially postmodern interest in pastiche, in blending, contrasting, juxtaposing, and

"colliding" the architectural and decorative styles of historically specific
times and places (most notably those of classical Rome and of the reinvented Rome of Mussolini) with additional design initiatives that are either
meant to carry specific symbolic weight (e.g., the scarification of Tamora
and Aaron the Moor, newly invented Roman funerary rituals) or more
promiscuously drawn from the domains of high art and popular culture
to operate as floating signifiers. As with any strongly conceived design
initiative, particularly one as interested as hers is in symbolic imagery,
Taymor's (which is rooted in the concept-addled practices of the down-
town New York art and theater scene) risks reducing the film to an array
of too prominently distinguished signs and markers: the outsize throne
which always makes the diminutive Saturnine look like a spoiled boy at
play and which plays too glibly with Alan Cumming's *Cabaret* look; the
bleached hair and contemporary "Goth" looks of Tamora's androgynous
sons; color-coded costumes and backdrops; the girl-next-door prettiness
of Lavinia's initial presentation, which Taymor likens to that of Grace Kelly
and later overlays with allusions to Marilyn Monroe. It all no doubt seems
too calculated and not a little self-reflexive.[5] But I intend to argue here that
Taymor's more dramatically sustained interpolations—understood here as
both her explicit scenic additions to the play text and her interventions
in how the text itself gets cinematically expressed—draw the film into
the circuit of a postmodernity that both reiterates the play text's own
fluidly indeterminate fracturing of time and space and surrogates it to
considerable contemporary effect by effecting profound changes in "the
entire infrastructure of the art form."[6]

I will also argue that responses to the film that concentrate exclusively
on its preoccupation with symbolic signs and markers, highly stylized
renderings of sex and violence, and the attention-getting "look" of its architectural settings—and consequently see it primarily as an extraordinarily
beautiful but essentially hollow cinematic shell, or worse[7]—fail to note the
extent to which *Titus*'s responsiveness to the interethnic and anachronistic
conjunctions of Moors, Goths, and Romans in Shakespeare's play also
draws it inside the circuit of the ethnic rivalries, religious conflicts, and
imperial anxieties that beset both his and our own contemporary political
scene. The political, or more strictly speaking, humanistic unconscious
of *Titus* rises most obviously to the surface in its closing shots when the
walls that appear to enclose Titus's climactic bloody banquet suddenly
dissolve, and the dinner table is resituated in an unusually well-preserved

ruin of a provincial Roman coliseum in Croatia. The closing actions proceed before a rapt audience of silent latter-day Croatians whose witnessing of this primal event is no doubt meant to constitute an act of surrogation, "an ambivalent replaying" of fraternal and tribal slaughters in the Balkans, which effectively bridge the distance between the year 1 and late 1999 when this scene was shot, what Taymor terms "the last 2000 years of man's inhumanity to man."[8] It is here that Taymor stages her last and, for some parties, most questionable interpolation, having Young Lucius rescue Tamora and Aaron's son and carry him outside the walls of the coliseum and, by extension, outside the bounds of a history that expands and contracts but offers neither relief nor escape from established patterns of mutual predation. That this takes place as the elder Lucius reiterates the play's last lines, an order to "throw [Tamora] forth to beasts and birds to prey," indicates both the arguably utopian aspects of this final interpolation ("utopian" in that it gestures toward an ethos situated outside the bounds of history and any specific political persuasion) and why it might well be preferred to a more professedly "faithful" reiteration of the Shakespearean text.[9]

The most pronounced and sustained of the many "additions" Taymor makes to the play text, and the one that has the most obvious ethical, if not quite, political valence, is her already noted deployment of Young Lucius as participant-witness throughout the film's unraveling. She deploys Lucius in a manner that recalls Derek Jarman's deployment of the young Edward, future Edward III, in his 1991 film version of Marlowe's *Edward II,* a work to which Taymor's film seems deeply, if silently, indebted. As in the Jarman film, the Boy (in this case, Lucius) often quietly shadows the actions and activities of the film's more prominently featured protagonists, serving variously as companion, witness, interrogator, and reflecting mirror of the various twists and turns of their fortunes and swings of their moods and attitudes. Taymor often positions Lucius in purely visual patches of unscripted, interpolated scenes where he functions less to advance the plot than in the interest of providing a reflection on it, as does Jarman's young Edward when, for example, he wanders outside the castle walls at night to silently witness a circle of naked men engaging in what looks like a rugby scrum.[10] Like young Edward, Young Lucius emerges at other times as something like an antidote or hybridized alternative to the manically vengeful energies that destroy both his family and their opponents. In a remarkably suggestive moment in *Titus,* for example, Young Lucius enters a workshop that would appear to specialize in the manufacture of artfully contrived wooden prostheses (which Taymor assembled out of a warehouse where dismantled carvings of saints and other figures employed in nativity scenes are stored between seasonal displays) and returns with a pair of wooden hands, which he gives to Lavinia. While the scene does little to advance the plot, it conveys Young Lucius's active sympathy for his disabled cousin, which we will later see extended to Aaron's child, and effort to compensate her for the lost "effects" of her hands, at the same time as it provides an unsettling insight into how thriving an enterprise a prosthesis workshop might prove in a world so abundant in acts of arbitrary terror and mutilation.[11]

Young Lucius, of course, also figures prominently in the dramatically unscripted "induction" to the film proper where we find him playing with wild and destructive abandon in a kitchen filled with all manner of toy soldiers and model weaponry and wearing a paper bag "helmet" over his head, the headgear at once suggesting his childishly willed emulation of the "real" soldiers into whose orbit he will soon tumble. His subsequent abduction by the Clown and introduction to the frighteningly "real" war-torn world of *Titus* seems, in the context of the film's ending, to function in the interest of some broadly ethical plan that will effect a marked change in Lucius himself, who, as he walks forth out of the film's frame, surely can no longer think innocently (or playfully) about man's inhumanity to man. Taymor herself observes that "the journey of the young boy from childhood innocence to passive witness and finally to knowledge, wisdom, compassion, and choice" operates as *Titus*'s "counterpoint to Shakespeare's dark [presumably unredeemable] tale of vengeance."[12] Indeed, Young Lucius functions as the virtual "eyes" of the film and becomes the medium through which we ourselves witness, and may also decide to exit from, what the film constructs as history.[13]

Another way of conceptualizing the politics of Taymor's interpolations is to see her trying to bring a kind of clarifying balance to her representation of the film's competing atrocities (as well as to the play's privileging of Titus's patriarchal hold on our sympathies). While Taymor's film clearly sides with Titus's family in their struggle against Tamora and Saturninus and makes Titus appear (like Lear) a man more sinned against than sinning, it also attempts to balance the ledger of mutual recrimination and vindictiveness. For example, in the first of what Taymor calls her "penny arcade nightmares" (hereafter PANs), which function as both interpolations and extrapolations from the play text, Taymor has Titus and Tamora square off at the foot of the palace stairs in a rigidly ordered face-off, while between and behind them fiery images of the limbs and torso of Tamora's sacrificed son, Alarbus, shift and blend into each other in a powerfully surreal manner. While the first PAN appears to employ Alarbus's dismembered body mainly in the interests of illustration, signifying it as a bridge across which Titus and Tamora will engage in a struggle to the death, a second PAN appears to emanate from Titus's own guilty conscience, portraying as it does "Titus's youngest son [Mutius] whom he himself rashly and wrongly murdered . . . in the form of a sacrificial lamb, evoking the story of Abraham and Isaac."[14] Here in particular we witness a more evenhanded, balanced approach to the revenge motive than Shakespeare seems to be aiming at in the play text, as Taymor extrapolates from Shakespeare's own silence on the subject ("The narrative," Taymor notes, "never brings up the event of Mutius' death once it is done") to claim for Titus a nagging "inner torment and guilt" that he does not appear to feel in Shakespeare's play.[15]

David McCandless is no doubt correct in noting that "the ornate, static staginess of these images renders them implausible as post-traumatic flashbacks," but wrong to classify Taymor's PANs as "flashbacks" in the first place.[16] For example, the two PANs in question effectively operate as visually overdetermined forms of editorial interventions. Although they fasten on and replay the content of recently staged events, they do so in a radically displaced manner, disassembling and scrambling the "post-traumatic" imagery presumably stored in the psyches of the remembering subjects and surrogating it to a series of iconographic metamorphoses which it exceeds their capacity to generate. Both spatially and temporally situated outside the "lived" dramatic reality of the characters, the PANs impinge less on *their* consciousness than they do on *ours*. They thus allow us to speculate freely on the rage Tamora feels but does not clearly show, and on the grief Titus shows but does not necessarily feel. Although virtually every action Titus undertakes in the first movement of the play—electing Saturninus as Rome's emperor; allowing Saturninus to choose Lavinia for his wife; sacrificing Alarbus in the face of Tamora's passionate plea for mercy; murdering his own son—seems obviously wrongheaded, Shakespeare does not give Tamora's motive for revenge the same legitimacy with which he later invests Titus's claim. Taymor does. Moreover, she makes Titus's rejection of Tamora's plea seem so dismissively patronizing and coldly self-righteous that Tamora's answering indignation and contempt become far more humanly comprehensible than does Titus's pietistically inflexible observance of a rite of blood sacrifice, which, as performed by the elder Lucius under Titus's supervision, seems like the ritualized exercise of a male-dominated cult wedded to patriarchal authority. And though, like Shakespeare, Taymor soon positions her audience squarely on Titus's side, she never entirely lets us forget that both camps are, in their way, equally barbarous, equally fixated on the pursuit of agendas that, like the late civil wars and ethnic cleansings in the Balkans (and in Rwanda and Sierra Leone), admit to no constructively human or humane justification.

If the play *Titus Andronicus* provides no exit from the history of mutual predation, it does provide a fertile site for staging scenes of shocking cruelty and traumatic purgation, thereby offering the skilled postmodern practitioner a host of opportunities to display what we would all like to be saved from. Taymor has on this account been roundly criticized for doing what she, as an unusually gifted manufacturer of stage imagery, does better than virtually anyone now at work in theater and film, that is, offer richly reimagined representations of the already horrific subject matter lying in wait in the Shakespearean play text. Much of this criticism has focused on her casting of Anthony Hopkins as Titus, a choice she allegedly made to exploit Hopkins's notoriety for his performance in the role of Hannibal Lector in *Silence of the Lambs* (1993). As Richard Burt has claimed:

Because most audiences read backward from film to Shakespeare, Taymor's casting of Anthony Hopkins, given that Titus serves human flesh at his banquet, will inevitably call to the minds of many reviewers and other audiences the serial-killer cannibal, Hannibal Lector. The connection between Titus and Lector is underlined by Hopkins' quotation of his role in *Silence of the Lambs* when he sucks in his spit before slitting Chiron and Demetrius's throats. Perhaps Taymor had of necessity to cast Hopkins as the leading man because he was the only one with the star power and the ability willing to do it.[17]

The presumed transparency of this connection encourages Burt to render most additional references to Titus in a composite Lector/Titus format, as in "Lector/Titus' decision to side with Saturninus rather than Bassianus is not merely bad judgment but an act of psychotic destruction," a move informed by the penchant (increasingly noticeable in current writing on Shakespeare on film) for privileging the immediacy of pop-cultural allusiveness over other forms of information.[18] In the process, the skill, authority, and gravitas an accomplished Shakespearean actor like Hopkins brings to bear on the role of Titus, not to mention his capacity to disappear into it at will, are elided, as is the film audience's presumed access to Hopkins's other theatrical and filmic performances. Other critics of Taymor's cultivation of violent effects in *Titus* seem to assume that, in composing *Titus Andronicus,* Shakespeare was merely offering a faithfully lurid reproduction of his own sources instead of recognizing that apart from precedents mainly found in Ovid, he was, himself, both "author" of the many murders and mutilations put on display and inventor of their dramatic stylization. Hence, rather than contribute here to the debate about Taymor's approach to violence, I would prefer to concentrate on the subject of interpolated imagery as well as on further examples of unscripted dramatic material that Taymor "adds" to the play text. Two examples in particular will suffice, both of which demonstrate how Taymor's film exploits blank spaces in the Shakespearean play text to enhanced dramatic effect and surrogates Shakespearean stage practice to the multimediated "language" of postmodern film art and technology.

I begin with the sequence that starts with Aaron's request for Titus's hand and that ends with the delivery of his two sons' heads (which roughly occupies the second half of act 3, scene 1, the first half of which dramatizes Titus's unregarded pleas for mercy for his condemned sons in Taymor's powerful Crossroads scene). The first movement of this sequence involves the darkly comedic competition of Titus, Lucius, and Marcus over whose hand will be cut off and the oddly conspiratorial interplay between Aaron and Titus as Titus beats the others to the punch and Aaron drops the "lopped" hand into a plastic Baggie, which he hangs on the mirror of his Maserati as he drives away. The brief, moving encounter between Titus and Lavinia that ensues functions like a bridge from one inconsolable injury to another. This is followed by an interpolated Felliniesque scene in which the Clown and his young, red-haired girl assistant drive a motorcycle van (which Burt suggestively associates with the strongman Zampano's truck in Fellini's *La Strada*)[19] into Titus's yard, set out campstools for what looks to be an impromptu theatrical performance, and then, with an alacrity entirely at odds with the reluctant speech spoken by a compassionate messenger in the play text, "discover" the heads of Titus's sons eerily looking out from two large "specimen jars," while Titus's severed hand sits pillowed between them on a black velvet cushion like a rarefied piece of anatomical sculpture. (I wonder here about the effects on the infinitely suggestible Taymor of the recent British art world vogue for the stylized representation of human and animal body parts.) The film lingers very briefly over this tableaulike effect, the composition managing to present both the bottled heads and pillowed hand and the stunned witnessing of the Andronici in one abruptly becalmed frame.

Apart from the highly stylized nature of this scene—which Taymor identifies as the fourth of her PANs and the first that directly invades the space of the film's construction of dramatic reality—most notable here are: the film's substitution of the rough-edged Clown for the play's compassionate Messenger; the cutting of three of the latter's most sympathetic lines, which read, "Thy grief their sports, thy resolution mocked, / That woe is me to think upon their woes / More than remembrance of my father's death" (3.1.239-41); and Taymor's addition of three harshly barked lines of Latin to the Clown's speech, which few auditors would be able to decipher as speech, much less understand.[20] (They read in translation as "The aim of the law is to correct those it punishes, or make others better through the example of the sentence it inflicts, or else to remove evil so that the others can live more peacefully.")[21] Taymor's interpolations aim here to transform what passes in the play text as an inexplicable bout of arbitrary cruelty into a much more cleverly crafted exercise of cinematically choreographed terror. Even the surviving residue of compassion in the lines that Taymor maintains from the Messenger's cropped speech—"Worthy Andronicus, ill art thou repaid / For that good hand thou sent'st the emperor. / Here are the heads of thy two noble sons; / And here's thy hand in scorn to thee sent back" (3.1.235-38)—are reproduced by the Clown with a flatness that belies their message. He delivers them in a detached Brechtian manner as if he is quoting something he, himself, has no stake in. (This is, it should be noted, the same character who "rescues" Young Lucius from his exploding kitchen in the film's opening shot and displays him aloft to the ghostly applause of the invisible spectators in the coliseum). This move raises some interesting concerns regarding the complex workings of Taymor's rendering of the play text, which, even when superficially faithful, partakes of the same appropriative drive that animates her interpolations. In this case, for example, the Clown's flat line reading generates a powerfully unsettled relationship between what the words say and how the words mean. The sympathy that the excised messenger felt for Titus is, as it were, put into quotation marks; it's cited (or re-cited) but not really stated or delivered. It haunts but no longer inhabits its scene of inscription.

In the aftershock of the Clown's horrific delivery, the film rather jarringly resumes its reproduction of dialogue drawn from the play text, which makes no provision for so sustained or stylized a presentation of the heads of Titus's sons. A revealing consequence of the transition between the interpolated material and the resumption of dialogue is how slow, stodgy, and out of keeping with the pace, panache, and black humor of the former the dramatic interactions of Titus and his family members seem. We have here one of several moments in Taymor's film that highlight the virtues and limitations of different forms of representational practice as the multilayered crosscuttings of cinema and the more measured, single-framed focus of theater "collide" with one another. The sequence that begins with Aaron's entrance is fast-paced to the extreme. It starts with Aaron's arrival being glimpsed from an upstairs window of Titus's house by the ubiquitous Young Lucius, functioning both as "our eyes" and as the object of our (and Aaron's) gaze. The camera speeds up as Titus responds to Aaron's misleading offer of mercy, making quick cuts between the wrangling Andronici and providing a picturesque glimpse into Titus's kitchen where the beautifully composed, hanging bodies of fowl complement Titus's laying of his hand on the chopping block as Aaron chooses between a pair of poultry scissors and a meat cleaver in playfully silent collaboration with Titus. The frenetically distorted mix of Elliot Goldenthal's jazz and circus music, which attends Aaron's quick-paced departure—executed in a face-on tracking shot as Aaron speaks directly into the camera on his return to his Maserati—and accompanies the Clown's arrival, evokes a carnivalesque mood that suddenly dissolves upon the display of the severed heads and hand, which returns us to a drama that has no more than talking heads and profoundly subdued and wounded bodies to speak for it. (In Taymor's sequencing of events, Marcus and Titus are just returning home with the ravished and mutilated Lavinia as Aaron arrives with his request for a hand. The umbrella that Aaron carries to protect himself from the rain functions here as a designedly cruel device in contrast to the Andronici's naked exposure to the elements and arbitrary violence alike.) The somberness of the mood is the result not just of the tragic turn of circumstance but of the cessation of the playful approach to cinematic reproduction that managed to sustain a frenetically comedic edge throughout the hand-cutting scene. Indeed, it might be said that until or unless Titus and his family themselves begin to generate the kind of manic energy and resourcefulness exercised by Aaron and the Clown in these scenes, they will remain victims of their attachment to older, primarily rhetorical modes of expression and representation.

Interestingly enough, this embrace of the surreal and the absurd begins apace when Titus responds to Marcus's mournful speech by laughing and then calmly supervising his family's collection of the bottled heads and pedestaled hand, ordering Lavinia to "Bear thou my hand, sweet wench, between thy teeth" (3.1.265, 283). In her persuasive reading of this action, Katherine Rowe indicates that Lavinia's effort here both highlights her own and Titus's loss of "effect" and agency and signals the beginning of their resurgence.[22] Taymor seems intuitively drawn to Rowe's argument in her ensuing interpolation where Lucius, motivated by sympathy for Lavinia's plight, retrieves the pair of wooden hands to serve as prostheses for his aunt. While these hands do nothing practical for Lavinia, her donning of them prepares us for the empowerment Lavinia and the other Andronici will feel once the identities of her ravishers are made known and Titus begins (however uncertainly) to make motions toward revenge.

Rather than push on from here to explore or examine other related sequences in the film, I would prefer to consider briefly the question of agency Rowe addresses and see how it works in concert with Taymor's repositioning of the play's political import. The first consequence visited on the Andronici by the violence of Tamora's sons and the villainous manipulations of Aaron is a kind of disabling passivity that employs rhetoric as its preferred mode of expression, most famously in the oft criticized speech of Marcus in act 2, scene 3, as he successively discovers and witnesses the ravished Lavinia, but also in the moving but ineffectual speech Titus delivers as much to himself as to the Roman senators in what Taymor presents as her "Crossroads" scene (the first half of act 3, scene 1 in the play text). Rhetoric is, of course, the primary dramatic and expressive medium of Shakespeare's play; Marcus and Titus "unpack [their hearts] with words" because that is all they can do under the circumstances. What they require to move to the level of action are scenes of suffering so intense that words formally ordered into elaborate rhetorical displays will no longer serve; or, as Taymor would have it, scenes that bring the shock of disordered perceptions into the orbit of "lived" dramatic experience. Such scenes effectively free the Andronici from the closed circuit of stylized lamentation and commiseration and resituate them in a dramatic mode that is more consistent with Taymor's cinematic preference for the playfully ironic, manically purposive, and intensely sardonic style that has heretofore been the stock-in-trade of Aaron. In so doing, the effectivity that has solely been Aaron's to command (on the basis of his dramatic energy, cunning, and imagination) slowly migrates into the compass of the Andronici themselves.

In the director's notes section of her *Illustrated Screenplay,* Taymor categorizes the scene begun by the arrival of the Clown and his assistant as another of her five penny arcade nightmares but distinguishes this one from all but the last on the basis of its operation on the level of "stark 'reality.'" As Taymor observes:

Unlike the other P.A.N.s, which were abstract or symbolic representations of an event or psychic state, this P.A.N. is actually happening. This "still life" P.A.N. signals the turn in the play where the nightmares are now reality and madness can be confused with sanity. Order has been replaced with chaos and the road to justice is paved with revenge.[23]

Although we are at this point of both the film and the play text still quite far from the moment when Titus will take effectual action against his enemies, Taymor's interpolation—which turns what seems in the play text an entirely arbitrary exercise of cruelty on the part of Aaron into something much more purposeful and premeditated, an act of "state-sponsored terror," if you will—has the effect of reorienting Titus's response to his enemies. Marcus responds to the display of heads and hand in much the way he responds to the display of the "ravish'd" Lavinia and calls for Titus to "die," to "rend" off his hair, to "gnaw" his other hand, and "to storm," that is, to display his grief in all the prescribed manners of histrionic expression.[24] But Titus, in what Jonathan Bate terms "the play's pivotal indecorum,"[25] *laughs* and then turns the occasion of their grief into an opportunity to reorder and reconstitute the dismembered family. He first stares into the faces of "these two heads [which] do seem to speak to me" and charge him with the imperative to revenge, then has his remaining family members "circle [him] about," as he places "his palm on either the head or heart of each one of them"[26] and finally allots to each duties that range from Lavinia's taking his hand in her mouth to Lucius's charge to raise an army of the Goths against Saturninus. The ritualized nature of this scene echoes with crucial differences the earlier scene at the family mausoleum as we watch the remaining Andronici gather together dismembered parts of their familial body as a first stage toward reinventing their relationship both to themselves and to the Roman state. Though much that they do or say from this point forward will remain ineffectual, and virtually all that Titus does will generate the pity and skepticism of the more rational Marcus, a corner has been turned in Taymor's representation of their plight that will fill them with some of the same anarchic energy and force heretofore invested primarily in Aaron and, to a lesser extent, in Tamora and her sons.

A brief look at two additional (and related) moments in Taymor's film should clinch at least this part of my argument. In what Taymor calls the third, but which is chronologically the fourth, of her PANs, we watch as (in Taymor's words) "a bolt of electric shock seems to run through [Lavinia's] body" which prompts the intercutting of her "ferocious writing in the sand" with "a bombardment of surreal images of her rape and dismemberment."[27] These images reproduce the scene of her ravishment in both broadly symbolic terms (Lavinia is figured as an innocent "doe-girl" trying to ward off the rabid attack of Chiron and Demetrius's "tiger-boys") and in more culturally promiscuous (and problematic) ways, with Lavinia sculpturally displayed on a columned pedestal in an allusion to Degas' preening *Little Dancer* while she also "quotes," in a decidedly more anxious fashion, the erotically iconographic abandon of Marilyn Monroe allowing a draft of air to puff up her summery dress in *The Seven-Year Itch* (1955).[28] While these allusions prompt troubling questions regarding what exactly Taymor wants us to draw from such iconically crossed references (are we supposed to be turned on or turned off by the fact that what alluringly lifts Lavinia's skirts and, by extension, the little dancer's tutu, is radically unlike the desired draft of air in which Monroe's skirt bellows?), the action which generates, or is cogenerative with, the nightmare—that is, Lavinia's resolute embrace of the stick which enables her writing in the sand—is considerably less ambiguous. The "ferocious" nature of Lavinia's writing serves as an incommensurate but effectual answer to the ferocious attack against her by Chiron and Demetrius, and it underwrites the energy and resolve with which Marcus and Titus engage in yet another ritual vow of revenge, this one aimed against "these traitorous Goths." Lavinia's extradramatic reliving of her ravishment and mutilation appears to operate on her with the force of primal therapy, as she transforms the trauma of memory into a cathartic expression of renewed agency.[29] And it prompts the first effort on Titus's part to meet terror with terror, as he sends Young Lucius over to the apartment of Chiron and Demetrius to deliver a bundle of "archaic weapons from the dark ages"[30] laced with an ironically apt quotation from Horace.

I use the word "terror" here because however ineffectual this gesture may seem, it marks the first time in the film and play text alike that Titus becomes master of the kind of activated dramatic irony that has heretofore been exclusively Aaron's medium of manipulation and control. I also use the term because of the panicked response Titus's second exercise in kind—his showering of the imperial palace with letters of complaint to the gods—elicits from Saturninus. Taymor notably stages and choreographs this scene (act 4, scene 3) with a carnivalesque panache that makes Titus seem more divinely inspired than mad, as he assembles his followers by moving from house to house with Young Lucius following along pulling a red Radio Flyer wagon filled with tools and weapons. Although Titus's extended family participates in his exploits solely to "feed" the "humour" of a "noble uncle thus distract" (4.3.26), Taymor presents the action in a manner that somewhat belies the family's presumed misgivings and the pathos that normally attends this scene in production, both by emphasizing the pleasure and solidarity the Andronici experience in the act itself and by providing us with direct access to the immediate effect the shower of arrows has on Saturninus and his decadent court. Taymor pointedly suppresses the comparatively static Clown and pigeons scene that follows the discharge of arrows in the play text, choosing instead to have our eyes follow the arrows' descent into an ongoing scene of orgy and banqueting where they operate like a siege of avenging angels.

We soon catch up with the elided play text in a sequence that again surrogates something new to something textually established, as news of the shower of arrows awakens Saturninus, who has been contentedly sleeping naked as a baby on the breast of his wife-mother. At this point, Taymor plays dramatically fast and loose both with the text and with our expectations of "reality" as the nighttime arrows find Saturninus asleep and push him from his bed, into a dressing gown, out to a courtyard brimming with daylight, and then fully dressed into the Senate chamber in a montage of six cleverly edited tracking shots. The abruptness with which Saturninus moves from childlike calm to hysterical abandon is made to appear the direct result of an action that, on the face of it, could not seem more ineffectual (and whose momentum in the play text is first eroded by Titus's charge to the Clown and later by the Clown's delivery of the message and his summary condemnation) but which has the effect of turning Titus into the aggressor and Saturninus into prey.

The effectual terror Titus and his cohorts unleash in this space of the film—and go on to burnish considerably in the playfully cold-blooded abandon with which Titus successively undertakes the roles of butcher, cook, dinner host, sacrificer, and revenger in the play's last two scenes— suggestively resonates with two scenes that flank it which concentrate on Aaron. In the first of these, Aaron effectively removes himself from the contention between the Andronici and Saturninus by dedicating himself to the survival of his newborn child, an act which is cued by his shocking murder of the nurse who has functioned as the intermediary between Aaron and Tamora. That this act is performed with a suddenness and resolve that recalls but stylistically transcends Titus's earlier murder of his son Mutius is, I believe, very much Taymor's point, which she proceeds to embellish and elaborate in the succeeding scene where Aaron is taken captive by Lucius but exercises an impressive degree of control over what Lucius can do with him. In each instance, we watch Aaron casually exceed the limit of behaviors that seem reasonable, turning his associates and enemies into the same kind of awestruck witnesses that we all eventually become as we witness Titus's own gathering assurance and empowerment. Indeed, the confrontation between Lucius and Aaron is arguably the most powerful and, in its way, irrecuperable moment in Taymor's film, turning the film's (and the play's) reigning monster into the most recognizably human presence within it.

While Taymor presents the dialogue of this scene in full fidelity to the text of act 5, scene 1, her direction and filming of it forcefully elaborate on the text's established disproportion of line assignments, which give Aaron twenty lines for every one line uttered by Lucius. Jonathan Bate's recent edition of the play has stage directions that read "*A Goth brings a ladder, which Aaron is made to climb*" and, later, "*to climb down*" but offers no prompts for actions undertaken during Aaron's interrogation. In *Titus* Harry Lennix's Aaron pridefully sustains a vicious blow from Lucius for every self-congratulatory claim he makes ("I trained / I wrote / I played") and then chooses to climb the ladder himself and place the noose around his own neck before unexpectedly removing it in order to leap down upon the unsuspecting Lucius. In each instance, Taymor cues the aggressor in Aaron to rise against his newly established status as victim and captive and in the process, makes the characteristically aggressive Lucius seem progressively more ineffectual and even implicitly acknowledge how unconquerable Aaron's spirit is. When we join to this directive Aaron's earlier (and successful) effort to have Lucius swear "To save my boy, to nurse and bring him up" (5.1.84), we may well register a more deeply (and darkly) ironic mingling of the roles of villain and victim than the play text alone would encourage, one that anticipates (and possibly conditions) Titus's own erratic evolution from rigorous militarist to Joblike victim to cold-blooded butcher to "homicidal merry prankster."[31] For even as the film's momentum shifts in Titus's favor as he develops an Aaron-like command over his enemies and cinematic resources alike, the certainty that we are about to surfeit on another course of ultraviolence somewhat qualifies the pleasure we arguably feel as Titus ambles around the banquet table in white chef's attire to serve up his pasty of crushed bones and blood to Tamora and Saturninus.

Indeed, the further elisions and interpolations Taymor makes in her filming of the last section of act 5, scene 3 make it even harder to sustain an unalloyed regard for Titus, who becomes, at the moment he breaks Lavinia's neck as if she were more a wounded sparrow than a woman, more "psycho-killer" than "merry prankster."[32] By cutting close to thirty lines of moving farewells to the dead Titus spoken in the play text by Marcus, Lucius, and, most crucially, Young Lucius, who, in Shakespeare's text, wishes that he, himself, were dead "so you [i.e., Titus] did live again" (5.3.172); by maintaining the elder Lucius's closing condemnation of the "beastly" and pitiless Tamora; and by adding Young Lucius's carrying off of Aaron's child through the once-closed gates of history into what appears to be a new dawn, Taymor affiliates the offspring of the ravenous Moor and Goth with a character who, in this surrogation of *Titus Andronicus,* has supplanted his grandfather as *our* surrogate, witness, and point of reference and who has discernibly learned things that his father and grandfather could not teach him.[33] Whereas the Young Lucius of the play text demonstrably promises to do everything in his power to *emulate* the fallen Titus, the Young Lucius of the film demonstrably promises to *differentiate* himself from the patriarchal mold of his grandfather and father alike. While Aaron and Titus have been paired sharers in the manic theatrical energy which, in this film, signals agency and command, Aaron's child and Titus's grandson are paired at the end in a very different form of agency, one that involves the deliberate choice and effort to move outside the frame of the film itself and also out of what that film has represented as "the last 2000 years of man's inhumanity to man." Although the politics of this gesture may no doubt be construed as "soft" and hardly an effectual answer to the horrors that the film puts on display, it operates as the most distinct and sustaining of Taymor's postmodern interpolations, offering an undeniable ethical counterpoint to the continued reign of mutual predation the elder Lucius proclaims at play's end.

Coda

This, as noted earlier, is decidedly not the judgment of two of the best earlier assessors of Taymor's film, who consider Young Lucius's slow-motion walk into a "computer-generated sunrise" a "wish-fulfillment fantasy . . . uncomfortably comparable to a Hollywood Happy Ending" and sufficiently "schlocky" as to beg comparison to a " 'Kids Raising Kids' episode of Rikki Lake," respectively.[34] I take both judgments seriously and have reservations of my own, both about the ending and about Taymor's explanation of its operation as a "counterpoint to Shakespeare's dark tale of vengeance."[35] I also see Taymor's decision as contextually linked to certain artistic tendencies of the last ten years or so which seek at least to pose alternatives to what I have, pace Taymor, perhaps too glibly identified as "history," or, in her words, as "the last 2000 years of man's inhumanity to man."

One of the earliest, and most defensible, examples of this tendency is the alternate, or double, ending that Derek Jarman appends to his 1991 film version of *Edward II* in which the play's executioner, Lightborne, casts his hot poker away and embraces Edward as a lover, thereby "making fantasy seem the preferred medium of resistance in the battle for homosexual rights."[36] Sounding only slightly less dismissive of Jarman's choice than Burt and McCandless do regarding Taymor's, I claimed, in my 1998 essay on the film, that Jarman's apparent "decision to delegate Edward's actual execution to the province of nightmare . . . magically elides the very relation between past and present oppressions that he otherwise seeks to document."[37] At the same time, I attempted to account for Jarman's provision of what is, after all, only a possible ending (and not the most plausible one) by contending that "Jarman seems specifically unwilling to allow a too powerful imaging of the material oppression of homosexuals to carry over into the present without simultaneously providing a way out."[38] In this enterprise, Jarman could have found a powerful ally in Tony Kushner, whose "gay fantasia on national themes," *Angels in America: Part One; Millenium Approaches,* would generate a second part, *Perestroika,* in which its presumably doomed protagonist, Prior Walter, is allowed to outlive the same AIDS virus which took Jarman's life.

However, even if we grant the authority to flaunt realism to such politically charged antecedents, what authorizes Taymor's attempt to prevent darkness from maintaining its grip over Shakespeare's "dark tale of
vengeance"? How do we differentiate her "Hollywood Happy Ending"
from the happy ending Nahum Tate appended to *King Lear* two hundred-
odd years ago? We do so not by reproducing Tate's argument that he
was simply naturalizing (that is, restoring a natural perspective to) the
unnaturally horrid prospects Shakespeare was compelling his audiences
(and readers) to swallow but, possibly, by doing the opposite and accepting
the artificiality of Taymor's "computer-generated sunrise" as an admittedly
strained solution to but needed departure from the seemingly insoluble
problem of mutually predatory human relations. As Jarman might say, why
take on such a "musty play" in the first place if you don't intend to "violate
it"? Victoria Nelson offers a somewhat different take on the problem in
her brilliant account of the Lars von Trier film *Breaking the Waves* (1996),
which ends with the ringing of enormous heavenly bells (visible to the
film viewer from on high, no less) that seemingly confirm the "holiness" of
the film's sexual martyr, Bess. To radically abbreviate her argument, Nelson
seeks to rescue the ending of von Trier's film from its detractors who find
in it "an unholy alliance of 1940s movie kitsch with organized religion."[39]
She does so by claiming that, absent "the metaphysical level on which
the bells operate . . . *Breaking the Waves* would be just another example
of the sort of art Westerners have happily consumed for a hundred and
fifty years: social realism shading into modernism that steadfastly upholds
a rational-empirical worldview."[40] And she concludes:

To the adherents of this sensibility, the demand for "realism" is as narrow and
two dimensional as the bells are to detractors of *Breaking the Waves*. In New
Expressionist terms, the bells represent a Shakespearean ending in which the moral
order has been restored by a message from those inner areas of reality coincident
with a transcendental reality we do not experience with our five senses—and it
is a defiant message in the face of all sensible judgment as rendered by the well-
intentioned, both within the film and in the audience.[41]

Taymor would no doubt discern some slippage between Nelson's effort to
recuperate the space of the spiritual or uncanny for Western art and her
own effort to generate— "as if redemption were a possibility"[42]—an ethical
alternative to the very different kind of "Shakespearean ending" with which
she was contending in *Titus*. For Taymor, the idea of a possibility—of release, escape, redemption—is about as far as it gets. However, the solution

she arrives at through the medium of Young Lucius uncannily anticipates the way Nelson brings her own scholarly production to a close, observing that "it is precisely the moment when we become completely conscious of the boundaries of the worldview we have comfortably inhabited for several centuries that is also, inevitably, the moment we abandon it: we see the door in the sky, and we walk through it."[43]

Notes

1. Julie Taymor, *Titus: The Illustrated Screenplay, Adapted from the Play by William Shakespeare* (New York: Newmarket Press, 2000), 178.

2. Director's Commentary, *Titus*, DVD, directed by Julie Taymor (New York: 20th Century Fox Home Entertainment, 1999), disc 1.

3. I employ the term "iteration" here and elsewhere in this essay as W. B. Worthen employs it in a recent article which treats the similarly provocative Baz Luhrmann film, *William Shakespeare's Romeo + Juliet*. Worthen writes, "Citing the text—the verbal text of a play, the cultural text of Shakespeare—Luhrmann's film undertakes a shrewd reflection of the relation between classic texts and their performances, presenting this version of Shakespeare's work not as a performance of the text and not as a translation of the work but as an iteration of the work, an iteration that necessarily invokes and displaces a textual 'origin' by performing the text in a specific citational environment—the verbal, visual, gestural, and behavioral dynamics of youth culture, of MTV." W. B. Worthen, "Drama, Performativity and Performance," *PMLA*, 113, no. 5 (1998): 1104. Worthen has borrowed this term from Joseph Grigely who, Worthen notes, "deploys the notion of 'iteration' to characterize not only the transmission of texts but also the ongoing negotiation of the meaning of artworks in culture" (1101). According to Worthen, "Grigely argues that textual studies frequently misunderstands the nature of iteration: insofar as texts are products of the working of culture at a given moment in history, copies of texts produced under new conditions do not iterate the original text" (1101). From this perspective, "the transmission of art . . . necessarily involves surrogation, a continual 'process of being unmade (as an object) and remade (as a text and as memory),' a kind of performance [Grigely] calls 'textualterity' " (Worthen 1101). See Joseph Grigely, *Textualterity: Art, Theory, and Textual Criticism* (Ann Arbor: University of Michigan Press, 1995), 1, 33.

4. This is the first of many places in this essay in which I engage in dialogue with Richard Burt's chapter on *Titus*, "Shakespeare and the Holocaust: Julie Taymor's *Titus* Is Beautiful, or Shakesploi Meets (the) Camp," in *Shakespeare after Mass Media*, ed. Richard Burt (New York: Palgrave, 2002), 295–329. In a passage that focuses on the film's ending, Burt claims that Shakespeare's own cultivation of "aesthetic excess" through "the media of theater and print narrative" effectively "destabilizes precisely the kinds of oppositions Taymor wants to affirm and correlate: between high art (film) and trash (blockbuster); Shakespeare and Shakesploitation; a critique of violence and an embrace of violence; modesty versus sexual perversion; and sacred and profane" (312–13). Despite Burt's compelling argument to the contrary, it isn't clear to me why Taymor's own obvious cultivation of aesthetic excess shouldn't effect the same kind of destabilization Burt describes, unless we conclude that

Taymor remains captive to the circularity of the binaries she sets up. This seems to be David McCandless's point when he contends that Taymor "aimed to make a violent movie that would deconstruct movie violence," which evokes the image of a cat chasing its tail ("A Tale of Two *Tituses*: Julie Taymor's Vision on Stage and Screen," *Shakespeare Quarterly* 53, no. 4 [2002]: 489).

5. Burt notes that Cumming wore his *Cabaret* haircut to the filming of his scenes in *Titus* (315-16) in the process of noting Taymor's implied linkage of homosexuality to perversion to Fascism. Michael Anderegg makes much the same point, adding, "Although [Cumming's] Saturninus is not necessarily constructed as 'gay' . . . he is thoroughly associated with a homosexual aesthetic," in *Cinematic Shakespeare* (Lanham, Md.: Rowman and Littlefield, 2004), 186. Anderegg instructively adds, "The danger of the kind of postmodern allusiveness Taymor practices is that the associations evoked will not be those the artist intends. Too many allusions to a diverse mix of external signs can result in a work that has no ultimate center, no 'base' from which the allusions can be launched and controlled" (186). While I share many of Anderegg's reservations about Taymor's free-floating postmodernity, I also think that if postmodernity is about anything, it involves the promiscuity of the relationship between signified and signifier. Searching for an example of Taymor's "fidelity" to anything beyond the Shakespearean play text (which Anderegg accounts "a virtue" in this case), much less a fixed "center" or "base," is apt to prove disappointing.

6. Grigely, *Textualterity*, 100.

7. See Burt, "Shakespeare and Holocaust," 295-300.

8. "Surrogation" is a term most closely identified with the work of Joseph Roach, who defines and elaborates on it in the first pages of *Cities of the Dead: Circum-Atlantic Performance* (New York: Columbia University Press, 1996), 2-3. Cf. Worthen: "To Roach, performance can be described as surrogation, an uncanny replacement acting, an ambivalent replaying of previous performers and performances by a current behavior. An act of memory and an act of creation, performance recalls and transforms the past in the form of the present" ("Drama, Performativity and Performance," 1101). In this case, the "form of the present," Taymor's film, performs a surrogation of the recent past through its iteration of an early modern play that surrogates itself to an anachronistic vision of ancient time and space.

9. While I plan to revisit this subject later, it bears noting now that Taymor's tampering with the ending of Shakespeare's play has evoked a hostile reaction among even avowedly postmodern critical practitioners. As Richard Burt writes, "In the final, prolonged, and schlocky shot of the film, Young Lucius walks with the baby out of the arena into a sunrise much as the boy Eliot carried the alien E.T. when they rode together on a bike off into the sky in Spielberg's *E.T.* Young Lucius, of course, cannot possibly know how to care for Aaron's baby" ("Shakespeare and Holocaust," 311). Although Burt also admits that the "early violence [to which Young Lucius is exposed], including the opening scene of the boy playing with his war toys, throws Lucius's later pacifism into bold relief" (311), he later adds that "some critics may . . . fault the film . . . for having a white child pick up the baby in a way that makes the exit from the colosseum appear to be the introduction of a new, racialized hierarchy, as if Young Lucius were taking up the white boy's burden" (315). David McCandless takes a similarly double-edged stance toward the film's ending. McCandless first claims, "This climactic rejection of violence constitutes the film's final decisive instance of

trauma management. In exiting the Colosseum, Young Lucius breaks the cycle of violence that the stage production portrayed as unbreakable. To the extent that the boy's violent play called the world of violence into being, his absence from it signifies its collapse" ("Tale of Two Tituses," 509). However, he later concludes, "Young Lucius's triumphant exit from the Colosseum" fortifies "the Symbolic against the Real by staging a wish-fulfillment fantasy, a denouement uncomfortably comparable to a Hollywood Happy Ending. . . . What the boy heads toward is an illusion, a haven provided by the fiats of aesthetic escapism. Rather than traumatize the audience, Taymor seems rather to release them from trauma, playing the quasi-therapeutic role of positioning her viewers to reexperience trauma in a safe environment, to obscure events evocative of contemporary terrors in order to achieve imaginative control over them" (510). The notion that Taymor's film is involved in trauma management and that the film's ending is integral to her designs is much more favorably addressed in Lisa Starks, "Cinema of Cruelty: Powers of Horror in Julie Taymor's Titus," in The Reel Shakespeare: Alternative Cinema and Theory, ed. Lisa S. Starks and Courtney Lehmann (Madison, N.J.: Fairleigh Dickinson University Press, 2002), 121–42.

10. Throughout his film, Jarman treats young Edward as a character whose questions, perceptions, observations, and experiments in gender displacement speak eloquently on behalf of subjects and sexualities still in the process of formation. Particularly effective is Jarman's inspired imaging of the future in the cross-sexed persona of the newly crowned Edward III who, at the end of the film, orchestrates the demise of the caged Mortimer and Isabella to the tune of "The Sugar Plum Fairy." For a more in-depth discussion of this and related subjects, see Thomas Cartelli, "Queer Edward II: Postmodern Sexualities and the Early Modern Subject" in Marlowe, History, and Sexuality: New Critical Essays on Christopher Marlowe, ed. Paul W. White (New York: AMS Press, 1998), 213–23; reprinted in Avraham Oz, ed., Marlowe: Contemporary Critical Essays (New York: Palgrave, 2003), 200–212.

11. If, as Grigely notes, "works are ontologized—that is to say, contextualized semantic-ally—by the temporal history that surrounds their composition" (Textualterity, 103), then Taymor's intervention gains added resonance from events like the widespread practice of arbitrary mutilation in the recently concluded civil war in Sierra Leone and from the efforts reportedly undertaken there by enterprising prosthesis suppliers to fit and sell "surrogate" legs and arms to its victims. This sequence may also be contextualized in terms of the disabling injuries which are increasingly occasioned by buried mines in places like Afghanistan. Such dismemberments are tragicomically treated in a central scene in a recent Iranian film, Kandahar (directed by Mohsen Makhmalbaf, 2001), which is set in a desert oasis in Afghanistan where people who have lost limbs due to the explosion of buried mines gather to be fitted for prosthetic arms and legs which are dropped from the sky by UN relief planes. A more recent report in the New York Times (June 22, 2004, A13) focuses on highly expensive state-of-the-art advances in prosthetic technology which have been generated by the U.S. government's effort to compensate young soldiers for their loss of arms and legs while stationed in Iraq.

12. Taymor, Titus: Illustrated Screenplay, 185.

13. See Starks ("Cinema of Cruelty," 134), who also notes that Taymor may have borrowed the idea of channeling her film through Young Lucius's point of view from Jane Howell's 1985 BBC production of Titus Andronicus. As Starks notes, "Taymor first incorporated it in

the off-Broadway stage-production she directed in 1994" (140, n. 56). Courtney Lehmann provocatively discerns a difference between Young Lucius's fate and our own at the end of the film, claiming that "if young Lucius gets to take up the living at the end of *Titus* while we are left to take up the dead, it is because we have not shown that we can consume with the care necessary to *preserve* life—not just imitate it." Courtney Lehmann, "Crouching Tiger, Hidden Agenda: How Shakespeare and the Renaissance Are Taking the Rage Out of Feminism," *Shakespeare Quarterly* 53, no. 2 (2002): 278.

14. Taymor, *Titus: Illustrated Screenplay*, 184.

15. Ibid.; cf. Burt, "Shakespeare and the Holocaust," 310.

16. McCandless, "Tale of Two *Tituses*," 501.

17. Burt, "Shakespeare and Holocaust," 308.

18. Ibid., 309.

19. Ibid., 312.

20. All quotations from the text of *Titus Andronicus* are drawn from Jonathan Bate's Arden edition, 3d series (London: Thomson Learning, 2000).

21. Taymor, *Titus: Illustrated Screenplay*, 107.

22. Rowe observes that "when Lavinia carries Titus's hand off stage, and . . . when she writes with a stick, she redefines her mouth as a grasping part in a way that complicates its earlier identification with the passive bubbling fountain and the 'Cocytus's mouth' of the scene of her rape. Taking up the severed hand as a supplement to her lost tongue, Lavinia converts herself from a figure of dismemberment into a figure of agency." Katherine Rowe, *Dead Hands: Fictions of Agency, Renaissance to Modern* (Stanford, Calif.: Stanford University Press, 1999), 78.

23. Taymor, *Titus: Illustrated Screenplay*, 185.

24. See Joseph Roach, *The Player's Passion: Studies in the Science of Acting* (Ann Arbor: University of Michigan Press, 1993).

25. Bate, *Titus Andronicus*, 204, n. 265.

26. Taymor, *Titus: Illustrated Screenplay*, s.d., 109.

27. Ibid., 117.

28. Cf. Lehmann, "Crouching Tiger, Hidden Agenda," 274–75; and Burt, "Shakespeare and Holocaust," 315.

29. Negatively comparing the film's PANs with the PANs in Taymor's earlier stage production, considering them "merely extravagant exhibitions[,] cut loose from the exhibitionistic context in which they formerly cohered as abstract commentary," McCandless asks, "Why should Lavinia, remembering her rape, imagine herself as a pedestal-bound doe-girl beset by rapacious tiger-boys?" (501–2). The question, I think, is misplaced. Lavinia needn't, shouldn't, imagine herself a "doe-girl." The imagery of "doe-girl" and "tiger-boys," like the allusion to Marilyn Monroe's skirt being lifted by the draft from subway vents, operates (as before) as "visually overdetermined editorial interventions," manufactured and screened for *our* benefit, not for hers. What Lavinia "experiences," I would submit, has little to nothing to do with imagery, even *should* she imagine herself in the figurative likeness of a doe beset by tigers. Rather, it has to do with the sense of renewed agency she achieves in the process of inscribing the names of her assailants in the dirt.

30. Taymor, *Titus: Illustrated Screenplay*, 121.

31. Cf. McCandless, "Tale of Two *Tituses*": "The emasculated patriarch is reborn as homicidal merry prankster, exploiting his abject status to destroy his enemies and restore some coherence to his world" (492).

32. Burt contends, "Resistance to fascism becomes in the film a kind of massive death-drive, and honor-killing in the play is transformed into psycho-killing in the film" ("Shakespeare and Holocaust," 309). He later adds, "Antifascism in *Titus* is not collective rational resistance to a tyrannical state, but is located in the subjectivity of a hero who is both sadistic and masochistic and whose acts of violence do not respect distinctions between people who are in or out of his family" (310).

33. For our purposes here, it may be said that "surrogation involves not the replaying of an authorizing text, a grounding origin, but the potential to construct that origin as a rhetorically powerful effect of performance" (Worthen, "Drama, Performativity, and Performance," 1101).

34. McCandless, "Tale of Two *Tituses*," 510; Burt, "Shakespeare and Holocaust," 311.

35. Taymor, *Titus: Illustrated Screenplay*, 185.

36. Cartelli, "*Queer* Edward II," 220. This conclusion was mine, not, assuredly, Jarman's. It should also be noted here that Jarman supplies footage of the play's "real" ending as well (i.e., having Lightborne drive a hot poker up Edward's anus) but intercuts the two in a way that privileges neither, thereby providing his audience with a double perspective, one which "channels" the past, the other the "best-case" present or, at worst, anticipated future.

37. Ibid.

38. Ibid.

39. Victoria Nelson, *The Secret Life of Puppets* (Cambridge: Cambridge University Press, 2001), 229.

40. Ibid.

41. Ibid., 230.

42. Taymor, *Titus: Illustrated Screenplay*, 185.

43. Nelson, *Secret Life of Puppets*, 290. Special thanks to Linda Charnes for introducing me to *The Secret Life of Puppets*.

Thanks to Brad Greenburg, Heather James, and Katherine Rowe, who read and commented on an earlier version of this essay.

School for Scandal?
New-Media Hamlet, *Olivier,*
and Camp Connoisseurship

DENISE ALBANESE

R ECENT WORK ON Shakespeare and media has tended to equate its object with novelty: the explosion of nonce coinages—"Shakespop," "Shake-sploi," "ShaXXXspeares"—used to delimit the phenomenon suggests an ever-mutating hybrid, a formation whose very innovativeness beggars linguistic, let alone interpretive, ability to play catch-up.[1] The emergence of new interactive technologies for the presentation of cultural goods might well necessitate rethinking acts of apprehension, especially when objects of great social authority, like Shakespeare, might be inflected thereby. Equally, however, the discursive challenge of a new form ought not to blind us to the possibility that the novelty of medium serves as a screen, a site of projection: what is then obscured is an overfamiliarity, even conservatism, in the focus of transmission. When it comes to this phenomenon, not all new bottles hold new wine.

The issue needs to be stated more expansively. The development of digitized media has occasioned prophetic manifestos about their potential to provide new forms of interaction and new modalities of pleasure; symmetrically, it has given rise to fears about human defenselessness in the face of such sirenic novelty. Yet more analytically precise theorists have pointed out that futurological enthusiasms tend in their celebratory haste to overemphasize the epistemic or perceptual break digitization brings about, in part because of an imprecision about the architecture and language of new media. Lev Manovich, for instance, suggests that cinema

185

form has more in common with computerized images than is generally acknowledged and that most of what has been claimed for technologies of data transmission since the 1990s is better cast back one hundred years, to the emergence of mass-entertainment forms as such.[2]

Given such historically minded correctives, it follows as a general proposition that new-media instantiations of Shakespeare may present themselves so as to throw into question any imputation that their hybridity marks something distinctively new, simply as a by-product of form. Consider DVD: as a comparatively recent format for the delivery of visual information, it offers the general possibility of a number of different features in addition to the main cinematic event. Some of these features are commercial by-products, as with trailers, but some, such as director's comments, interviews with actors, and, more radically, alternative camera angles and endings, can potentially destabilize the text under consideration and allow home viewers to construct their own preferred objects of interaction, objects which moreover might vary with repeated viewing. Yet in general, it is far from clear what relationship exists between the recombinational potential of the format and the mass of viewing habits—if, that is, the aim of analysis is to move away from generating new readings and into a broader interest in understanding how new technological modalities refract on Shakespeare as public object. Manovich suggests that much discussion of heightened media "interactivity" (stirred, perhaps, by the homology between these new technologies and the discourse of the postmodern) ignores the extent to which technologies that privilege the forging of new links simply turn a form of cognitive labor that was always available to the private discerning subject—the labor, that is, to read sequentially or not, make conclusions, fill in blanks or discern subtexts, juxtapose, and so on—into the objectified associations generated by a programmer.[3] Correspondingly, there is much about DVD format that looks backward, rather than ahead to new forms of enjoyment: that many menus break the digitized film down into "chapters" suggests the covert reterritorialization of the visual by a coding system dependent on textuality and willing to call on its older associations by way of interface.

Moreover, if Shakespeare films prove impossible to generalize about, the same must surely be true when it comes to how DVD and Shakespeare intersect. Not only do the films as productions and interpretations of Shakespeare differ in their relationship to script, author, performance, audience: as DVDs, which is to say both as commodities and as technologically mediated re-presentations of prior cinematic releases for private viewing, they offer an as yet limited basis for generalization.[4] Some widely discussed Shakespeare movies have yet to appear on DVD, such as Kenneth Branagh's 1996 *Hamlet* and Peter Greenaway's 1991 *Prospero's Books,* which one might reasonably expect to come accompanied by elaborate digital apparatuses—a shorter, alternative cut of Branagh's four-hour epic, for instance; or information about Greenaway's own digitally inflected composition process. At the present moment, however, few DVD issues of Shakespeare movies can begin to match mainstream releases in the number and kinds of peripheral texts they put on offer. *Titus* (directed by Julie Taymor; 2000), for instance, appears to be all but unique in its elaborateness: it has been issued in a special two-DVD set, with the first disc containing, in addition to the film, a commentary by Taymor and a separate music track with remarks by composer Elliot Goldenthal, and the second disc a documentary on the making of the film, a question-and-answer session with Taymor, a costume gallery, and trailers.[5] The DVD's producer, 20th Century Fox Home Entertainment, is a major force in the home DVD market; although the movie itself was not a mainstream Hollywood production, the corporation seems to have been involved with *Titus* from its initial cinematic release, via its Fox Searchlight Pictures division. The right to reproduce the DVD and an atypical wealth of ancillary material, therefore, might well have been part of the original funding deal.[6] As this instance evinces, the political economy of film—within which contractual relations, backlist, and the general profile of the company that issues the DVD are all operant terms—constitutes a significant means of defining and circumscribing new-media Shakespeare: business arrangements are as pertinent to reading the DVD as the fact that the film digitized connects to Shakespeare. This is not to argue that readings are unimportant. Rather, it is to do for digital Shakespeare what recent essays into editorial practice have done for print Shakespeare: make overt, and therefore available for critical reflection, the tacit productive factors behind the manifest text.

And for every viewer who wishes to take in the extra nuance offered by the two-disc release of *Titus* or would embrace an enhanced version of *Prospero's Books,* there is surely another who relishes the less technologically intricate pleasures on offer with the Criterion Collection's 2000 release of Laurence Olivier's 1948 *Hamlet,* the focus of this essay. As the preceding discussion suggests, if it is hard to offer any sort of comprehensive argument about the difference technological form makes, it is equally hard to generalize about the circuit of exchange, given that it encompasses the movement from the specific potentiality of a Shakespearean film on DVD to an equally specific act of reception, itself a complex and variable phenomenon. Yet without acknowledging the problematic of audience, all pronouncements on new-media Shakespeare risk becoming the phantasmatic projections of a reading subject writing her own perceptions large.[7]

In what follows, therefore, I will stick close to a particular text and substantiate a particular viewing context within which alternative reading might occur, the better to make good on the skeptical premise with which I began: that new-media Shakespeare does not always respond to the privilege we accord its novelty. When it comes to Olivier's *Hamlet,* there exists a convergence between the discourse of the DVD and a cinematic production more than fifty years old: each in its own way is a backward-looking text, and each reveals a similar, albeit historically distinct, investment in the potential of its medium to re-present canonical works. Perhaps most important, in each case the discourse of medium and canon works to foreground the pedagogical potentiality of the object. The liner notes on Criterion's disc make the (surely plausible) case that this version of *Hamlet* claims sustained attention as a piece of filmmaking; however, it is surely possible to read those notes as reproducing an agenda with respect to audience that resembles the modes of address to be found in the film production itself. In both cases, didacticism abounds, which manifests itself in the desire to take something of historical currency and render it, via a medium whose discourse is restoration, as timeless as Shakespeare himself is presumed to be.

But if that is the intention, it does not, of course, dictate the contours of reception. In this essay I will juxtapose a more disciplined and properly interpellated sense of how to read *Hamlet,* engendered both by Olivier's pedagogical imperative within the film and by the redoubling of that imperative by Criterion, with the carnivalesque moments of reception I've encountered in teaching. In that more formally, less phantasmatically pedagogical venue, certain moments of the film—most particularly Olivier's staging of "To be or not to be"—have, more than once, occasioned derisive, uncomfortable, challenging amusement. Among other things, that laughter is both naive and knowing: uninformed about how to read the historicity of performance practices, yet all too attuned to how Olivier's staging of masculinity in crisis can be recuperated to a viewing pleasure that bears more than a passing relationship to camp connoisseurship—and thus to a historically discrete relationship to cultural forms whose very obliquity reveals midcentury presumptions about film's vexed place in the panoply of cultural goods. As I'll argue, the bodily decorum characteristic of Olivier's performance seems, at this historical remove, to offer a text for interpretation in itself, the pleasures of which might have as much to do with redeeming the outmoded for present uses, and inverting the sign of high seriousness that attends on cinematic Shakespeare, as with the understanding of the play text the performance constitutes.

The Criterion Collection

Criterion first emerged in 1984 as an important agent in the laserdisc market, and it persists as a highly regarded independent company manufacturing DVDs. From the first, the company has been identified with careful and thorough restorations of historically significant films.[8] As its Web site proclaims, "Criterion began with a mission to pull the treasures of world cinema out of the film vaults and put them in the hands of collectors. All of the films published under the Criterion banner represent cinema at its finest."[9] The firm is well known to film instructors and to a segment of the home DVD audience, that most interested in what used to be known as art-house cinema, a formation once widely supported by theaters like the Thalia in New York and the Biograph in Washington, D.C., but now more likely the purview of museums and cinema-studies programs. One might even say that Criterion's role in making art-house films available to the home viewer represents an important development in the history of cinephilia, comparable to the economic transformations in urban spaces that rendered public theatrical venues commercially untenable. That the films are represented as dormant and all but forgotten, lying "in vaults," elides the importance of a prior historical formation even as it suggests the company is the natural extension of it: where once films were screened to metropolitan audiences influenced by *Cahiers du Cinema* and the burgeoning of film criticism in the United States, now private collectors, not united by propinquity but forming a community nevertheless, are the beneficiaries of Criterion's curatorial interest in world cinema.

Evidence abounds that the sense of community I have sketched is more than a phantasmatic projection. The Web site reveals a sense of audience, encouraging suggestions for new titles fitting the Criterion profile, and its list of frequently asked questions (FAQs) indicates a great awareness of the reputation its productions have among consumers. The resale market is another indication: although Criterion has lost many of the rights it once owned as studios developed home entertainment branches of their own and as larger firms have beaten out specialty companies for the right to issue rereleases, there exists an active (and at times suspect) resale market for out-of-print titles on such sites as eBay: if imitation is the sincerest form of flattery, then the appearance of counterfeit Criterion discs is surely a sign of the exchange value of the originals. As is the allure of comprehensiveness: when extensive Criterion DVD runs are put up for auction, the initial bidding price is several hundred dollars.

It follows that the company casts itself in the role of cultural intermediary. In October 2003, for instance, the Criterion Web site carried notification of a conference on Japanese filmmaker Yasujiro Ozu, timed to coincide with the forty-first annual New York Film Festival; via its "Focus" features, it regularly runs miniessays on such topics as experimental film, national cinemas, and actor-director collaborations.[10] But as befits its kinship to an earlier foundational moment in cinema studies, when discourses around the auteur began to coalesce, Criterion's understanding of film promotes the director as the producer of meaning. Hence the pride it takes in listing Renoir, Cocteau, Fellini, Tarkovsky, Ozu, and Buñuel, among others, as constituting the basis of its collection. And all steps taken to prepare its issues are informed, materially or ideologically, by directorial intent:

Each film is presented uncut, in its original aspect ratio, as its maker intended it to be seen. For every disc, we track down the best available film elements in the world, use state-of-the-art telecine equipment and a select few colorists capable of meeting our rigorous standards, and take time during the film-to-video digital transfer to create the most pristine possible image and sound. Whenever possible, we work with directors and cinematographers to assure that the look of our releases does justice to their intentions.[11]

As its words suggest, Criterion regards the potentiality of new media as a paradoxically conservative, even scholarly force: digital technology becomes the medium of recovery and rehabilitation, and all restorations are, "whenever possible," submitted to the review of those considered most responsible for the films' artistry and meaning in the first place. Even when the releases contain extra materials akin to those found on more mainstream DVDs, the emphasis is not on supplementarity in any theoretically revealing sense but rather on what Criterion calls "context," with audio commentaries, storyboards, shooting scripts, and the like subsumed to an all-governing purpose: presenting the film "as its maker intended it to be seen."

Of course, as I have already suggested, there is no guarantee that that is how any such additional material would be used by a given home viewer. But the very framing of the process of disc making suggests an important discursive continuity between 1960s cinephilia, within which the model of a director's creative control is central, and the home market of the 1990s and beyond. Indeed, even to refer to it as a market is to fail to notice the care with which Criterion employs the language of "collecting," which effects a commonality of intent between collection and collector, between those who make the discs and those who purchase them. At both ends there is a high regard for "cinema at its finest" and for building up a scholarly archive that enables home cinephiles to immerse themselves in its protocols. Hence the importance of comprehensiveness, entailed both in the idea of Criterion's "Collection" and in the fight to maintain its backlist against larger competitors. Criterion understands itself to be as much curator and conservator as business, with a concomitant effect on its prices: just as scholarly editions of texts cost more than mass-market versions, so too do Criterion issues tend to average ten dollars more per title at retail prices, because its painstaking restoration process cannot be done cheaply and thus adds value (a subject addressed in its FAQs).

And yet the evidence of how the market interpenetrates with Criterion's sense of its mission is not far to seek. Comparing the list of laserdisc offerings with the list of DVDs reveals a substantial divergence between them; Criterion has lost rights to a great number of important or popular American films, among them *Citizen Kane* (numbered first among its laserdisc releases), *It's a Wonderful Life* (disc no. 18), *The Wizard of Oz* (no. 59), and *Singin' in the Rain* (no. 52)—not to mention films by Steven Spielberg, John Singleton, and Woody Allen. The more temporally remote directorial roster which Criterion celebrates and on which it depends is determined, in part, by the question of continuing access, by the quite material right to keep something in the collection on offer to the home viewer. That is to say, Criterion's canon is a function not simply of judgment, whether local or inertial, but also of the vicissitudes of competition in a hyped-up market.

Notwithstanding this tacit circumscription, the discourse of collecting employed by Criterion connotes connoisseurship, the process, as much

ideological as educational, of acquiring sufficient cultural capital to recognize why the films that Criterion issues have made the cut. While such
capital might be acquired in the way that other competencies are—through
educational institutions, for example, or through the sort of public cinema
practices that were once more pervasive—it seems possible, even likely,
that the collection itself occasionally functions as both source of expertise
and confirmation of its possession. In effect, Criterion is a canon-building
institution within capital whose historical dependency on prior formations
doing similar work is not materially crucial to the continuation of that work.
"Criterion," a name brand and a term that suggests a discerning standard
of value, might be as much to the point as "Collection." One need not have
been a film major or a habitué of art houses in order to appreciate what
Criterion puts on offer, via its issues and its Web features. The Criterion
Collection is sufficient in itself, however much its recourse to "cinema at
its finest" risks falling back on mystified criteria of judgment, subtended
by a set of market relations to which the growth and continuation of the
list are subject.

Criterion's incarnation as an adjudicator of value has important consequences for the development of what I earlier referred to as the home-
pedagogical market. According to industry categories, DVDs are considered "infotainment"—a hybrid of, or perhaps a collision between, knowledge and leisure.[12] Taking the overtones of that category and amplifying
them, one winds up with the Criterion Collection. Criterion's DVDs take
the concept of entertainment as information into a newly formalized realm,
in which perfecting the text is crucial: the labor put into improving the
image, the color, and the sound reinforces, indeed materially secures, the
significance of the cinematic text thus attended to. That is why its relationship to bygone public interest in cinephilia matters: Criterion undertakes
a historically distinct extension of the pedagogical issues that, as we shall
see, have hovered around the history of the medium, and it installs this
prior dispensation in local and potentially more private venues.

This is not to say, of course, that there no longer exists a public discourse
about quality in film. It has, however, concentrated by and large on two
related formations, the "indie" film and the Sundance Festival, both of
which are generally considered to be hot markets (witness, for instance,
the way that Miramax Studios has gone from being a boutique company to
a "major" minor on the strength of its successful, well-promoted releases).
Criterion's version of "world cinema at its finest" is generally not identical

with the discourse of American independent cinema, and a few recent releases—like Steven Soderbergh's *Traffic* (2000)—and a few anomalies—such as Michael Bay's *The Rock* (1996) and *Armageddon* (1998) as well as the Beastie Boys Video Anthology (2000)—trouble, at the very least, my overall description of its profile. However, it seems clear that Criterion Collection looks backward in its list even as its technical standards for DVDs are cutting edge. On the evidence, its innovations are above all a way to serve the interests of the old, of traditional notions of intent, creators, and quality—and of the cultivation to appreciate them.

Hamlet: Film and the Pedagogical Imperative

The DVD of Olivier's *Hamlet* available as of this writing is one of Criterion's leaner productions.[13] It adds nothing specifically contextual by way of augmentation: there are no outtakes, eliminated scenes, or director's commentary—all of which are perhaps unavailable, given the age of the film and the comparative lack of value and, indeed, meaning, such ephemera once had. If the issue is remarkable, it is because of the quality of the reproduction Criterion has undertaken, described via technical data that refer back to the large screen as its point of origin: "*Hamlet* is presented in its original theatrical aspect ratio of 1.33:1. This digital transfer was created from a 35mm duplicate negative. The sound was mastered from a 35mm optical soundtrack print."[14] As it happens, that original aspect ratio means the film is perfectly suited to the proportions of the average TV screen; notwithstanding this nice coincidence between original release format and the technology of many home viewers, however, it is clear that Criterion means to invoke the film-theatrical experience as definitive. That is to say, the company indexes a prior representation as a way to legitimate the continued existence of that representation in different species, a translation of medium that both calls attention to its difference and effaces that difference via the prominence it gives to filmic, indeed, large-screen theatrical, image conditions. The DVD of *Hamlet,* then, is a text that indexes an older text, not only to constitute it as point of origin but to re-present that origin in optimized conditions made possible only by a later technology. In its relationship to a prior text, the DVD aligns up with the filmic model it realizes, since Olivier's movie, as is well known, is itself the triangulation of two texts: the script of *Hamlet,* certainly, but also the text of Ernest Jones's *Hamlet and Oedipus.*[15] Even further, however, in the foundational priority it accords to film as an earlier and original medium, Criterion's DVD echoes the relationship Olivier's film establishes with theater as a mode of experience, as I shall demonstrate later. In each case, a classic is reimagined, a different sense of audience is negotiated, a rapprochement is reached between old and new.

Through its cover image, for instance, the DVD works to position the film within the discourse of the classic. The tinted cover of the earlier VHS release, showing a full-figure image of Olivier on the battlements of Elsinore, has been banished, to be replaced by a tightly cropped black-and-white close-up of the star cradling Yorick's skull against his cheek.[16] The velvety luminosity of this black-and-white image is synecdochic for the status of the release as a restoration, an attempt to correct a visual text corrupted by time and dispersal. Nor is the particular choice of image insignificant: in epitomizing *Hamlet* via a highly familiar, and highly theatrical, staging of introspection, Criterion signals its desire to summon forth a normative sense of character and staging associated with the play, while also granting increased prominence to Olivier as auteur as well as actor. That the cover image is in close-up aligns it visually with the typical head shot of the star; that Olivier's name as director appears in gray tones just above the movie title (which appears in large white letters), and just below the image of his face, coalesces his two roles into one. This is, after all, "Laurence Olivier's *Hamlet*," not Shakespeare's, an actor-director's production, rather than strictly a playwright's. (The image just inside the DVD packages reinforces the effect of the cover: another brooding shot of Olivier in black and white, another variation on the director and title graphic of the cover, only this time oriented vertically rather than horizontally.)

If Criterion's DVD commodity is made to look like a classic for the home viewer, it is also made to read as one in the discourse of the insert, which consists of an appreciative essay by journalist Terrence Rafferty as well as the list of disc chapters. Rafferty's main task seems to be to teach viewers how to appreciate a *Hamlet* that has, paradoxically enough at first glance, *not* withstood the test of time: "this *Hamlet,* once so celebrated, has taken on the quality of a forlorn and nearly forgotten thing, like Yorick's skull." Given the myriad ways in which Olivier's *Hamlet* has had a vigorous afterlife (not least in officially pedagogical sites, as I'll suggest at the end of this essay), Rafferty's claim seems a bit misplaced. But since he is making the case for the film as an outstanding instance of directorial skill, for an actor-director who considered himself better suited to "character roles, such as Hotspur or Henry V," the hyberbole sets up a justification that summarily highlights the film's formal virtues: the "restless" yet oddly unlocatable gaze of the camera that haunts—spies on—every scene; the deep focus and remote framing; the austere chiaroscuro. For that matter, Rafferty suggests that any bad fit between the actor and the role might have allowed him to discern a hidden potential for vigor in a role often typed as lyric and poetic: "Olivier may be the only actor who has fully recognized that Hamlet's irresolution has its own fierce energy, and that his morbidity is, at heart, a kind of ardor." Indeed, Olivier's acting in the film was renowned at the time for its masculine athleticism; as will be apparent, it is precisely that aspect of his performance that has become illegible to many contemporary viewers. Still, aligning the film with the resonant memento mori of the skull, however provisional the rhetoric, does not summon forth an energetically idiosyncratic performance by association. Nor does it really argue by implication for the film itself's having been consigned to oblivion: after all, we know Yorick's skull as well as we do because Hamlet rescues it from that very oblivion by reminiscence. Instead, Rafferty's words identify the film with the skull as endlessly revivified touchstone against which Hamlet, both play and character, are launched in the public imaginary. That is, Yorick's skull, precisely as a familiar image meant to epitomize Hamlet's subjectivity and used in this way on the cover, samples the film in instantly apprehensible, "classic" terms.

The disc's chapter titles further the sense of sampling the text, providing a roster of well-known utterances as a key to the action of the film. Witness: "Something is rotten in the state of Denmark"; "Frailty, thy name is woman"; "To thine own self be true"; "Get thee to a nunnery"; "To be or not to be"; "The play's the thing"; "Alas, poor Yorick!"; and, finally, "Good night, sweet prince." Of course, almost all of these chapters link the viewer to scenes in which the eponymous line is given context. But using them as chapter titles reduces the scenes they index to an already familiar tagline, a free-floating quotation whose overfamiliarity obscures, perhaps even replaces, its dramatic function. Like Yorick's skull, these lines "stand in" for *Hamlet* (it is worth noting that cinematic trailers for Branagh's *Hamlet* used much the same strategy to advertise the movie, intercutting recognizable quotations with snippets of dramatic action). At the same time, however, they also offer to interpret the action of *Hamlet* for the home viewer: thus "Frailty," which links one to Hamlet's soliloquy "O, that this too too solid flesh," teases out his relationship to Gertrude (and, of course, to Ophelia) as the apparently unique cause of his distress.

Given that this particular chapter, the fifth, succeeds the scene in which Eileen Herlie's Gertrude notoriously kisses Hamlet passionately and on the mouth, in keeping with Olivier's Oedipal interpretation of the play, that Criterion's title for it underscores the importance of the event is perhaps unexceptionable. But what, for instance, of the displaced line, "Something is rotten in the state of Denmark," which introduces not Horatio's musings on the Ghost but the initial moments of the film—the moments, that is, when an unidentified voice (Olivier's) is heard intoning lines never claimed as part of *Hamlet* (1.4.23-36), transposed to the movie's opening and removed from the diegesis? In context, the passage functions foremost as the basis for an analogy Hamlet draws between the faults of an individual and the faults of the Danish nation in excessive revelry, as he and Horatio wait for the reappearance of the Ghost. In the movie, however, they are offered as an interpretive preface, whose force as significant articulation is further secured by the scrolling of the lines as they are read aloud. Placed out of context, like the DVD's first chapter title, they offer to assimilate the play to the exigencies of classic (and classical) tragic discourse, with its emphasis on a single individual and a single, determining flaw:

> So, oft it chanceth in particular men,
> That for some vicious mole of nature in them . . .
> By the o'ergrowth of some complexion,
> Oft breaking down the pales and forts of reason, . . .
> Carrying, I say, the stamp of one defect,
> His virtues else be they as pure as grace,
> As infinite as man may undergo,
> Shall in the general censure take corruption
> From that particular fault.[17]

The "rottenness" in Denmark, it appears, is nothing other than Hamlet himself, the implied "particular man" of the lines. Thus the DVD seems to reinforce the film's interpretive discourse, as my previous claims about Criterion's submissiveness to directorial agendas might suggest. Nevertheless, the difference between the DVD's didacticism and that of the film is worth attending to. The former, which I've already termed sampling, reveals the DVD's imbrication, via Criterion, in a balancing act between informed cinephilia, within which the director is a significant guarantor of meaning, and the Shakespeare function at the present moment, which often deals with selectively reduced packets of signification as discursive stand-ins for a more complex engagement with the demands of the corpus. Hence the vague claims of rottenness at Denmark's core, which if taken in diegetic context might countermand the focus on individual agency highlighted by the opening shots they index. The pedagogical imperative enshrined in Olivier's film is in some ways more transparent, even coercive, as befits its having been produced at an earlier historical moment, before cinema was introduced as an object for serious intellectual reflection and connoisseurship. Consider again the words from the play with which the film commences: as a version of disembodied and potentially universal wisdom—what "is known" to apply to Shakespeare's play—and not even identified in the film as part of the text, the scrolled passage and voice-over interpellate the spectator as someone who might need to be prompted in how to read the film to follow and above all to understand the lines as an articulation of the Aristotelian tragic flaw. This interpretation is driven home by the next words Olivier speaks, over a shot of the dead Hamlet on battlements that literalize the "pales and forts" of the preceding lines, which summarily interpret the Shakespearean passage already adduced as interpretive: "This is the tragedy of a man who could not make up his mind."

The focus on individuality and decisiveness to be found in this interpretive frame is in one sense unsurprising, given the relationship I've already noted between Olivier's understanding of the text and Jones's work conjoining Oedipus and Freud, which has been amply investigated by Peter Donaldson.[18] But the film's complex melding of Viennese psychopathology and classical discourse has more than characterological significance. The Freudianized realization of *Hamlet* that ensues can be conjoined with other signs of elite cultural capital the movie puts on display; by these means it signals its relationship to theater as an originary site of significance, rather as the DVD signals its indebtedness to wide-screen conditions and directorial control. Aristotle, after all, emblematizes popular understanding of tragedy; when Aristotle gives way to Freud—when, that is, the interpretive prologue is succeeded by the camera that searches the vacancies of Elsinore and thereby establishes a series of visual relationships that are the equivalent of the analyst's ear—the succession brings Aristotle up-to-date while couching the discourse of the tragic flaw in terms that had some purchase on midcentury bourgeois formations around Freud.[19]

More immediately, those frames may be read as one further realization of a cultural project of popularization and dissemination that over the course of the twentieth century has often conjoined Shakespeare and film with messianic, or rather missionary, zeal. That Olivier's film offers itself for didactic purposes can be related to the fact that it thematizes drama against the horizons of film, in a manner reminiscent of cultural debates that emerged with the emergence of the medium. In such debates, as may be familiar, mainstream film was demonized as a form of easy and debased consumption, a medium that pandered to quasi-literate or non-Anglophone masses, or as a form mirroring the industrialized relations of production that kept them in ideological mystification.[20] Cinematic renditions of classic literary texts not only redeemed the nascent industry from bourgeois contempt from the left and the right; they were seen as providing a form of mass-cultural uplift, whose political overtones, viewed retrospectively, are decidedly reactionary. William Uricchio and Roberta E. Pearson, for example, have shown that the New York firm Vitagraph's "Quality Films," dedicated to representing literary and historical classics in the new medium of film, were produced during a crisis in Anglo-Saxon hegemony occasioned by shifting patterns of immigration in the United States. Thus, they argue, the films interpellated a diverse mass population into bourgeois aesthetic and cultural norms; witness a 1910 review in *Moving Picture World* of Vitagraph's *Twelfth Night,* which claims the film

elevates and improves the literary taste and appreciation of the greatest mass of the people, performing in this way a service which cannot be measured in material terms. Such work is the nature of an educational service which is deserving of the heartiest support of all who are working for the improvement of humanity.[21]

The situation in Britain, where Olivier's film was produced, was inescapably different—yet, as John Collick has suggested, early British cinematic versions of Shakespeare were effectively responses to an American industry already considered distasteful and vulgar, even as they were also influenced by the comparative success of the Vitagraph series.[22] And, like Vitagraph's productions, they were also influenced by stage conventions then regnant. Although the nationalist thrust of its productions posited indigenous discourses of quality against those from the United States, the fact remains that even in 1948 Britain, film as a medium for presenting Shakespeare had a long history of opportunistically drawing upon stage conventions as a signal for quality cinema's aspirations. Indeed, Collick demonstrates that the stage-inflected pageantry typical of early Shakespeare films left its traces on Olivier's earlier film, *Henry V,* produced for the War Office.[23]

It is perhaps no surprise, then, that Olivier might produce another film that bears the traces of this formation, not via its image repertory, however, which is expressive and modernist, but via an earnest optimism about the power of film to interpellate mass viewers into a version of Shakespeare symbolized by the stage. In place of the demonized articulations typical of mass-cultural debates, *Hamlet* effectively proposes the film commodity as means by which lofty ideas, elite cultural forms, may be disseminated and made available, the better to "elevate and improve the literary taste of the greatest mass of people."[24] Like the earliest Shakespeare films, it also introduces the film commodity by reference to conditions of performance and thus to a history that precedes it as point of reference. Strictly speaking, the contingent vagaries of that performance tradition are representationally incommensurate with the invariant iterability of film. Hence the important auditory sign with which the film begins, which precedes any visual information: it is of an orchestra tuning up, and it signifies the film's status as elite offering by displacing what cannot be shown cinematically within a moderately realist diegesis onto a conventional auditory cue that a performance is about to commence. That the music was composed by the eminent Sir William Walton and played by an ensemble identified as the "Philharmonia Orchestra," and that the image that immediately succeeds offers a stylized assemblage of banners, props, and tragic and comic masks, all reinforce the sense that Olivier's film means to invoke a prior aesthetic dispensation to condition audience expectations. In order to appreciate the bodily decorum of Shakespearean theatricality that Olivier puts on offer, the film seems to suggest that audiences take on a corresponding, and corporeal, discipline, the better to receive the propositions—concerning Aristotelian tragedy, Shakespeare, and Hamlet's vexed interiority—that follow.

Such, at least, appear to be the aims of the film with respect to its audience. But of course audiences might refuse to be so interpellated, refuse, that is, to be the subjects thus addressed by Olivier's directorial and performance choices. When audiences refuse—when the cultural field has shifted to the extent that derisive laugher rather than hushed anticipation is the response engendered by these and other cues—then high seriousness teeters on the edge of pretension, with risibility as a potential result.

Pedagogical Realities and Sissified Shakespeare

It is not my purpose here to argue with the analysis by Peter Donaldson to
which I have already referred, but rather to set up his nuanced articulation
of *Hamlet* as one pole of a rhetorical dichotomy. Donaldson's essay is
an example of a sympathetic, collaborative response to the film; precisely
because it is, it cannot but reveal its prior acceptance of the film's premises
as a disciplining precondition for analysis. However factitiously, then, it
can be said to embody the stance of the "good student"—the one who
learns what the film wants him to and who extends the argument in such
a way as to respect the directorial agenda while producing new insights.
Donaldson's reading of *Hamlet* is not, of course, merely a slavish school
lesson. At the same time, however, it can usefully be contrasted with
actually occurring pedagogy—my students' derisive response to Olivier's
staging of his soliloquy, "To be or not to be"—the better to flesh out, and
counter, the fantasies of didacticism differentially proposed by DVD and
film.

As may be remembered, Donaldson's essay closely demonstrates the
varied means by which Olivier's choices in the film realize the Oedipal
subtext the actor-director wished to convey: as Donaldson summarily
suggests, "the phallic symbolism of rapier and dagger, the repeated dolly-in
down the long corridor to the queen's immense, enigmatic, and vaginally
hooded bed, the erotic treatment of the scenes between Olivier and
Eileen Herlie as Gertrude all bespeak a robust and readily identifiable, if
naïve, Freudianism." Indeed, Donaldson's reading of the long introductory
scene to which I've alluded recognizes the camera as seeking a sort of
psychoanalytic solution, as recognizing that "literal vacancy suggests an as
yet unspecified symbolic function." However, his reading both of actor and
film redoubles the psychological model Jones's Freud seems to offer as an
overt compositional strategy for Olivier and accepts it both as an index
of the film's success and a register of the conventions within which close
reading must occur. That is, Donaldson fills the space of literal vacancy with
a psychological analysis that takes its agenda from the preferred reading
of *Hamlet*. Most tellingly for my purposes, he locates the performance
of gender ambiguity in only a few privileged scenes: although Donaldson
claims that Hamlet's abeyance in front of the Ghost stages a biographically
inflected passivity in the face of peremptory male desires, fusing the ghost-
father with a schoolboy who approached Olivier with sexual aggression

at school, he contains the resonances of his own argument. Hence his characterization of Olivier's acting of Hamlet, which was, from its first performances in 1937 through to the film realization some ten years later, a radical departure from the "delicate souled dreamers and thinkers of nineteenth century tradition"; moreover, the actor's reckless, indeed masculine, athleticism set him particularly apart from his peers.[25]

That may be so in a documentary sense. Yet in class after class, at universities both elite and public, I have been taken aback by the snorts of ridicule at what students have variously termed Olivier's "affected," "exaggerated," "self-indulgent," "overtheatrical," and "wimpy" mannerisms, which show up most clearly in the famous soliloquy. Although these reactions seem to undermine the historical assessment of Olivier's performance style offered by Donaldson, it is easy enough, on one level, to correct what seems like pure misapprehension, or (better) a gap in historical knowledge that Method naturalism has never been the only game in town. As anyone who has occasion to teach performance knows, acting crystallizes not simply the compact between individual agent and text—which includes what is cognitive and volitional *and* what is not consciously available to the acting subject as subtext. It also embraces the subject's own internalization of an acting regime, in this case a classical one, in which propositions about what is "properly" Shakespearean cannot but condition the corporeal habitus.[26]

So far, so good. A corollary to the preceding point is thus that any proposition about what is proper to the performance of Shakespeare is also a proposition about how elite culture is to be staged, embodied, represented. A transaction is at work here, an assertion of the relationship between bodily modes and cultural worth—a transaction whose very historicity is brought into relief by the fact that it is itself a translation of Freud, and hence of a cultural discourse gaining, at midcentury, an increasing purchase on bourgeois attention, into the terms of the Shakespearean, and vice versa. Hence the film constitutes a series of mutually reinforcing articulations: of Freud as a way to understand a problem of agency; of an interpretation that makes agency the privileged realm of masculinity; of a text that itself problematizes male agency; and, finally, of one elite text—Freud—as a way to understand another—*Hamlet*—and to serve as the sign of that understanding in mass-cultural form. Presumably, the prestige of both texts—the validity that is seen to accrue to both with respect to their psychological and aesthetic propositions about masculinity—is increased thereby.

And yet there remains the students' intransigently undisciplined response. In my efforts to understand those reactions as meaningful and so to
avoid simply correcting them, something became clear: what I was initially
claiming was their naively experienced unfamiliarity with a temporally
distant instantiation of British classical training was, inevitably, more than
that. Especially when viewed as part of a discursively privileged scene in
a mass-cultural form, one moreover constructed to enforce a particularly
didactic reading of perhaps *the* fetish object of the high-cultural panoply,
and especially when received and experienced (then and now) as a British
import brought before an American audience and so working with and
against a native Anglophilia, Olivier's *Hamlet* could not but speak to issues
more far-reaching than acting style.

Indeed, under persistent questioning, it emerged from my students that
there was something "unmanly" about Olivier's performance that induced
their discomfiture, something approximating homophobic hysteria. At
the same time, however, the students' discomfiture had to be weighed
against prior engagements with similar material: they'd had no trouble
acknowledging homoerotic subtexts in Branagh's *Henry V,* for instance,
and appeared to appreciate the ending of Jarman's *Tempest* without apparent anxiety or resistance. In the latter case, at least, it is possible
that Jarman's queer sailors swooning while Elisabeth Welch's Ertesque
diva sings "Stormy Weather" preserves intact a stereotypical distinction
between marked and unmarked, which thus can safely be ghettoized as
exotic. And although Branagh's passionate attack on his treacherous "bed-
fellow" Scrope is framed in close-up shots and countershots that betoken
the intimacy of the boudoir, by and large both male actors establish a
safe performative distance from the homoerotic desire that the formal
shots urge on them: that is, Branagh's direction makes a contrary reading
available as a structural subtext, but it does not challenge heteronorma-
tivity as such. (The fact that Katherine is played by Branagh's then wife,
Emma Thompson, further secures the always already quality of his Henry's
straightness.) Were my students' potential anxieties more readily bought
off by these instances than by Olivier's more ambiguous, more historically
remote performance?

Certainly, there is an aspect to their amusement that cannot be readily
passed off as something other, particularly at the current moment, when
American ambivalence about gender institutions is echoed by a mass
culture that is at best contradictory in its relation to queerness.[27] Even

so, the classroom laughter I have encountered did not simply encompass moments of studied—and, arguably, nonheteronormatively gendered—self-consciousness in Olivier's portrayal; it also took in other moments, notably the directorial framing of Shakespeare's most famous soliloquy.[28] That is to say, much student reluctance to accept Olivier's *Hamlet* as interpellating them lies in the realm of viewing practices and is worth considering insofar as it registers a habit of consumption rather than a disposition toward identity, performative or otherwise. To put it more baldly: part, at least, of their response seemed like a gleeful refusal to read Olivier's Shakespearean enterprise straight.

As is well known, Susan Sontag has suggested that camp is what happens to dandy connoisseurship in the age of mass culture, when an aesthetic response undefiled by mass appreciation is no longer possible.[29] Clearly, the history of camp formations, and their shifting inflection of gender positions, roles, and tastes, is beyond the scope of this essay.[30] Nevertheless, it seems possible to claim that what was once a dandified, coterie response has, at the moment, a different and wider valence—it has migrated, that is, from its shoring in certain consuming practices historically associated with a metropolitan subculture of gay men, and become mainstream. Camp formations old and new use gender norms to transcode and recuperate a form of pleasure from a commodity that has otherwise come to seem discardable because of its signifying excesses, its indecencies, or its tritenesses. At its worst, this habit of consumption resembles a perimillennial cynicism that has been critiqued as reactionary, and Sontag herself averred that camp was largely an apolitical response to aesthetic stimuli.[31] But camp reveals a politics of culture in the very work of perception it enshrines, and in the collision between an object whose time has come and gone and a viewer whose interest in the text is constrained—as students' viewing of Shakespeare films so often is—by institutional imperatives about value. Sontag's essay is in fact a meditation on the historicity of viewing: it posits not only that mechanical reproduction has left its trace on an aesthetic pleasure heretofore defined by scarcity of access to experience, but that the distance from the mechanically reproduced object bequeathed by the passage of time is all but necessary for a camp response to be possible in the first place:

It is not a love of the old as such. It's simply that the process of aging or deterioration provides the necessary detachment. . . . When the theme is important or

contemporary, the failure of a work of art may make us indignant. Time can change
that. Time delivers the work of art from moral relevance, delivering it over to the
Camp sensibility. . . .

Thus things are campy, not when they become old—but when we become less
involved in them, and can enjoy, instead of be frustrated by, the failure of the
attempt.[32]

Based on Sontag's positioning of camp in the historical problematic of
the mass-produced cultural object, I would aver that my students were
reading Olivier as camp intellectuals do, and finding perverse pleasure
in what seemed, to them at least, a banal, unoriginal—not to say equally
mass-produced—interpretation. As Sontag argues, "The whole point of
Camp is to dethrone the serious. . . . Sincerity can be simple philistinism,
intellectual narrowness."[33]

And that the serious interpretation in question travels under the sign of
Freudianism as it has already been exhaustively dispersed in pedagogical
practice is very much at issue here: not so much the "naive" Freudianism
that Donaldson describes, but an enforcedly didactic and narrow one, at
this remove lacking the power of innovation, and so retrospectively war-
ranting the charge of naïveté. The didactic imperative further illuminates
the risibility of my students, since their laughter is a sign of their distance
from the historical moment of production and spectatorship implied by
Olivier's film text, when Freud might possibly have seemed a thrilling, even
"dangerous," extension of Aristotelian claims about tragic heroes and their
flaws into the realm of psychopathology. Witness the fact that some of their
resistance to Olivier's climactic staging of interiority could be located in
what students saw as the crudeness of its symbolism—the way, for instance,
the rather small dagger is introduced, deployed, made to bear what is, for
them, an oppressive interpretive burden, and quite an obvious burden at
that. What was all too available to my students as a phallic symbol, even
without having read Donaldson, becomes a way to register how Freudian-
inflected modes of reading have gone from potentially avant-garde to risibly
obvious, in the space of some fifty years.

That it should be *the* soliloquy that most amused my students makes
an immediate kind of sense: just as the "to be or not to be" speech is
the distillation of *Hamlet*—indeed, of all of Shakespeare in the popular
imaginary—it is inevitable that it be made to bear the largest freight of
interpretive excess in the film. The pulsating camera focusing and unfo-
cusing, the juxtaposition of a whorled pattern of hair on Olivier's head with

a whirling sea which represents the objective correlative of what's going on beneath Hamlet's Scandinavian blondness, are argumentative assertions of meaning and as such restrictions of the field of interpretation and signification. These images mean, in all earnestness, to tell you what to think, how to understand. They are of a piece with the languid, studied moves Olivier makes: his gestures are the corporeal equivalent of the didactically symbolizing camera, propositions about masculinity and agency as staged by and through Shakespeare that find a certain reduction to banality in the phallic imagery and that cannot—precisely because that imagery summons forth a seemingly infinite number of subsequent pedagogical moments in which students "discover" the secret of masculine signification (that it's always about the penis) in literary texts—fail to convince at this remove.

To displace Donaldson's reading, as I have done, is not to deny the potential cogency of his insights insofar as they yield a persuasive explication of the film, taken on its own terms. But it is also, as I have noted, to round again on the question of pedagogy. Abetted by the responses of any number of students who piously avow that film enables Shakespeare "to be brought to the masses" at the same time they admit their own jaundiced reactions to such high seriousness in cinematic form, I have begun to wonder about the unacknowledged persistence of pedagogical imperatives structuring public formations around Shakespeare. As Uricchio and Pearson have demonstrated, such imperatives seem coextensive with a residual (and suspect) sense that the vehicle is less than its tenor and that Shakespearean cinema can serve as a model of mass uplift. Given the tendentious predictability that some, at least, of some of these productions have assumed, is it perhaps no wonder that Sontag closes by suggesting that "the relation between boredom and Camp taste cannot be overestimated."[34]

It is also perhaps no wonder that mass culture has brought the decidedly guilty pleasure of John McTiernan's 1993 movie *Last Action Hero,* in which a decidedly unvacillating Arnold Schwarzenegger is offered as the phantasmatic corrective for Olivier's incapacity to follow through.[35] In contrast to the littleness of Olivier's accouterments, Schwarzenegger embodies a prosthetic masculinity so exaggerated, so unambiguously large in scale, that it needs no signifying sword. As the prince who is anything but "sweet," Schwarzenegger rampages anarchically, taking out the trash of rotten Denmark and leaving the languor of Olivier's Hamlet behind, the better to offer its audience the frisson of a different kind of revenge fantasy. Although it nominally belongs to Danny Madigan, the boy whose absorption with Schwarzenegger's film character transmogrifies Olivier's Hamlet into a pumped-up commando, that diegetic fantasy takes place in a classroom—and speaks, even if only in passing and even if only in potential, to precisely the issues I've examined here. For the student subject interpellated by the extravagantly heightened sensations of late twentieth-century mass culture, and bored with the unrelenting effort to redeem mass forms from demonizing discourse by putting them in the service of Shakespearean pedagogy, camp irreverence has its attractions.

Notes

This essay began as a lecture at Fordham University in 2001. I wish to thank Kim Hall and Mary Bly for their comments on that occasion.

1. The first term comes from Douglas Lanier, *Shakespeare and Modern Popular Culture* (Oxford: Oxford University Press, 2002); the next two terms are Richard Burt's from his *Unspeakable ShaXXXspeares: Queer Theory and American Kiddie Culture* (New York: St. Martin's, 1998).

2. Lev Manovich, *The Language of New Media* (Cambridge, Mass.: MIT Press, 2001), 49–61.

3. Ibid., 61.

4. The question of privacy is material: DVDs and VHS tapes are sold for limited use, and owners are legally restricted from screening them in public for large audiences.

5. Technically, *Titus* is now available in two different issues: the earlier version, produced by Fox-Lober, is generally considered inferior to the more recent release from Fox Home Entertainment.

6. Funding for film projects has become extremely elaborate; trans- and multinational deals dominated by Hollywood corporations are increasingly the norm, particularly for nondominant national cinema industries. For a detailed account of the political economy of cinema in the world market, see Toby Miller, Nitin Govil, John McMurria, and Richard Maxwell, *Global Hollywood* (London: British Film Institute, 2001).

7. This is a question theorized at great length in cultural studies. For a useful critique of reception work, see John Frow, *Cultural Studies and Cultural Value* (Oxford: Clarendon, 1995).

8. My account of Criterion has been informed by discussions with Peter Brunette and David Levy.

9. Criterion Collection Database, http://criterionco.com ("About Criterion"; accessed March 10, 2004).

10. "Focus," http://criterionco.com/asp/focus_toc.asp (for Ozu conference; accessed October 23, 2003).

11. "About Criterion," http://criterionco.com/asp/about.asp.

12. I owe this information to Caroline Bassett.

13. I express myself with caution not only because Criterion's continued right to Olivier's film is not guaranteed but also because Criterion occasionally remasters and repackages titles

to which it has retained rights, as it has recently done with *Charade* (directed by Stanley Donen; 1963).

14. Criterion Database, *"Hamlet,"* http://criterionco.com/asp/release.asp?id=82.

15. Ernest Jones, *Hamlet and Oedipus* (1949; New York: Doubleday and Company, 1954). Although Jones's text was published two years after the release of Olivier's film, it had been in progress since 1910 and was published in provisional form a number of times before 1949.

16. My discussion of packaging was spurred by Barbara Hodgdon's argument about the cover art for the VHS release of Zeffirelli's 1990 *Hamlet;* see Barbara Hodgdon, "The Critic, the Poor Player, Prince Hamlet, and the Lady in the Dark," in *Shakespeare Re-Read: The Texts in New Contexts,* ed. Russ McDonald (Ithaca, N.Y.: Cornell University Press, 1994), 275–93.

17. William Shakespeare, *Hamlet,* ed. Harold Jenkins (London: Methuen, 1982), 1.4.23–36.

18. Peter S. Donaldson, "Olivier, Hamlet, and Freud," in *Shakespearean Films/Shakespearean Directors* (Boston: Unwin Hyman, 1990), 31–67. Marjorie Garber has a provocative essay on Freud's constitutive repression of *Hamlet* in the making of his theory of the Oedipus complex; see her "Hamlet: Giving Up the Ghost," in *Shakespeare's Ghost Writers: Literature as Uncanny Causality* (New York: Methuen, 1987), 124–76.

19. On the increasing popularity of a sexual liberalism inspired by Freud, see Estelle Freedman and John D'Emilio, *Intimate Matters: A History of Sexuality in America,* 2d ed. (Chicago:University of Chicago Press, 1997), 239–74.

20. The literature addressing debates concerning the debilitating effects of mass culture is extensive. I can do no more than gesture to a few sources: Max Horkheimer and Theodor Adorno, "The Culture Industry: Enlightenment as Mass Deception," in *Dialectic of Enlightenment,* trans. John Cumming (1944; New York: Continuum, 1972), 120–67; Andreas Huyssen, *After the Great Divide: Modernism, Mass Culture, Postmodernism* (Bloomington: Indiana University Press, 1986), 44–81; Paul R. Gorman, *Left Intellectuals and Popular Culture in Twentieth Century America* (Chapel Hill: University of North Carolina Press, 1996), 137–85; and Stanley Aronowitz, "Culture between High and Low," in *Roll Over Beethoven: The Return of Cultural Strife* (Hanover; N.H.: Wesleyan University Press, University Press of New England, 1993), 63–84.

21. Quoted in William Uricchio and Roberta E. Pearson, *Reframing Culture: The Case of the Vitagraph Quality Films* (Princeton, N.J.: Princeton University Press, 1993), 71.

22. John Collick, *Shakespeare, Cinema and Society* (Manchester: Manchester University Press, 1989), 39–47.

23. Ibid., 47–51.

24. *Moving Picture World* quotation from 1910; quoted in Uricchio and Pearson, *Reframing Culture,* 71.

25. Donaldson, "Olivier, Hamlet, and Freud," 31, 52, 33.

26. Although the concept of habitus is most usually associated with Pierre Bourdieu, I use it in the sense Marcel Mauss has in mind in his work on "body techniques": see Marcel Mauss, *Sociology and Psychology: Essays,* trans. Ben Brewster (London: Routledge and Kegan Paul, 1979), 97–122. For the ideological ramifications of acting style, see W. B. Worthen, *Shakespeare and the Authority of Performance* (Cambridge: Cambridge University Press, 1997), 95–150.

27. *Queer Eye for the Straight Guy* and *Will and Grace* have certainly made homosex-

uality visible on broadcast TV, although principally they have further secured an already hoary relationship between white urban gayness and (consumerist) aesthetics. Additionally, a number of straight entertainers, notably Conan O'Brien, circle around "gayness" in a way that ironizes both homophobia and the putative object of its fear. O'Brien, for instance, uses comic performance so as to distance (or perhaps rescue?) himself from "meaning"—which is to say inhabiting—either pole. Such a performance seems to take as its precondition that "real" homophobia is safely in the past, but this might be a distance without a difference. The unreconstructedly negative implications of O'Brien's occasional claims to be gay are reinforced by the obsessive recurrence of the discourse, as well as by the privilege homosexuality holds as an acceptable object of male comic anxiety.

28. Marjorie Garber has argued that Olivier's defining characteristic as an actor is a gender ambiguity that places him in a third zone, somewhere between binary genders; see her *Vested Interests: Cross-Dressing and Cultural Anxiety* (New York: Routledge, 1991), 32–34. Although in this essay I am unconcerned with what Laurence Olivier's possible sexual orientation might have been, it is nevertheless interesting that both Garber and Donaldson characterize Olivier as decidedly heterosexual even while their analyses depend on a public discourse that reads him "otherwise." For an alternative take on Olivier's erotic dispensation, see Donald Spoto, *Laurence Olivier: A Biography* (New York: HarperCollins, 1992), esp. 70–71; 275–78.

29. Susan Sontag, "Notes on 'Camp,' " *Against Interpretation* (New York: Dell, 1967), 275–92. My sense of how camp, capital, and the labor of perception are intermingled is indebted to Matthew Tinckom, *Working Like a Homosexual: Camp, Capital, Cinema* (Durham, N.C.: Duke University Press, 2002).

30. In addition to Tinckom's study, see Andrew Ross, *No Respect: Intellectuals and Popular Culture* (New York: Routledge, 1989), 135–70.

31. In addition to Sontag, see Peter Sloterdijk, *Critique of Cynical Reason,* trans. Michael Eldred (1983; Minneapolis: University of Minnesota Press, 1987).

32. Sontag, "Notes on 'Camp,' " 285.

33. Ibid., 288.

34. Ibid., 289.

35. I was introduced to this parody by Eric Mallin; see his "You Kilt My Foddah; Or, Arnold, Prince of Denmark," *Shakespeare Quarterly* 50, no. 2 (1999): 127–51. Mallin's essay largely focuses on the McTiernan film as a retelling of *Hamlet.*

Notes on Contributors

DENISE ALBANESE teaches English and cultural studies at George Mason University. She is the author of *New Science, New World*, as well as articles on Shakespeare and contemporary culture, and on mathematics and scientific and textual practices in the early modern period. She is completing a book on Shakespeare in the peri-millennial United States entitled *Extramural Shakespeare*.

THOMAS CARTELLI is the NEH Professor of Humanities at Muhlenberg College. He is author of *Repositioning Shakespeare: National Formations, Postcolonial Appropriations*; *Marlowe, Shakespeare, and the Economy of Theatrical Experience*; and, with Katherine Rowe, the forthcoming *New Wave Shakespeare on Screen*.

ANNE HENRY is a fellow and a lecturer in English at Trinity College, Cambridge.

BARBARA HODGDON is a professor of English at the University of Michigan. Her books include *The Shakespeare Trade: Performances and Appropriations*; *The First Part of King Henry the Fourth: Texts and Contexts*; *Henry IV, Part Two* in the Shakespeare in Performance series; and *The End Crowns All: Closure and Contradiction in Shakespeare's History*. She is the coeditor of *A Companion to Shakespeare and Performance* and is currently editing *The Taming of the Shrew* for the Arden 3 Shakespeare series.

COURTNEY LEHMANN is an associate professor of English and film studies and the director of the Humanities Center at the University of the Pacific. She is the author of *Shakespeare Remains: Theater to Film, Early Modern to Postmodern* and coeditor, with Lisa S. Starks, of *Spectacular Shakespeare: Critical Theory and Popular Cinema* and *The Reel Shakespeare: Alternative Cinema and Theory*. She is currently completing a manuscript on Shakespeare, film, and feminism.

STEPHEN ORGEL is the J. E. Reynolds Professor in the Humanities at Stanford. His most recent books are *Imagining Shakespeare* and *The Authentic Shakespeare and Other Problems of the Early Modern Stage*.

RICHARD PREISS received his doctorate from Stanford University and is currently an assistant professor of English at the University of Utah. He is revising a dissertation on the discursive exchanges between stage clowning and dramatic authorship in early modern theater. Another article recently appeared in *From Performance to Print in Shakespeare's England*.

RICHARD W. SCHOCH is a professor of the history of culture at Queen Mary, University of London. His books include *Not Shakespeare: Bardolatry and Burlesque in the Nineteenth Century*; *Shakespeare's Victorian Stage: Performing History in the Theatre of Charles Kean*; and *Queen Victoria and the Theatre of Her Age*.